Illustrated Battles of the
Napoleonic Age

Illustrated Battles of the
Napoleonic Age
Volume 1—1800-1811

Marengo, Copenhagen, Egypt,
Janissary Rebellion, Laswaree & Asaye,
Pulo Aor, Austerlitz, Trafalgar, Jena,
Maida, Walcheren and Albuera

C. J. Cutcliffe Hyne, D. H. Parry
and Others

LEONAUR

Illustrated Battles of the Napoleonic Age: Volume 1—1800-1811:
Marengo, Copenhagen, Egypt, Janissary Rebellion, Laswaree & Asaye,
Pulo Aor, Austerlitz, Trafalgar, Jena, Maida, Walcheren and Albuera
by C. J. Cutcliffe Hyne, D. H. Parry and Others

Leonaur is an imprint of Oakpast Ltd

Material original to this edition and presentation of the
text in this form copyright © 2014 Oakpast Ltd

ISBN: 978-1-78282-241-7 (hardcover)
ISBN: 978-1-78282-242-4 (softcover)

http://www.leonaur.com

Publisher's Notes

The views expressed in this book are not necessarily
those of the publisher.

Contents

JUNE 14 1800

The Battle of Marengo

Montgomery B. Gibbs

At the time of Napoleon's return from the Egyptian expedition the legislative bodies of Paris were divided into two parties, the Moderates, headed by Sieyes, and the Democrats, by Barras. Finding it impossible to remain neutral, Bonaparte took sides with the former. Lucien, his brother, had just been elected president of the Council of Five Hundred; the subtle and able Talleyrand and the accomplished Sieyes were his confidants, and he determined to overwhelm the imbecile government and take the reins in his own hands. He had measured his strength, established his purpose, and, as France stood in need of a more energetic and regenerated government, he now went calmly to its execution.

During his absence in Egypt France had cause to deplore the loss of his military genius, and had hailed his return with rapturous acclamations. Napoleon's intentions were no sooner suspected than he was surrounded by all those who were discontented with the

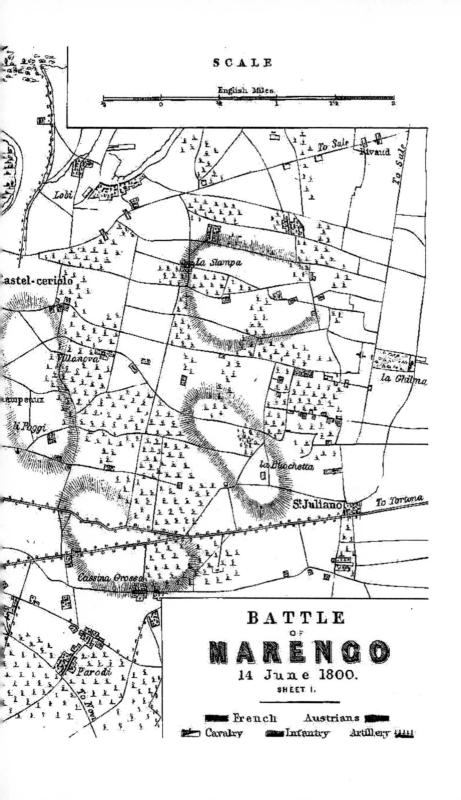

SCALE

English Miles.

BATTLE
OF
MARENGO
14 June 1800.
SHEET I.

French   Austrians
Cavalry   Infantry   Artillery

established government, and who found in him such a leader as they had long looked for in vain.

He soon opened negotiations with Sieyes who commanded a majority in the Council of Ancients, and had no sooner convinced him that the project of overturning the Directorial government was his object, than he was regarded as the instrument destined to give France that "systematic" constitution he had so long deliberated on and desired. Napoleon's overtures were therefore cordially met, and Sieyes gave all the weight of his influence to the impending revolution. Two men whose names have since been known all over Europe, were also added to the number of his adherents, Talleyrand, who had been recently deposed from a place in the ministry; and Fouché, minister of police. The talents of both were actively employed in his service and materially promoted his success. He had no faith in Fouché and used him without giving him his confidence. Lucien Bonaparte held the important post of president of the Council of Five Hundred; a circumstance highly advantageous to his brother at this juncture. It was there that the greatest opposition would be made to any attempt which was hostile to the Constitution of the Year Three.

A large portion of the army was certain to side with Napoleon. His house was now the resort of all the generals and men of note who had served under him in his campaigns in Italy and Egypt, Bernadotte alone standing aloof.

A meeting took place between Napoleon and Sieyes on the 6th of November 1799, in which it was finally determined that the revolution should be attempted on the 9th. This date, called in the history of the period, the 18th *Brumaire*, was exactly one month from the day of Napoleon's landing at Fréjus on his return from Egypt. The measures resolved upon were as follows: The Council of Ancients, taking advantage of an article in the constitution, which authorized the measure, were to decree the removal of the legislative bodies to St. Cloud, beyond the walls of the city. They were next to appoint Napoleon commander-in-chief of their own guard, of the troops of the military division of Paris, and of the National Guard. These decrees were to be passed at seven in the morning; at eight Napoleon was to go to the Tuileries, where the troops should be assembled, and there assume the command of the capital.

The Council of Ancients at length gathered in the Tuileries at an early hour, every arrangement having been made in accordance with these resolutions, declared that the salvation of the State demanded

vigorous measures, and proposed through its president, (one of Napoleon's confidants)—the passage of the decrees already agreed upon. The decrees were at once adopted without debate and Napoleon notified. All had occurred as had been prearranged. Early on the morning of the 18th *Brumaire*, the house of Napoleon in the Rue de la Victoire was crowded with a large assemblage of officers. It was too small to hold them all and many were in the courtyard and entrances. Numbers of these were devoted to him; a few were in the secret, and all began to suspect that something extraordinary was soon to happen. Everyone was in uniform except Bernadotte who appeared in plain clothes. Displeased at this mark of separation from the rest Napoleon said hastily: "How is this? You are not in uniform!"

"I never am on a morning when I am not on duty," replied Bernadotte.

"You will be on duty presently," rejoined Napoleon.

"I have not heard of it; I should have received my orders sooner," came the answer quickly.

Napoleon now drew him aside, disclosed his plans and invited him to take part with the new movement against a detested government. Bernadotte's only answer was that "he would not take part in a rebellion," and with some reluctance made a half promise of neutrality.

The moment the decrees of the Council of Ancients arrived Napoleon came forward to the steps of his house, read the documents, and invited them all to follow him to the Tuileries. The enthusiasm of those present was now at the highest pitch and all the officers drew their swords, promising their services and fidelity. Napoleon instantly mounted, and placed himself at the head of the generals and officers. Attended by one thousand five hundred horse, he halted on the boulevard at the corner of the street Mont Blanc; he then dispatched some confidential troops under Moreau to guard the Luxembourg, and the Directory ceased to exist, although Barras entered a mild protest and then retired to his country residence to live upon the great spoils of his office.

The Council of Five Hundred, an hour or two afterwards, assembled to learn its fate. Resistance would have been idle, and adjourning for their next session at St. Cloud, they mingled with the enthusiastic people shouting, "*Vive la République!*" When they assembled at St. Cloud the next morning they found that beautiful chateau completely invested by the brilliant battalions under the orders of Murat.

At about one o'clock on the 19th *Brumaire* Napoleon appeared at St. Cloud attended by Berthier, Lefebvre, Lannes and all the generals in his confidence. Upon his arrival he learned that a heated debate had commenced in the Council of Ancients on the subject of the resignation of the directors and the immediate election of others. Napoleon hastily entered the hall accompanied only by Berthier and Bourrienne who attended as his secretary. He addressed the body with much difficulty and after many dramatic interruptions, told them that it was upon them he relied, declaring his belief that the Council of Five Hundred—corresponding in part with the lower house of Congress—would restore the Convention, popular tumults, the scaffold, the Reign of Terror. He said:

"I will save you from all these horrors, I and my brave comrades, whose swords and caps I see at the door of this hall; and if any hireling traitor talks of outlawry, to those swords will I appeal. You stand over a volcano. Let a soldier tell the truth frankly. I was quiet in my home when this Council summoned me to action. I obeyed: I collected my brave comrades, and placed the arms of my country at the service of you who are its head. We are repaid with calumnies—they talk of Cromwell—of Caesar. Had I aspired to power the opportunity was mine ere now. I swear that France holds no more devoted patriot. Dangers surround us. Let us not hazard the advantages for which we have paid so dearly— Liberty and Equality!" Rallying at the uproar which pursued him to the door, Napoleon turned round and called upon the Council to assist him in saving the country; and with the words, "Let those who love me follow," he passed quickly out, reached the courtyard where he showed the soldiers the order naming him commander-in-chief, and then leaped upon his horse, shouts of "*Vive Bonaparte!*" resounding on all sides.

In the meantime the hostile Council of Five Hundred had assembled, and there a far different scene was passing. With the same steadiness of purpose and calmness of manner, Bonaparte walked into the chamber with two grenadiers on either side, who halted at the doors that were left open, while the general advanced towards the centre of the chamber.

At the sight of drawn swords at the passageway, and the presence of armed men at the doors of that deliberative body, loud cries of "Down with the traitor!" "Long live the Constitution!" etc., broke forth. Several of the members rushed upon Napoleon, some seized him by the collar and one is said to have attempted his life with a dagger. In an instant the grenadiers rushed forward exclaiming, "Let us save our general," and bore their commander from the hall.

Napoleon was quickly in the midst of his soldiers and found ready ears and enthusiastic spirits to listen to his excited words. "Soldiers," he said, "I offered them victory and fame—they have answered me with daggers."

It was at this moment that Augereau, whose faith in his former general's fortune began to waver, is said to have addressed him with the words, "A fine situation you have brought yourself into!" Upon which Napoleon answered, "Augereau, things were worse at Arcola; take my advice, remain quiet; in a short time all this will change."

Meanwhile the commotion in the Council of Five Hundred rose to the highest pitch, a scene of the wildest confusion was taking place in the Assembly, and the grenadiers sent by Napoleon once more entered and bore Lucien, the president, from his colleagues. They had charged him with conspiracy and were about to vent their fury upon him, when he flung off the insignia of his office and was rescued.

13

Lucien found the soldiery without in a high state of excitement. He mounted a horse quickly that he might be seen and heard the better, and dramatically addressed the assembled troops: "General Bonaparte, and you, soldiers of France," he said, "the President of the Council of Five Hundred announces to you that factious men with daggers interrupt the deliberations of the Senate. He authorizes you to employ force. The Assembly of Five Hundred is dissolved." The soldiers received his harangue with shouts of, "*Vive Bonaparte!*" Still there was an appearance of hesitation, and it did not seem certain that they were ready to act against the representatives of the people, till Lucien drew his sword, and vehemently exclaimed, "I swear that I will stab my own brother to the heart, if he ever attempts anything against the liberty of Frenchmen."

This statement roused the soldiers to action and they were now ready to obey any order from Napoleon. At a signal from him, Murat, at the head of a body of grenadiers, at once started to execute the order of the president. With a roll of drums and levelled pieces, Lucien followed the detachment, mounted the tribune, and dispersed the Council of Five Hundred. The deputies were debating in a state of wild indecision and anxiety when the troops slowly entered. Murat, as they moved forward, announced to the council that it should disperse. A few of the members instantly retired; but the majority remained firm. A reinforcement now entered in close column headed by General Leclerc, the commanding officer, who said loudly, "In the name of General Bonaparte, the Legislative Corps is dissolved; let all good citizens retire. Grenadiers, forward!" The latter advanced, levelling their muskets with fixed bayonets and occupying the width of the hall. Most of the members at once made their escape by the windows with undignified rapidity; in a few minutes not one remained.

Lucien immediately assembled the "Moderate" members of the council who resumed its session, and in conjunction with that of the Ancients, a decree was passed investing the entire authority of the State in a Provisional Consulate of three—Napoleon, Sieyes and Roger-Ducos who were known as "Consuls of the French Republic." Thus ended the 18th and 19th *Brumaire*, (November 10th and 11th, 1799) one of the most decisive revolutions of which history has preserved any record; and, so admirable had been the arrangements of Napoleon, that it had not cost France a drop of blood. "During the greater part of this eventful day," says Bourrienne, "he was as calm as at the opening of a great battle."

The next day the three consuls met at Paris, and France once more began to make progress. At this meeting, Sieyes, who had up to this moment conceived himself to be the head, and the others but the arms of the new constitution, asked, as a form of politeness, "Which of us is to preside?"

"Do you not see," answered Ducos, "that the general presides?"

Sieyes had expected that Napoleon would content himself with the supreme command of all the armies, and had no idea that he was conversant with, or wished to interfere in profound and extensive political affairs and projects. He was, however, so astonished at the knowledge displayed by Napoleon in questions of administration,

SCALE.

English Miles

BATTLE
OF
MARENGO
14 June 1800.
SHEET 2

French   Austrians
Cavalry   Infantry   Artillery

even to the minutest details, and in every department, that when their first conference was concluded, he hurried to Talleyrand, Cabanis, and other counsellors, assembled at St. Cloud, exclaiming, "Gentlemen, you have now a master. He knows everything, arranges everything, and can accomplish everything."

Those persons must know the character of Napoleon very imperfectly, who consider him great only at the head of armies; for he was able to acquit himself of the various functions of government with glory, shining equally as conspicuous in the cabinet as in the field.

Napoleon guided and controlled everything; humane laws were enacted; Christianity was again restored, and upwards of 20,000 French citizens now came forth from the prisons to bless his name. Many who had been exiled because they did not approve of the Reign of Terror and the despotism of the directory were recalled, and many other salutary reforms at once stamped the new government with the seal of public approbation and the confidence of Europe. In everything that was done the genius of Napoleon was visible. A great man was at the helm, and the world saw that his creative genius was regenerating France. The new constitution met the approval of the people, and in February 1800 the First Consul took up his residence in the Tuileries, the old home of the monarchs of France. Shortly afterwards Napoleon reviewed the Army of Paris, amounting to 100,000 men. When the 96th, 43rd and 50th demi-brigades defiled before him he was observed to take off his hat and incline his head, in token of respect at the sight of their colours torn to shreds with balls, and blackened with smoke and powder.

For the first time in modern history the world saw the greatest general of the age the civil chief of the most brilliant state in Europe. The First Consul now held frequent and splendid reviews of the troops. He traversed the ranks, now on horseback, now on foot; entered into the minutest details concerning the wants of the men and the service, and dispensing in the name of the nation, distinctions and rewards. A hundred soldiers who had signalized themselves in action, received from his hand the present of a handsome sabre each, on one of these occasions.

The Parisians received the new constitution with delight. The inhabitants also viewed the pomp and splendour of the Consular government with surprise and self-complacency. They reasoned little and hoped much. Napoleon was their idol, and from him alone they expected everything. The constitution continued the executive power in the hands of three consuls, who were to be elected for the space of ten years, and were then eligible to re-election. The First Consul held powers far superior to his colleagues. He alone had the right of nominating all offices, civil and military, and of appointing nearly all functionaries whatsoever. Napoleon assumed the place of First Consul without question or debate. He then named Cambacérès and LeBrun as Second and Third Consuls respectively.

It was about this time that Napoleon learned of the death of Washington. He forthwith issued a general order commanding the French army to wrap their banners in crape during ten days in honour of "a great man who fought against tyranny, and consolidated the liberties of his country." He then celebrated a grand funeral service to the memory of Washington in the council-hall of the Invalides. The last standards taken in Egypt were presented on the same occasion; all the ministers, the counsellors of state and generals, were present. The pillars and roof were hung with the trophies of the campaign of Italy and the bust of Washington was placed under the trophy composed of the flags of Aboukir.

"From this day," says Lockhart, "a new epoch was to date. Submit to that government, and no man need fear that his former acts, far less opinions, should prove any obstacle to his security—nay, to his advancement." In truth the secret of Bonaparte's whole scheme is unfolded in his own memorable words to Sieyes: "We are creating a new era—of the past we must forget the bad, and remember only the good."

During the absence of Bonaparte in Egypt the tri-colour which he had left floating on the castles along the Rhine, and from the Julian Alps to the Mediterranean, had been humbled, and England and Austria, with the allies they could bring into the coalition, were preparing once more to compel the French to retire to their ancient boundaries, and ultimately offer the crown to the exiled Bourbons.

But Napoleon knew that France needed internal repose, and he desired universal peace in Europe. He even went so far, in order to bring this about, as to address a letter to George III. in which he said:

"Your Majesty will see in this overture only my sincere desire to contribute effectually, for a second time, to a general pacification—by a prompt step taken in confidence, and freed from those forms, which, however necessary to disguise the feeble apprehensions of feeble states, only serve to discover in the powerful a mutual wish to deceive. France and England, abusing their strength, may long defer the period of its utter exhaustion; but I will venture to say that the fate of

fectly in accord with the principles which guided the rulers of England at that period. They had joined the other governments of Europe in commencing war against France, in order to restore its legitimate sovereign, contrary to the will of the French people.

When Napoleon read the letter he said: "I will answer that from Italy!" and immediately called his generals together and ordered them to get ready for another campaign beyond the Alps. It is said that on receiving the reply from England Napoleon exclaimed to Talleyrand, "It could not have been more favourable," but this is credited by but few historians as it appears that his sincere convictions were that peace was best for France.

Three days after the Grenville letter, the First Consul electrified France by an edict for an army of reserve embracing all the veterans then unemployed, who had ever served the country, and a new levy of 30,000 recruits or conscripts as they were termed; and the most active preparations were rapidly made. At this time four great armies were already in the field—one on the North coast was watching Holland, and guarding against any invasion from England; Jourdan commanded the Army of the Danube, which had repassed the Rhine; Massena was at the head of the Army of Helvetia, and held Switzerland; and the fragment of the mighty host that Napoleon had himself led to victory, still called the Army of Italy.

Upwards of 350,000 men were now marched to various points of conflict with the European powers—England, Austria and Russia, together with Bavaria, Sweden, Denmark, and Turkey, which made a formidable array of enemies with whom Napoleon had to contend. The operations were conducted with the utmost secrecy. Napoleon had decided to strike the decisive blow against Austria in Italy, and to command there in person. An article in the new constitution forbade the First Consul taking the command of an army but he found a ready way to evade it. Berthier was superseded by Carnot as minister of war and given the nominal command of the Army of Italy. It was generally believed that the troops were to advance upon Italy. Meantime, while Austria was laughing with derision at the French conscripts and "invalids" then at Dijon and amused itself with caricatures of some ancient men with wooden legs, and little boys twelve years old entitled "Bonaparte's Army of Reserve," the real Army of Italy was already formed in the heart of France and was marching by various roads towards Switzerland and was commanded by officers of recognized ability and courage. The artillery was sent piecemeal from different arsenals; the provisions, necessary to an army about to cross barren mountains, were forwarded to Geneva, embarked on the lake, and landed at Villeneuve, near the entrance of the valley of the Simplon.

The daring plan of Napoleon was to transport his army across the Alps; surmounting the highest chain of mountains in Europe, by paths which are dangerous and difficult to the unencumbered traveller; to plant himself in the rear of the Austrians, interrupt their communications, place them between his own army and that of Massena who was in command of the 12,000 men at Genoa, cut off their retreat and then give them battle under circumstances which must necessarily render one defeat decisive.

After dispatching his orders Napoleon joined Berthier at Geneva on May 8th, 1800. Here he met General Marescot, the engineer, who by his orders had explored the wild passes of the Alps. He described to the First Consul most minutely the all but insuperable obstacles that would oppose the passage of an army.

"Difficult, granted; but is it possible for an army to pass?" Napoleon at last impatiently inquired.

"It might be done," was the answer.

"Then it shall be; let us start," said the First Consul, and preparations for that most herculean task were at once made, the commander intending to penetrate into Italy, as Hannibal had done of old, through all the dangers and difficulties of the great Alps themselves.

For the treble purpose of more easily collecting a sufficient stock of provisions for the march, of making its accomplishment more rapid, and on perplexing the enemy on its termination, Napoleon determined that his army should pass in four divisions, by as many separate routes. The left wing, under Moncey consisting of 15,000 men, detached from the army of Moreau, was ordered to debouch by the way of St. Gothard. The corps of Thureau, 5,000 strong, took the direction of Mount Cenis; that of Chabran, of similar strength, moved by the Little St. Bernard. Of the main body, consisting of 35,000 men, although technically commanded by Berthier, the First Consul himself took charge, including the gigantic task of surmounting, with the artillery, the huge barriers of the Great St. Bernard. Once across he expected to rush down upon Melas, cut off all his communications with Austria, and then force him to a conflict.

The main body of the army marched on the 15th of May from Lausanne to the village of St. Pierre, at the foot of the Great St. Bernard, at which point all traces of a practicable path entirely ceased.

25

civilized nations is concerned in the termination of a war, the flames of which are raging throughout the whole world. I have the honour, etc., etc., Bonaparte."

If the king himself had had an opportunity to reply to this letter, as he afterwards admitted, it would have saved England millions of money, and Europe millions of lives; but in a very short-sighted letter,

Lord Grenville, then Secretary of State, replied to Talleyrand, France's minister of Foreign Affairs, in which he said: "The war must continue until the causes which gave it birth cease to exist. The restoration of the exiled royal family will be the easiest means of giving confidence to the other powers of Europe." The refusal of England to treat with the Consular Government of France was to be expected, being per-

Field forges were established at St. Pierre to dismount the guns. The carriages and wheels were slung on poles and the ammunition boxes were to be carried by mules. To convey the pieces themselves a number of trees were felled, hollowed out, or grooved, and the guns being jammed within these rough cases, a hundred soldiers were attached to each whose duty it was to drag them up the steeps. All was now in readiness to commence the great march.

Botta in his description of this campaign says:

"The First Consul set forth on his stupendous enterprise, his forces being already at the foot of the Great St. Bernard. The soldiers gazed on the aerial summits of the lofty mountains with wonder and impatience. On the 17th of May the whole body set out from Martigny for the conquest of Italy. Extraordinary was their order, wonderful their gaiety, and astonishing also, the activity and energy of their operations. Laughter and song lightened their toils. They seemed to be hastening, not to a fearful war, but a festival. The multitude of various and mingled sounds were re-echoed from hill to hill, and the silence of these solitary and desolate regions, which revolving ages had left undisturbed, was for the moment broken by the rejoicing voices of the gay and warlike. Precipitous heights, strong torrents, sloping valleys, succeeded each other with disheartening frequency. Owing to his incredible boldness and order, Lannes was chosen by the First Consul to take the lead in every enterprise of danger. They had now reached an elevation where skill or courage seemed powerless against the domain of Nature. From St. Pierre to the summit of the Great St. Bernard there is no beaten road whatever, until the explorer reaches the monastery of the religious order devoted to the preservation of travellers bewildered in these regions of eternal winter. Every means that could be devised was adopted for transporting the artillery and baggage; the carriages which had been wheeled were now dragged—those which had been drawn were now carried. The largest cannon were placed in troughs and on sledges, and the smallest swung on sure-footed mules. The ascent to be accomplished was immense. In the windings of the tortuous paths the troops were now lost and now revealed to sight. Those who first mounted the steeps, seeing their companions in the depths below, cheered them on with shouts of triumph. The valleys on every side re-echoed to their voices. Amidst the snow, in mists and clouds, the resplendent arms and coloured uniforms of the soldiers appeared in bright and dazzling contrast: the sublimity of dead Nature and the energy of living action thus united, formed a spectacle of surpassing wonder.

"The consul, exulting in the success of his plans, was seen everywhere amongst the soldiers, talking with military familiarity to one and now another, and, skilled in the eloquence of camps, he so excited their courage that, braving every obstacle, they now deemed that easy which they had adjudged impossible. They soon approached the highest summit, and discerned in the distance the pass which leads from the opening between the towering mountains to the loftiest pinnacle. With shouts of transport they hailed this extreme point as the termination of their labours and with new ardour prepared to ascend. When their strength occasionally flagged under excess of fatigues, they beat their drums, and then, reanimated by the spirit-stirring sound, proceeded forward with fresh vigour.

"At last they reached the summit and there felicitated each other as if after a complete and assured victory. Their hilarity was not a little increased by finding a simple repast prepared in front of the monastery, the provident Consul having furnished the monks with money to supply what their own resources could not have afforded for such numbers. Here they were regaled with wine and bread and cheese, enjoyed a brief repose amid dismounted cannon and scattered baggage, amidst ice and conglomerated snow; while the monks passed from troop to troop in turn, the calm of religious cheerfulness depicted on their countenances. Thus did goodness and power meet and hold communion on this extreme summit."

The troops made it a point of honour not to leave their guns in the rear; and one division, rather than abandon its artillery, chose to pass the night upon the summit of a mountain, in the midst of snow and excessive cold.

Thus did this brave army reach the Hospice of St. Bernard, singing amidst the precipices, dreaming of the conquest of that Italy where they had so often tasted the delights of victory, and having a noble presentiment of the immortal glory which they were about to acquire; as they climbed up and along airy ridges of rock and eternal snow, where the goatherd, the hunter of the chamois, and the outlaw smuggler, are alone accustomed to venture; amidst precipices where to slip a foot is death; beneath glaciers from which the percussion of a musket-shot is often sufficient to hurl an avalanche.

The labour was not so great for the infantry, of which there were 35,000 including artillery. As for the 5,000 cavalry, these walked, leading their horses by the bridle. There was no danger in ascending but in the descent, the path being very narrow, obliging them to walk before the horse, they were liable, if the animal made a false step, to be dragged by him into the abyss. Some accidents of this kind, not many, did actually happen, and some horses perished but scarcely any of the men.

After a brief rest at the hospice the army resumed its march and descended to St. Remy without any unpleasant accident. Napoleon rested and took a frugal repast at the convent, after which he visited the chapel, and the three little libraries, lingering a short time to read a few pages of some old book. He performed the descent on a sledge, down a glacier of nearly a hundred yards, almost perpendicular. The whole army effected the passage of the Great St. Bernard in the space of three days.

The transfer of the gun carriages, ammunition wagons and cannon was the most difficult of all, but the genius of Napoleon accomplished even this seemingly impossible feat. The peasants of the environs were offered as high as a thousand *francs* for every piece of cannon which they succeeded in dragging from St. Pierre to St. Remy. It took a hundred men to drag each; one day to get it up and another to get it down.

It has been said that Napoleon had his fortune to make at this period; but, at the moment of crossing Mount St. Bernard, he had fought twenty pitched battles, conquered Italy, dictated peace to Austria,— only sixty miles distant from Vienna,—negotiated at Rastadt, with Count Cobentzel for the surrender of the strong city of Mentz, raised nearly three hundred millions in contributions,—which had served to supply the army during two years,—created the Cisalpine Army, and paid some of the officers of the government at Paris. He had sent to the museum three hundred *chef d'oéuvres*, in statuary and painting; added to which he had conquered Egypt, suppressed the factions at home and totally eradicated the war in La Vendée.

Napoleon has been pictured crossing the Alpine heights mounted on a fiery steed. As a matter of fact he ascended the Great St. Bernard in that gray *surtout* which he usually wore, sometimes upon foot, and again upon a mule, led by a guide belonging to the country, evincing even in the difficult passes the abstraction of mind occupied elsewhere, conversing with the officers scattered on the road, and then, at intervals, questioning the guide who attended him, making him relate the particulars of his life, his pleasures, his pains, like an idle traveller who has nothing better to do. Thiers says:

"This guide, who was quite young, gave him a simple recital of the details of his obscure existence, and especially the vexation he felt because, for want of a little money, he could not marry one of the girls of his valley. The First Consul, sometimes listening, sometimes questioning the passengers with whom the mountain was covered, arrived at the hospice, where the worthy monks gave him a warm reception. No sooner had he alighted from his mule than he wrote a note which he handed to his guide, desiring him to be sure and deliver it to the quartermaster of the army, who had been left on the other side of the St. Bernard. In the evening the young man, on returning to St. Pierre, learned with surprise what powerful traveller it was whom he had guided in the morning, and that General Bonaparte had ordered that a house and a piece of ground should be given to him immediately, and that he should be supplied, in short, with the means requisite for marrying, and for realizing all the dreams of his modest ambition."

This mountaineer lived for a number of years, and when he died was still the owner of the land given him by the First Consul. The only thing remembered by this attendant in after years of the conversation of Napoleon during his trip was, when shaking the rain-water from his hat he exclaimed, "There! See what I have done in your mountains—spoiled my new hat!—Well, I will find another on the other side."

The passage of the Alps had been achieved long before the Austrians knew Napoleon's army was in motion. So utterly unexpected was this sudden apparition of the First Consul and his army, that no precaution whatever had been taken, and no enemy appeared capable of disputing his march towards the valley of Aosta. After a brief engagement at the fortress of St. Bard and other minor battles in which the French were victorious, they now advanced, unopposed down the valley to Ivrea which was without a garrison. Here Napoleon remained four days to recruit the strength of his troops.

Napoleon now took the road for Milan. The Sesia was crossed without opposition; the passage of the Tesino was effected after a sharp conflict with a body of Austrian cavalry, who were put to flight; and, on the 2nd of June, the First Consul entered Milan, amidst enthusiastic acclamations of the people, who had all believed that he had died in Egypt and that it was one of his brothers who commanded this army. He was conducted in triumph to the ducal palace, where he took up his residence. He remained six days in Milan during which time he gained the most important information, all the dispatches between the court of Vienna and General Melas falling into his hands. From these he

learned the extent of the Austrian reinforcements now on their way to Italy; the position and state of all the Austrian depots, field-equipages, and parks of artillery; and the amount and distribution of the whole Austrian force. Finally, he clearly perceived that Melas still continued in complete ignorance of the strength and destination of the French army. His dispatches spoke with contempt of what he called "the pretended army of reserve," and treated the assertion of Napoleon's presence in Italy as a "mere fabrication." Possessed of all this valuable information Napoleon knew how to proceed with clearness and precision.

The eyes of the Austrian general were at length opened and he was preparing to meet the emergency with all the energy that the orders from Vienna and his great age of eighty years permitted; but his delay had been sufficient to render his situation critical. His army was divided into two portions, one under Ott near Genoa; the other, under his own command at Turin. The greatest risk existed that Napoleon would, according to his old plan, attack and destroy one division before the other could form a junction with it. To prevent such a disaster, Ott received orders to march forward on the Tesino, while Melas, moving towards Alessandria, prepared to resume his communications with the other division of his army.

Napoleon now advanced to Stradella where headquarters were fixed. On the 9th of June, Lannes, who continued to lead the vanguard of the French Army was attacked by an Austrian division superior in numbers and commanded by Ott. The battle, though severely contested, ended in the complete defeat of the Austrians, who lost three thousand killed and six thousand prisoners. The Battle of Montebello was won by sheer hard fighting, there being little opportunity for skill or manoeuvre, the fields being covered with full-grown crops of rye. The shower of balls from the Austrian musketry was at one time so intense, that Lannes, speaking of it afterwards, described its effect with a horrible graphic homeliness. "Bones were cracking in my division" he said, "like a shower of hail upon a skylight." Lannes was subsequently created Duke of Montebello.

Napoleon remained stationary for three days at Stradella, employing the time in concentrating his army, in hopes that Melas would be compelled to give him battle in this position; he was unwilling to descend into the great plain of Marengo, where the Austrian cavalry and artillery which was greatly superior in numbers, would have a fearful advantage. Meanwhile he dispatched an order to Suchet to march on the river Scrivia, and place himself in the rear of the enemy.

General Desaix now joined the army with his *aides-de-camp* Rapp and Savary, he having returned from Egypt and landed in France almost on the very day that Napoleon left Paris, and had immediately received a summons from him to repair to the headquarters of the Army of Italy, wherever they might be situated. Desaix and Napoleon were warmly attached to each other and their meeting was a great and mutual pleasure. Desaix was appointed to the command of a division, the death of General Boudet having left one vacant, and was extremely anxious to signalize himself. Under the impression that the Austrians were marching upon Genoa, Napoleon dispatched Desaix's division in form of the van-guard upon his extreme left, while Victor, arriving at Marengo from Montebello, where he had assisted Lannes, routed a rear guard of four or five thousand Austrians and made himself master of the village of Marengo.

The French and Austrian armies finally came together on June 14th on the plains of Marengo, to decide the fate of Italy.

Marengo was a day ever to be remembered by those who participated in the stubborn struggle. Napoleon fought against terrible odds in numbers and position. A furious cannonading opened the engagement at daybreak along the whole front, cannon and musketry spreading devastation everywhere—for the armies were but a short distance apart, their pieces in some cases almost touching. The advance under Gardanne, was obliged to fall back upon Victor,—who had been stationed with the main body of the first line,—for more than two hours and withstood singly the vigorous assaults of a far superior force; Marengo had been taken and retaken several times by Victor ere Lannes, who was in the rear of him, in command of the second line, received orders to reinforce him. The second line was at length ordered by Napoleon to advance, but they found the first in retreat, and the two corps took up a second line of defence, considerably to the rear of Marengo. Here they were again charged furiously, and again after obstinate resistance, gave way. The retreat now became general, although Lannes fell back in perfect order.

The Austrians had fought the battle admirably. Their infantry had opened an attack on every point of the French line, while the cavalry debouched across the bridge which the French had failed to destroy, and assailed the right of their army with such fury and rapidity that it was thrown into complete disorder. The attack of the Austrians was successful everywhere; the centre of the French was penetrated, the left routed, and another desperate charge of the cavalry would have terminated the battle. The order for this, however, was not given; but the retreating French were still in the utmost peril. Napoleon had been collecting reserves between Garafolo and Marengo and now sent orders for his army to retreat towards these reserves, and rally round his guard which he stationed in the rear of the village of Marengo and placed himself at their head.

To secure a position more favourable for resisting the overpowering numbers of the enemy, Bonaparte now seized a defile flanked by the village of Marengo, shut up on one side by a wood and on the other by lofty and bushy vineyards. Here from the astonishing exertions of their commander the French made a firm stand, and fought bayonet to bayonet with Austrian infantry, whilst exposed at the same time to a battery of thirty pieces of cannon, which was playing upon them with deadly effect. Every soldier seemed to consider this the defile of Thermopylae, where they were to fight until all were slain. With a heroism worthy of the Spartan band they withstood the tremendous shock of bayonets and artillery, the latter not only cutting the men in pieces, but likewise the trees, the large branches in falling killing many of the wounded soldiers who had sought a refuge under them. At this awful moment Bonaparte, unmoved, seemed to court death, and be near it, the bullets being observed repeatedly to tear up the ground beneath his horse's feet. Alarmed for his safety the officers exhorted him to retire, exclaiming, "If you should be killed all would be lost." But the hero of Lodi and Arcola would not retire. Undismayed and unmoved amidst this dreadful tempest, he observed every movement and gave orders with the utmost coolness. The soldiers could all see the First Consul with his staff, surrounded by the two hundred grenadiers of the guard and the sight kept their hopes from flagging. The right wing, under Lannes, quickly rallied; the centre, reinforced by the scattered troops of the left, recovered its strength; the left wing no longer existed; its scattered remains fled in disorder, pursued by the Austrians. The contest continued to rage, and was obstinately disputed; but the main body of the French army, which still remained in order of battle, was continually, though very slowly, retreating.

The First Consul now dispatched his *aide-de-camp*, Bruyere, to Desaix, with an urgent message to hasten to the field of battle. Desaix on his part, had been arrested in his march upon Novi, by the repeated discharges of distant artillery; he had in consequence made a halt, and dispatched Savary, then his *aide-de-camp*, with a body of fifty horse, to gallop with all possible haste to Novi, ascertain the state of affairs

there, according to the orders of Napoleon, while he kept his division fresh and ready for action.

Savary found all quiet at Novi; and returning to Desaix, after the lapse of about two hours, with this intelligence, was next sent to the First Consul. He spurred his horse across the country, in the direction of Marengo, and fortunately met General Bruyere, who was taking the same short cut to find Desaix. Giving him the necessary directions, Savary now hastened towards Napoleon. He found him in the midst of his guard, who stood their ground on the field of battle; forming a solid body in the face of the enemy's fire, the dismounted grenadiers were stationed in front and the place of each man who fell was instantly supplied from the ranks behind.

Maps were spread out before Napoleon; he was planning the movement which was to decide the action. Savary made his report and told him of Desaix's position.

"At what hour did he leave you?" said the First Consul pulling out his watch. Having been informed he continued, "Well he cannot be far off; go, and tell him to form in that direction (pointing with his hand to a particular spot); let him quit the main road, and make way for all those wounded men, who would only embarrass him, and perhaps draw his own soldiers after them."

It was now three o'clock in the afternoon; had Melas pursued the advantage with all his reserve the battle was won to the Austrians; but that aged general (he was eighty years old) doubted not that he had won it already. At this critical moment, being quite worn out with fatigue, he retired to the rear leaving General Zach to continue what he now considered a mere pursuit.

Napoleon's army was still slowly retiring from the field, one corps occupying three hours in retiring three quarters of a league, when Desaix, whose division was now forming on the left of the centre, rode up to the commander, and taking out his watch, said in reply to a question: "Yes, the battle is lost; but it is only three o'clock; there is time enough to gain another!"

Bonaparte was delighted with the opinion of Desaix, whose division had arrived at a full gallop after a force march of thirty miles, and prepared to avail himself of the timely succour brought to him by that far-seeing general, and of the advantage insured to him by the position he had lately taken. Napoleon quickly explained the manoeuvre he was about to effect and gave the orders instantly. He now drew up his army on a third line of battle, and riding along said to the different corps: "Soldiers! We have fallen back far enough. You know it is always my custom to sleep on the field of battle." The whole army now wheeled its front up the left wing of its centre, moving its right wing forward at the same time. By this movement Napoleon effected the double object of turning all the enemy's troops, who had continued the pursuit of the broken left wing and of removing his right at a distance from the bridge, which had been so fatal to him in the morning. The artillery of the guard was reinforced by that which belonged to Desaix's division, and formed an overwhelming battery in the centre.

The Austrians made no effort to prevent this decisive movement; they supposed the First Consul was only occupied in securing his retreat. Their infantry, in deep close columns, was advancing rapidly, when at the distance of a hundred paces they suddenly halted, on perceiving Desaix's division exactly in front of them. The unexpected appearance of six thousand fresh troops, and the new position assumed by the French, arrested the battle: very few shots were heard; the two armies were preparing for a last effort.

The First Consul rode up in person to give the order of attack while he dispatched Savary with commands to Kellerman, who was at the head of about six thousand heavy cavalry, to charge the Austrian column in flank, at the same time Desaix charged it in front. Both generals effected the movement rapidly and so successfully that in less than half an hour the French had put the enemy to rout on nearly all sides. A final charge was now made, when Desaix, whose timely arrival with reinforcements had saved the day, and who was then in the thickest of the engagement, was shot dead, just as he led a fresh column of 5,000 grenadiers to meet and check the advance of Zach. But a few moments before Desaix said to Savary, "Go and tell the First Consul that I am charging, and that I am in want of cavalry to support me." As the brave man fell he said: "Conceal my death, it might dishearten the troops." Napoleon embraced him for an instant, and said, as his eyes filled with tears: "Alas, I must not weep now—" and mounting his horse again plunged into the thickest of the battle.

The whole army fought with renewed vigour on learning of Desaix's death, every soldier being bent on avenging individually the loss of their leader. The combined forces now concentrated themselves and hurled their invincible columns upon the Austrian lines, marching victorious at last over thousands of slain. General Zach, and all his staff, were here made prisoners. The Austrian columns behind, being flushed with victory, were advancing too carelessly, and were unable to resist the general assault of the whole French line, which now pressed onward under the immediate command of Napoleon. Post after post was carried. The terrified cavalry and broken infantry fled in confusion to the banks of the Bormida, into which they were plunged by the French cavalry who swept the field. The Bormida was clogged and crimsoned with corpses, and whole corps, being unable to effect the passage, surrendered. The victory, which had seemed quite secure to the Austrians at 3 o'clock was completely won by the French at six. Napoleon's conduct throughout the day and the bravery of his troops were beyond all praise; and it is no less a fact, that the appearance of victory in one or two parts of the extended field roused the courage of the Austrians to enthusiasm and in some cases fatal recklessness.

They pressed forward to complete their triumph when the Consular guard, called the "wall of granite," met and successfully resisted the shock. The eye of Napoleon fixed the fortune of the day: he foresaw that the enemy, in the ardour of success, would extend his line too far; and what he had conjectured happened. Then it was that Desaix's division rushed amidst the all but triumphant foe, divided his ranks, and finally completed his ruin.

In this sanguine engagement the Austrians lost about 8,000 men in killed and wounded, and 4,000 more were taken prisoners—one-third of their army. The life of Desaix was the sacrifice. The French loss amounted to 6,000 killed or wounded and about 1,000 of them were taken prisoners, a loss of about one-fourth out of 28,000 soldiers present at the battle.

In the estimation of the First Consul this loss was great enough to diminish the joy that he felt for the victory. When Bourrienne, his secretary, congratulated him on his triumph saying, "What a glorious day!" he replied: "Yes it would have been glorious indeed, could I but have embraced Desaix this evening on the field of battle. I was going to make him minister of war; I would have made him a prince if I could." The triumph of this decisive victory was poisoned by Desaix's death. It seems that he never loved, nor regretted, any man so much and he never spoke of him without deep feeling. Desaix met his death at the early age of thirty-three, and France lost in him a great general and a man of rare promise. Savary, who was much attached to him, sought for his body amongst the dead, and found him completely stripped of his clothes, lying among many others in the same condition. "France has lost one of her most able defenders and I my best friend," Napoleon said after the battle; "No one has ever known how much goodness there was in Desaix's heart; how much genius in his head." Then after a short silence, with tears starting into his eyes, he added, "My brave Desaix always wished to die thus; but death should not have been so ready to execute his wish."

Though the vast plain of Marengo was drenched with French blood, joy pervaded the army. Soldiers and generals alike were merited for their gallant conduct and were fully aware of the importance of the victory to France. Thus ended the Battle of Marengo, one of the most decisive which had been fought in Europe, and one which opened to Napoleon the gates of all the principal cities of northern Italy. By one battle he regained nearly all that the French had lost in the unhappy Italian campaign of 1799 while he was in Egypt. He had also shown that the French troops were once more what they had been when he was in the field to command them.

In talking with Gohier one day, Napoleon said: "It is always the greater number which defeats the lesser."

"And yet," said Gohier, "with small armies you have frequently defeated large ones."

"Even then," replied Napoleon, "it is always the inferior force which was defeated by the superior. When with a small body of men I was in the presence of a large one, collecting my little band, I fell like lightning on one of the wings of the hostile army, and defeated it. Profiting by the disorder which such an event never failed to occasion in their whole line, I repeated the attack, with similar success, in another quarter, still with my whole force. I thus beat it in detail. The general victory which was the result was still an example of the truth of the principle, that the greater force defeats the lesser." One of his favourite maxims is said to have been, "*God always favours the heaviest battalions.*"

The Austrians were completely enveloped, and had no alternative but to submit to the law of the conqueror. Melas sent a flag of truce to Napoleon at daybreak on the following morning, and peace negotiations were at once began. In the meeting which followed Bonaparte required that all the fortresses of Liguria, Piedmont, Lombardy and the Legations should be immediately given up to France, and that the Austrians should evacuate all Italy as far as the Mincio.

The surrender of Genoa was strongly objected to by Melas, but the conqueror would not waive this point. The baron sent his principal negotiator to make some remonstrances against the proposed armistice: "Sir," said the First Consul with some warmth, "my conditions are irrevocable. It was not yesterday that I began my military life; your position is as well known to me as to yourselves. You are in Alessandria, encumbered w ith dead, wounded, sick, destitute of provisions; you have lost the best troops of your army, and are surrounded on all sides. There is nothing that I might not require, but I respect the gray hair of your general, and the valour of your troops, and I require, nothing more than is imperatively demanded by the present situation of affairs. Return to Alessandria; do what you will, you shall have no other conditions."

The treaty of peace was signed at Alessandria, the same day, June 15th, 1800, as originally proposed by General Bonaparte. He then

started for Paris by way of Milan, where preparations had been made for a solemn *Te Deum* in the ancient cathedral, and at which the First Consul was present. He found the city illuminated, and ringing with the most enthusiastic rejoicings. The streets were lined with people who greeted him with shouts of welcome. Draperies were hung from the windows, which were crowded by women of the first rank and

who threw flowers into his carriage as he passed. He set off for Paris on the 24th of June and arrived at the French capital in the night between the 2nd and 3rd of July, having been absent less than two months. Massena remained as commander-in-chief of the Army of Italy.

To one of his travelling companions with whom he conversed on the journey to Paris about his remarkable victory at Marengo, he said:

43

"Well, a few grand deeds like this campaign and I may be known to posterity."

"It seems to me," said his companion, "that you have already done enough to be talked about everywhere for a time."

"Done enough," said Bonaparte quickly, "You are very kind! To be sure in less than two years I have conquered Cairo, Paris and Milan; well, my dear fellow, if I were to die tomorrow, after ten centuries I shouldn't fill half a page in a universal history!"

At night the city of Paris was brilliantly illuminated and the inhabitants turned out en masse. Night after night every house was illuminated. The people were so anxious to show their pleasure at Napoleon's miraculous victory that they stood in crowds around the palace contented if they could but catch a glimpse of the preserver of France. These receptions so deeply touched him that twenty years afterwards, in loneliness and in exile, a prisoner at St. Helena, he mentioned it as one of the proudest and happiest moments of his life.

On the day following his return to the capital the president of the Senate—the entire body having waited upon him in state—complimented the conqueror of Marengo in language such as kings were formerly addressed in, and in closing his address said: "We take pleasure in acknowledging that to you the country owes its salvation; that to you the Republic will owe its consolidation, and the people a prosperity, which you have in one day made to succeed ten years of the most stormy of revolutions."

In November following Napoleon's return to the capital he received a letter addressed to him by Count de Lille (afterwards Louis XVIII.) which the exiled prince of the House of Bourbon evidently believed would place him on the throne of France. He said: "You are very tardy about restoring my throne to me; it is to be feared that you may let the favourable moment slip. You cannot establish the happiness of France without me; and I, on the other hand, can do nothing for France without you. Make haste, then, and point out, yourself, the posts and dignities which will satisfy you and your friends."

The First Consul answered thus: "I have received your Royal Highness' letter. I have always taken a lively interest in your misfortunes and those of your family. You must not think of appearing in France—*you could not do so without marching over five hundred thousand corpses*. For the rest, I shall always be zealous to do whatever lies in my power towards softening your Royal Highness' destinies, and making you forget, if possible, your misfortunes. Bonaparte."

The Battle of Marengo was celebrated at Paris by a *fête* on the 14th of July, which presented a singularly interesting spectacle owing to the appearance of the "wall of granite," the members of which, just as the games were about to begin, marched into the field. The sight of those soldiers, covered with the dust of their march, sun-burned and powder-stained, and bearing marks of heroic deeds on the battle-field, formed a scene so truly affecting that the populace could not be restrained by the guards from violating the limits, in order to take a nearer view of those interesting heroes.

Copenhagen

Herbert Russell

The history of nations has plenty of instances to offer of the very trifling causes by which war may be brought about, but none, perhaps, of such utter insignificance in its import as the incident that was answerable for that great Baltic drama whose central brilliant feature was the Battle of Copenhagen. There were, of course, political motives at work influencing and urging on the plucky little Scandinavian Power: that mad and brutal Russian monarch the Emperor Paul secretly forced the Court of Denmark into an attitude of hostility, from which it would doubtless have far sooner refrained. But the direct *causa belli* was as follows:

On the 25th of July, 1800, a British squadron, consisting of three frigates, a sloop, and a lugger, fell in with a large Danish forty-gun frigate, the *Freya*, which was convoying two ships, two brigs, and two *galliots*. Denmark was at that period a neutral Power; England was engaged in conflict with very nearly half of Europe. Orders had been given for British officers to search the ships of neutral Powers for contraband of war, with which there was reason to suspect our foes were being liberally supplied from these sources. In the exercise of his undoubted right. Captain Baker, of the twenty-eight gun frigate *Nemesis*, the senior officer of the little British squadron, hailed the *Freya*, and stated his intention of sending boats to board the vessels under convoy. Captain Krabbe, of the *Dane*, replied with warmth that if any such attempt were made he should unhesitatingly open fire upon the boats. This attitude could, of course, be productive of but one result: both threats were put into execution, and a general action ensued. The *Freya* was overpowered by the superior force against which she had to contend, and was obliged to submit: and the whole of the vessels, including the convoyed ships, made sail for the Downs, where they anchored, the Danish frigate, by command of Admiral Skeffington Lutwidge, keeping her colours flying. Unhappily, the affair had not passed off without bloodshed. The British loss was two men killed and several wounded; the Danes likewise had two men killed and five wounded.

The episode was one to have been easily adjusted by a little political diplomacy, particularly as a tolerably good understanding had previously existed between the two nations. The British Government despatched Lord Whitworth to Copenhagen to arrange the matter: conferences resulted in the agreement that the *Freya* and her convoy were to be repaired at the cost of the English, and released, and the question of the right of British naval officers to search neutral ships was to stand over for discussion at a future period. And here the affair might very well have been allowed to rest. But Russia, the inherent foe of this country, even more than France, although actually deemed to be an ally of ours, seized the opportunity which the popular bitter feeling, briefly aroused in Denmark, gave to her. She established an armed neutrality between herself and Sweden, laid an embargo upon all the British ships then lying in her ports; coalesced with Prussia, and, as history has since shown, practically compelled, by secret pressure, the Court of Copenhagen to join in the general Northern confederacy against Great Britain.

This was an alliance in which Denmark was as a puppet in the hands of the Moscovite string-pullers. The hardy Norsemen, whose sympathies must assuredly have been far more with us at heart than with the bullying, hectoring nation which was urging them into unwilling hostility, were destined to bear the whole brunt of the strenuous conflict. But in those brave days of old the pulse of the British nation beat high, and the spirit of aggressiveness, born of long series of wars, ran strong; the Northern Powers had assumed a menacing posture, and with all her traditional swiftness, England was upon the offensive. On the 12th of March, 1801, there sailed from Yarmouth, under the command of that mild old admiral Sir Hyde Parker, a fleet of fifteen, shortly afterwards increased to eighteen, sail-of-the-line, with a large number of frigates, bombs, and other craft. A terrible disaster, however, weakened the British force at the outset of the voyage. The *Invincible*, of seventy-four guns, carrying the flag of Rear-Admiral

Totty, struck upon a shoal called Hammond's Knoll, where she lay beating for upwards of three hours, and then, gliding off, sank in deep water, taking with her four hundred people.

As second in command of this expedition went Lord Nelson, with his flag in the *St. George,* of ninety-eight guns. In a letter preserved amidst the voluminous correspondence and despatches collected by Sir H. N. Nicholas, Nelson thus describes his command, he wrote on February 9th, 1801:

"You cannot think how dirty the *St. George* is. . . . . The ship is not fitted for a flag. . . Her decks leaky, and she is truly uncomfortable; but it suits exactly my present feelings."

These "feelings," one deplores to discover, were melancholy,

caused by his separation from Lady Hamilton. Nelson hoisted his flag on February 12th, but, owing to the violence of the weather, he was unable to go on board until seven days later. A curious anecdote, illustrating the wonderful tactical genius of the great admiral, is narrated. Immediately prior to his departure for Copenhagen, he was visiting a friend of his, one Mr. Davidson. Speaking of the Baltic expedition he was about to enter upon, Nelson desired a chart of the Cattegat should be procured and brought to him, that he might study it and impress his memory with a knowledge of those waters. This was done, and in the presence of Mr. Davidson, Nelson studied the chart, musing awhile as he overhung it. Then, saying he

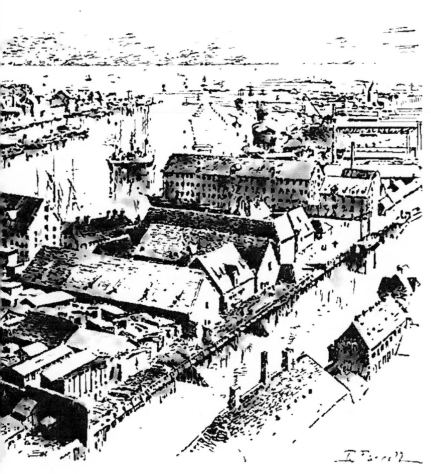

believed the government would spare only twelve ships-of-the-line, he marked out the situation in which he should dispose them, a prophetic indication which was exactly fulfilled.

Meanwhile, in the belief that Denmark, for all her hostile demonstrations, would be willing to enter into negotiations for the preservation of peace, the British Government had despatched the Honourable Nicholas Vansittart to Copenhagen, about a fortnight prior to the departure of the fleet, with full powers to treat. The issue of his mission was, of course, unknown at the time of the departure of Sir Hyde Parker's force. Strong winds prevented the British fleet from making the Naze of Norway before the 18th of March, and scarcely were they within sight of land when a heavy gale, lasting for two days, scattered the ships in all directions. One of these, the *Blazer*, gun-brig, was driven under the Swedish fort of Warberg, and there captured.

The fleet having again assembled, on the 23rd there arrived from Copenhagen the *Blanche* frigate, bringing back Mr. Vansittart and Mr. Drummond, the British *chargé d'affaires*; and the reply of the Danish Government, instead of being one tending towards conciliation, was a sheer message of defiance. On the 29th of March, Lord Nelson struck his flag from the cumbersome and unseaworthy *St. George*, and hoisted it afresh on board the *Elephant*, of seventy-four guns. The gallant spirit had been greatly vexed by Sir Hyde Parker's procrastination on the arrival of the fleet at Cronenberg, outside of which he proposed to anchor in order to give the British minister time to negotiate at Copenhagen. He writes in a letter to his friend Davidson:

"To keep us out of sight is to seduce Denmark into a war. I hate your pen-and-ink men: a fleet of British ships-of-war are the best negotiators in Europe; they always speak to be understood, and generally gain their point; their arguments carry conviction to the hearts of our enemies."

In truth, Sir Hyde Parker, though as brave and hearty an admiral as ever hoisted his flag on a British liner, was scarcely fitted to the command of such an expedition as this. Nelson fretted under the delays which accompanied every fresh move. His own theory was always one of instant action. It was his swiftness which paralysed the French at the Nile, which characterised his masterly manoeuvring at the Battle of St. Vincent, and which assured the success of his scheme at Trafalgar. Colonel Stewart, who commanded the troops in the fleet at Copenhagen, and who wrote a very full account of the battle, points out that Nelson's plan, had he been commander-in-chief, would have been to start immediately from Yarmouth with such ships as were in readiness, and made straight for the mouth of Copenhagen Harbour, leaving the remainder of the fleet to follow as rapidly as they could contrive. Such a dashing movement would have rendered it almost impossible on the part of the Danes to provide against the expected attack by preparations, which Sir Hyde Parker's lingering had enabled them to render formidable. As a specimen of the dallying which went on James in his Naval History writes:

"The pilots, who, not having to share the honours, felt it to their interest to magnify the dangers of the expedition, occasioned a few more days to be dissipated in inactivity. In the course of these. Admiral Parker sent a flag of truce to the Governor of Elsinore, to inquire if he meant to oppose the passage of the fleet through the Sound. Governor Stricker replied that the guns of Cronenberg Castle would certainly be fired at any British ships-of-war that approached."

What other answer could Sir Hyde Parker have anticipated? One may conceive, and sympathise with, the bitter impatience of Nelson at these protracted delays. "Time, Twiss, time," he once remarked to one of his favourite captains, in emphasising the value of instant action. The Danes themselves did not fail to appreciate, and make full use of, the long interval which was granted to them. Even Lord Nelson himself confessed to being astonished by the commanding and formidable appearance of the enemy's preparations. His sketch of the Danish hulks and ships-of-battle certainly exhibits a very powerful array: several towering, two-decked hulks, their sides a-bristle with the muzzles of cannon, and each equipped with a solitary pole-mast amidships; tall, fully-rigged liners, sloops and gun-brigs, and in perspective the great Crown Battery, with the masts of vessels moored within it showing above the walls.

Totally ignoring the threat of Governor Stricker, whose answer Sir Hyde Parker must certainly have accepted as an ultimatum, the British fleet, early on the morning of the 30th, got under way, and with a fine working breeze stood through the Sound in the formation of "line ahead," Nelson commanding the leading division, Sir Hyde Parker the centre, and Rear-Admiral Graves the rear. The Elsinore batteries opened fire, but not one of the ships was struck. Shortly after noon the fleet anchored a little way above the island of Hüen, distant about fifteen miles from the Danish capital; and Nelson, accompanied by Admiral Graves, went away in the *Lark* lugger to reconnoitre the enemy's defences. The preparations looked truly very formidable. Eighteen vessels, comprising full-rigged ships and hulks, were moored in a line, stretching nearly a mile and a half, flanked to the northward by two artificial islands called the Trekrona, or Trekroner batteries, mounting between them sixty-eight guns of heavy calibre, with furnaces for heating shot, and close alongside of these lay a couple of large two-deckers which had been converted into block-ships. Across the entrance of the harbour was stretched a massive chain, and batteries had also been thrown up on the northern shore commanding the channel. Outside of the harbour's mouth were moored two seventy-four gun ships, a forty-gun frigate, a couple of brigs, and some xebecs. To the south of the floating line of hulks and ships, upon Amag Island, several gun and mortar batteries had been erected, so that on the seaward

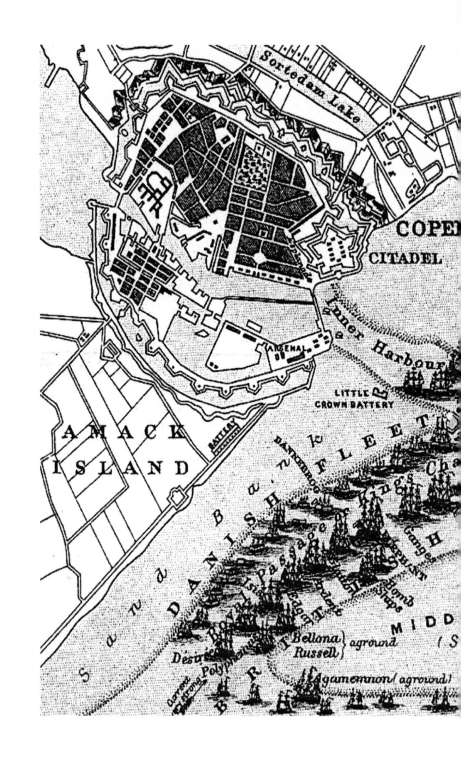

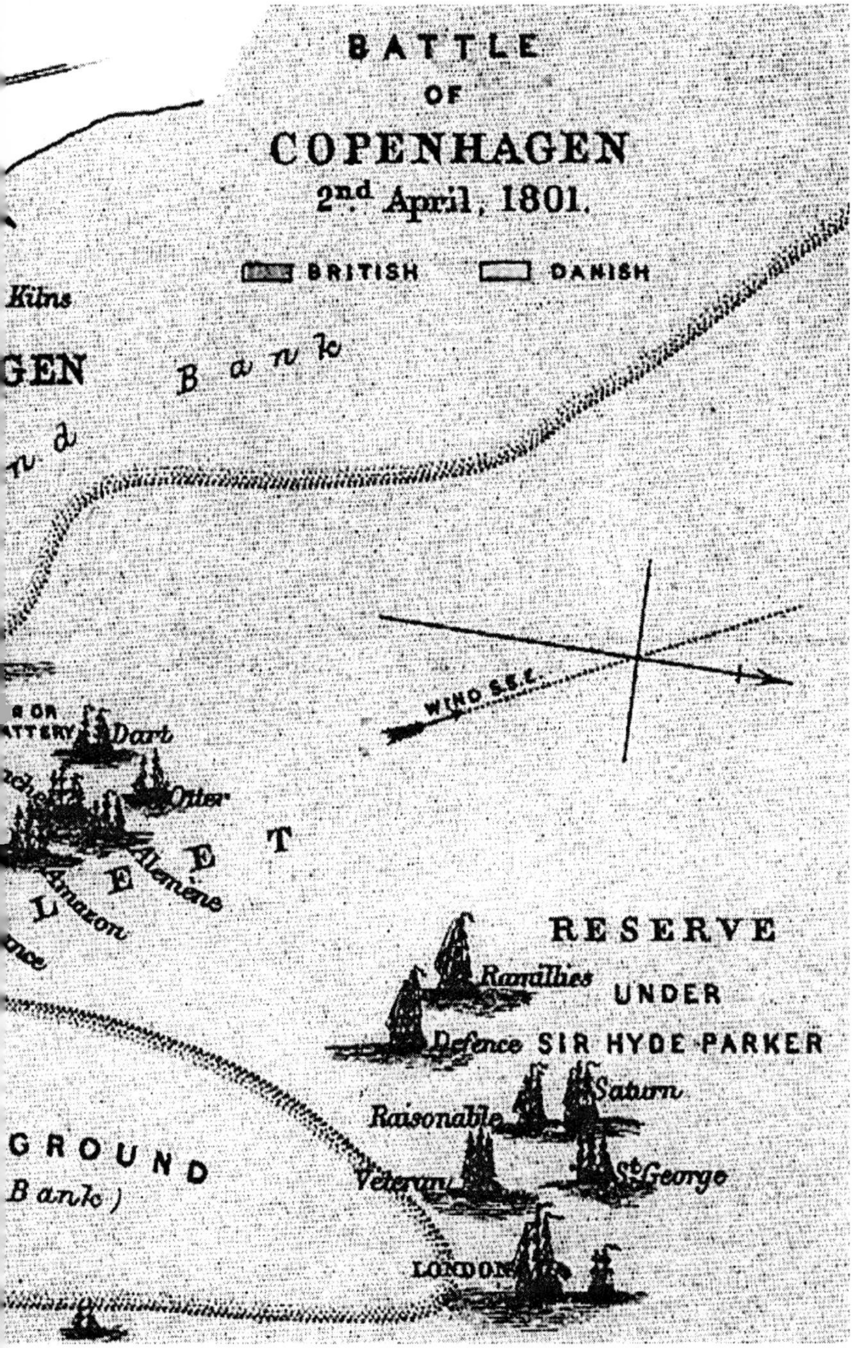

BATTLE
OF
COPENHAGEN
2nd April, 1801.

▩ BRITISH ▢ DANISH

Kilns

GEN

Bank

nd

WIND S.E.

**R OR
ATTERY** *Dart*

Otter

Amazon *Alcmène*

L E E T

RESERVE

Ramillies **UNDER**

Defence **SIR HYDE PARKER**

Saturn

Raisonable

Veteran *St George*

G R O U N D

Bank)

LONDON

side of it Copenhagen was protected by defences which, from end to end, stretched for nearly four miles. Added to these artificial defences, additional security was furnished to the enemy by the dangers of the navigation. The channel, hazardous at all times and beset with shoals, had been beaconed with false buoys, for the purpose of decoying our ships to destruction upon the sands.

Upon these elaborate preparations Lord Nelson gazed, not, we may be sure, with feelings of dismay, but, as he himself admits, with astonishment and admiration. What the Danes thought of the great British admiral is well exemplified by the following anecdote:— When our fleet lay at anchor outside Cronenberg an *aide-de-camp* of the Prince of Denmark came on board the *London*. Whilst seated in the admiral's cabin writing a note the pen spluttered, and the youthful officer exclaimed to Sir Hyde Parker, "If your guns are no better than your pens, admiral, you had better return to England!" He then inquired who commanded the different ships, and presently coming to the *Elephant*, Nelson's name was pronounced. "What!" exclaimed the *aide-de-camp*, "is *he* here? I would give a hundred pieces to have a sight of him. Then, I suppose, it is to be no joke if *he* has come!"

The British fleet having passed into the Sound on the 30th March, as has already been related, and Lord Nelson being returned from reconnoitring the enemy's defences, the commander-in- chief on the evening of this same day summoned a council of war. Sir Hyde Parker was for delaying the attack; Nelson was against losing another moment. "Give me ten sail-of-the-line. Sir Hyde," he exclaimed, "and I will undertake to carry the business through in a proper manner."

Knowing the character of his second, Admiral Parker cheerfully accepted Nelson's offer, and granted him two sail-of-the-line in addition to those for which he asked—that is to say, two fifty-gun ships, which the Danes always reckon as line-of-battle ships. The force at the disposal of Lord Nelson consisted of seven ships of seventy -four guns each, three ships of sixty-four guns, one of fifty-four, and one of fifty guns, five frigates, mounting in all one hundred and ten guns, and several sloops, bomb-vessels, fire-ships, and gun-brigs—a total of thirty-six sail of square-rigged vessels. In all, the British armament numbered seven hundred guns, of which one hundred and fifty-two pieces were carronades. The Danes, by their own accounts, had six hundred and twenty-eight guns, all heavy pieces, and no carronades.

With the indomitable energy which characterised all his manoeuvres, Nelson, accompanied by Captain Brisbane of the *Cruiser*, proceeded in a boat, under cover of darkness, on the night of Sir Hyde Parker's council of war, and explored the channel between the island of Saltholm and the Middle Ground, in order to acquaint himself with the navigation of that dangerous stretch of water. Foot by foot he groped his way over the darkling current through the biting March air and ice of that bitter Northern clime. He rebuoyed the channel, and ensured the safety of his ships, so far as the reefs and sandbanks were concerned, whose whereabouts was treacherously falsified by the Danes. Clark Russell in his *Life of Nelson*, says:

"How many admirals then afloat would have undertaken this duty for themselves? Most of them, possibly, would have applied to such a task Lady Nelson's theory of boarding, and 'left it to the captains.'"

On the 31st of March Nelson made another examination of the Danish fleet, with the result that he abandoned his original project to attack from the northward, and, the wind being favourable, he resolved to deliver the assault from the southward. Late on the morning of the 1st of April the British fleet weighed, leaving Sir Hyde Parker's division of eight sail-of-the-line at anchor in the Middle Ground. Lord Nelson had gone on board the Amazon frigate, in order to take a final view of the enemy's situation and disposition; and when he returned to the *Elephant* he ordered the signal to be made for all the vessels under his command to get under way. It is related that at sight of those colours the seamen of the fleet broke into a hurricane of cheering, which must have been borne to the ears of the Danes afar. The wind blew a light breeze, though from a favourable quarter, and the ships, in perfect line, led by the *Amazon*, threaded the smooth water of the narrow channel. Simultaneously with the weighing of Nelson's division the commander-in-chief's squadron of eight ships also lifted their anchors and floated into a berth a little nearer to the mouth of the harbour, where they again brought-up. And here, throughout that famous battle, lay Sir Hyde Parker, a passive spectator of the Titanic conflict, scarcely, perhaps, illustrating Milton's noble line—

"He also serves who only stands and waits."

At dusk Nelson's column anchored for the night within two miles of the tail of the enemy's line. Throughout the hours of darkness the English guard-boats were stealthily creeping hither and thither upon the narrow waters, sounding and testing the buoys. In one of these boats Captain Hardy, of the *St. George*—the man in whose arms Nelson

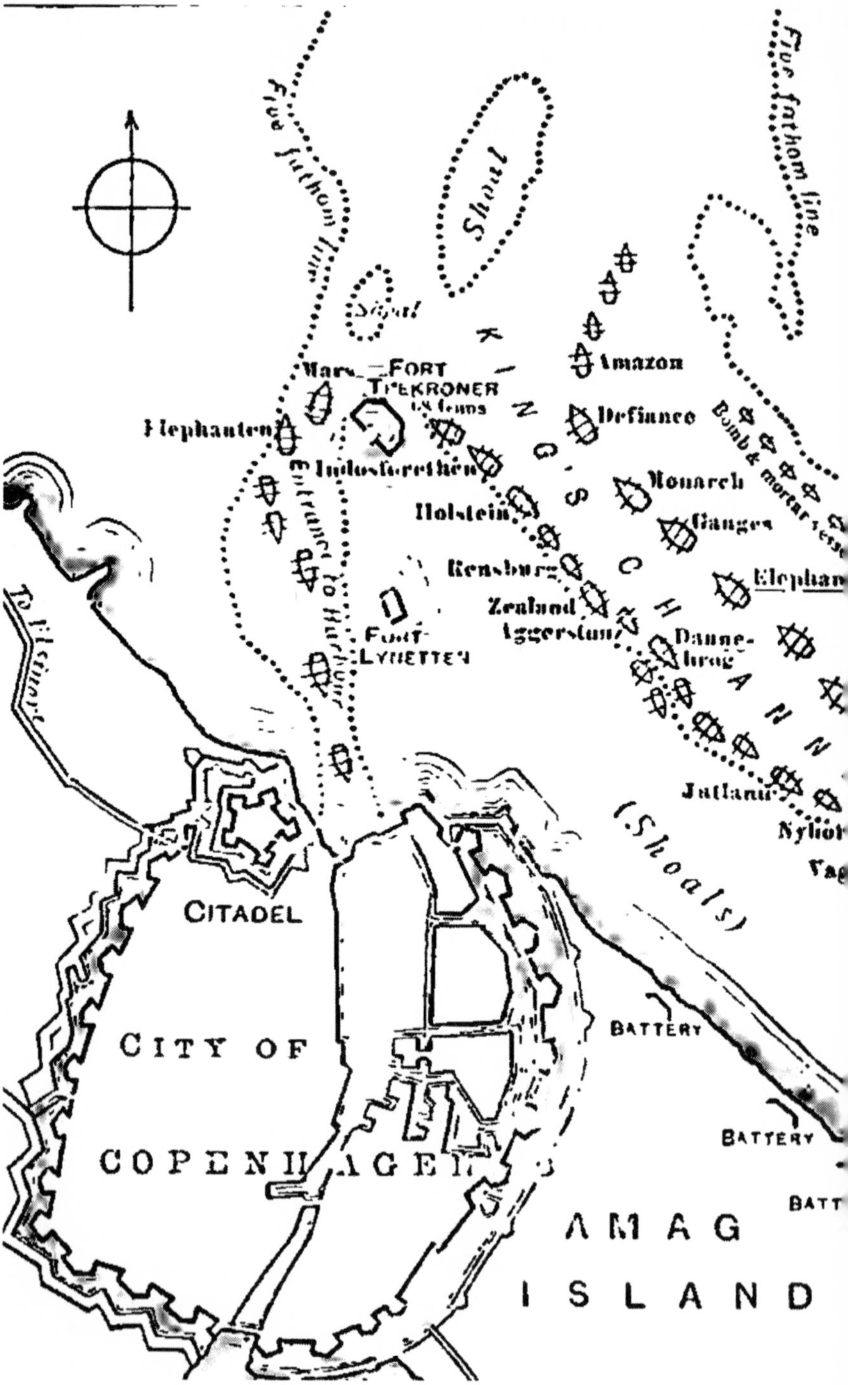

Five fathom line

Five fathom line

Shoal

Signal

Mars FORT TREKRONER
64 Guns

KING'S

Amazon

Elephanten

Defiance

Indusforethen

Monarch

Holstein

Ganges

Elephan

Rensburg

Entrance to Harbour

Zealand
Aggerstan

Danne-
brag

FORT
LYNETTEN

Jatland

CHANN

Nyhot

Vag

To Elsinore

CITADEL

(Shoals)

CITY OF

COPENHAGEN

BATTERY

BATTERY

BATT

AMAG

ISLAND

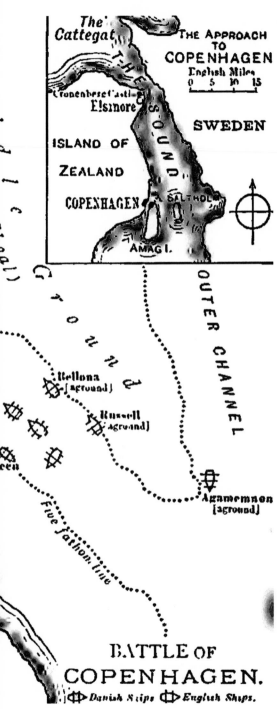

**THE APPROACH
TO
COPENHAGEN**

English Miles
0   5   10   15

The Cattegat

THE SOUND

Cronenbese Castle
Elsinore

ISLAND OF
ZEALAND

SWEDEN

COPENHAGEN

SALTHOL

AMAG I.

Ground

OUTER CHANNEL

Bellona
[aground]

Russell
[aground]

Agamemnon
[aground]

Five fathom line

**BATTLE OF
COPENHAGEN.**

⊕> *Danish Ships*   ⊕> *English Ships.*

died at Trafalgar—actually rowed to within the very shadow of the leading Danish ship and plumbed the water around her with a pole, so as not to be heard. On board of the *Elephant* on the eve of battle Lord Nelson was entertaining most of the captains of his division at dinner. The hero was in high spirits, and drank to *"a leading wind and to the success of the ensuing day."* Until one o'clock that night he was dictating his orders, and, although he retired to his cot, he did not sleep, but every half-hour called for reports of the direction of the wind. At six o'clock he was up and dressed, and at seven caused the signal to be made for all his captains to come on board. James, in his precise Naval History says:

"The day of the 2nd of April opened, as the British had hoped it would, with a favourable or north-easterly wind. The signal for all captains on board the flag-ship was hoisted almost as soon as it could be seen, and at 8 a.m. the several captains were made acquainted with the several stations assigned to them. As circumstances prevented the plans being strictly followed, it may suffice to state that all the line-of-battle ships were to anchor by the stern abreast of the different vessels composing the enemy's line, and for which purpose they had already prepared themselves with cables out of their stern-ports."

This system of mooring abreast of the enemy when the formation of the fleet permitted it, and engaging ship to ship, was a very favourite manoeuvre of Nelson's, and was brilliantly successful both at Aboukir and Copenhagen.

The battle began at ten o'clock. The *Edgar.*, a seventy-four, commanded by Captain Murray, was the first vessel to get into action, and for some while engaged the Danes unsupported. The block-ship *Provesteen* opened a heavy fire upon her the moment she came within range; but she held on all in grim silence until abreast of the craft she had been instructed to tackle, and then poured in a terrific broadside. So narrow was the channel that in bearing down to their respective stations the *Bellona* and *Russell* grounded. The *Elephant*, whose situation was very nearly amidships of the line, signalled for the two stranded ships to close with the enemy. As this order was not at once complied with, Nelson instantly guessed the reason, and with his marvellous promptitude and capacity of swiftly formulating his plans, he changed the intended mode of sailing, and starboarded his helm to provide against a like casualty, trusting to the vessels in his wake to perceive his reason, and follow his example. This they all did, and the rapid manoeuvre of the admiral's ship undoubtedly saved nearly two-thirds of the fleet from grounding.

The craft which Nelson had singled out as his particular opponent was the flagship of the Danish commander-in-chief, Commodore Fischer. This was a vessel named the *Dannebrog*, mounting sixty-two guns and carrying 336 men. When within a cable's length (120 fathoms) of her, the *Elephant* let go her anchor. Nelson wished to get still closer to his foe, but the pilots were afraid of the shoaling water, and when the lead indicated a depth of a quarter less five, they insisted upon bringing-up. The average distance at which the vessels engaged was 100 fathoms—terribly close quarters for such ordnance as the broadside metal of the liners. Lord Nelson had written to Sir Edward Berry in anticipating this fight:

"I hope we shall be able to get so close to our enemies that our shot cannot miss their object, and that we shall again give our enemies that hailstorm of bullets which is so emphatically described in the *Naval Chronicle*, and which gives our dear country the dominion of the seas."

For three hours the cannonade was sustained by each side with undiminished fury, and then the fire of the Danish block-ships, *praams*, and *rideaus* began sensibly to slacken. Still the contest could not be said to have shown symptoms of taking a decisive turn. The *Russell* and *Bellona* were flying signals of distress, and the *Agamemnon*, which had also grounded, had hoisted flags indicating her incapacity. The *London* lay a long way off, and it has been suggested by James that Sir Hyde Parker's view of the progress of the fight might have been imperfect. This is more than probable, when we consider the dense clouds of smoke that must have rolled from the broadsides of the contending ships. The Danes' fire was incessant and furious; nothing seemed yet to have been silenced, and the commander-in-chief, viewing the ceaseless spitting flames from every point of the ponderous looming line of defence, began to grow apprehensive for the British vessels, and to fear that the fire was too hot even for Nelson. The notion of a retreat must have been cruelly mortifying to the fine-spirited old Briton; but his sense of honour was foremost in the motive which prompted him to fly a signal of recall. He said:

"He was aware of the consequences to his own personal reputation; but it would be cowardly in him to leave Nelson to bear the whole shame of the failure, if shame it should be deemed."

And so, according to Southey, with all imaginable reluctance, Sir Hyde Parker, at about one o'clock upon that memorable day, hoisted the signal for the action to cease.

How that order, delivered by the bunting of the *London*, was received by Nelson is one of the immortal episodes of the hero's career. During the course of the battle down to this time, the admiral had been pacing the quarter-deck of the *Elephant*. He was clad in a blue coat, epaulettes of gold fringe, and a plain, small cocked-hat, whilst on his breast were several orders. Colonel Stewart, who was on board throughout the engagement, says "he was full of animation, and heroically fine in his observations." He had just remarked to the colonel that the fight was a warm one, and that any moment might be the last to either of them, and was adding "But, mark you, I would not be elsewhere for thousands!" when the flag-lieutenant reported the order from the *London*, and asked whether he should repeat the signal. "No," replied Nelson; "merely acknowledge it."

He then inquired if signal No. 16 was still flying—that being the order for "Close action." The lieutenant answered that it was. "Mind you keep it so," said Nelson sternly, but with the stump of his ampu-

tated arm working as it was wont to do when the admiral was agitated. Then turning abruptly to Colonel Stewart: "Do you know," said he, "what's shown on board the commander-in-chief, No. 39?"

The colonel inquired the purport of No. 39. "Why, to leave off action." A moment later he burst out: "Leave off action! Now damn me if I do!" Captain Foley stood near: Nelson turned towards him. "Foley," said he, "you know I have only one eye: I have a right to be blind sometimes." He levelled his telescope, and applying his blind eye, said: "I really do not see the signal." It was therefore merely acknowledged on board the *Elephant*, and not repeated, whilst on high, clear of the clouds of smoke, continued to stream the signal for "Close action."

It is only fair to Sir Hyde Parker, in reference to this signal of recall, to quote the statement of the Rev. Dr. Scott, who was chaplain on board the *London*. He affirms in his account of the battle:

"It had been arranged between the admirals (Parker and Nelson) that, should it appear that the ships which were engaged were suffering too severely, the signal for retreat should be made, to give Nelson the opportunity of retiring if he thought fit."

The frigates and sloops of the British fleet, however, obeyed Sir Hyde Parker's signal and hauled off. They were suffering cruelly, and their services were all but worthless. The gallant Captain Riou in the *Amazon*, who had been wounded by a splinter in the head, sat upon a carronade encouraging his men. A volley from the Trekroner batteries killed his clerk and laid low a file of marines. So close was the frigate, that, in rounding, her stern beam grazed the fort. Springing up, Riou exclaimed: "What will Nelson think of us? Come, my boys, let us all die together!" Scarcely were the words off his lips when a round shot cut his body fairly in half.

At about half-past one the fire of the Danes began seriously to slacken, and twenty minutes later it had ceased along nearly the whole of the line astern of the hulking *Zealand*. The enemy had suffered frightfully: the carnage had been terrific, the destruction enormous. Several of the lighter vessels had gone adrift owing to their cables having been shot through. Between the bulwarks the corpses lay strewn knee-deep, reinforcements continually coming off from the shore to serve the guns. Several of the Danish ships had surrendered; but there was much difficulty in taking possession of these prizes, partly on account of the ceaseless fire from the Amag batteries, and partly because of the shot discharged at the boats of the captors by the fresh drafts, who seemed not to heed that the vessels they reinforced had already struck. Particularly was this the case with the Danish admiral's ship, the *Dannebrog*. She was on fire; her colours had been lowered; the commodore had struck his pennant and left her; and still men from the shore continued to swarm into her, firing at the boats sent by the British to take possession, in all defiance to the right and custom of warfare. Enraged by this obstinate resistance. Nelson again directed the batteries of the *Elephant* to open upon her, and another vessel joined in the attack. When the smoke from the two ships' broadsides had cleared away, the *Dannebrog* was perceived to be drifting before the wind, ablaze fore and aft, with her men flinging themselves into the sea.

At about half-past two, the battle now having taken a decided turn in favour of the British, Lord Nelson sent ashore his *aide-de-camp*, Sir Frederick Thesiger, with a flag of truce to the crown prince and the celebrated letter, hastily written by him upon the rudder-head of his ship and addressed "To the brothers of Englishmen—the Danes." In this note he wrote:

"Vice-Admiral Lord Nelson has been commanded to spare Denmark when she no longer resists. The line of defence which covered her shores has struck to the British flag; but, if the firing is continued on the part of Denmark, he must set on fire all the prizes that he has taken, with- out having the power of saving the men who have so nobly defended them. The brave Danes are the brothers, and should never be the enemies, of the English."

Whilst Captain Thesiger was gone on shore with this letter, the destructive fire still kept up by the *Monarch*, *Ganges*, and *Defiance* silenced the fire of the *Indosforethen*, *Holstein*, and the adjoining ships of the Danish line. The *Defence* and *Ramillies*, from Sir Hyde Parker's division, which had heretofore been unengaged, were approaching, and things looked black for the Danes. But the great Trekroner battery, having had nothing but frigates and smaller craft to oppose it, was comparatively uninjured, and sustained a hot, destructive fire. Fifteen hundred men had been thrown into it from the shore, and it was considered too strong to carry by assault. It was deemed wise to withdraw the British ships from the dangerous intricate channel whilst the favourable wind gave them an opportunity of getting out, and signals were actually being made to that purpose when the Danish adjutant-general, Lindolm, came out, bearing a flag of truce, at sight of which the Trekroner and Crown batteries ceased fire; and the action, which had lasted for about five hours, during four of which it had been very fiercely contested, was brought to a close.

The crown prince, whom Captain Thesiger found standing in a sally-port, inquired Nelson's motive in sending a flag of truce. The reply was:

"Lord Nelson's object in sending on shore a flag of truce is humanity; he, therefore, consents that hostilities shall cease till Lord Nelson can take his prisoners out of the prizes, and he consents to land all the wounded Danes, and to burn or remove his prizes."

Formidable preparations had been made on board the British ships to provide against the non-acceptance of the terms of the truce. As Captain Thesiger left Nelson's ship, 1,500 of the choicest boarders of the fleet entered fifty boats, under the command of Colonel Stewart and Captain Fremantle. Clarke and M'Arthur's Life of Nelson says:

"The moment it should be known that the flag of truce had been refused, the boats were to have pushed for the batteries, and the fire of every gun in the fleet would have covered their approach."

Lindolm, on coming aboard the *Elephant* with his flag of truce, had been referred to Sir Hyde Parker; and about four o'clock in the afternoon of this eventful day, Nelson himself went on board the *London*. His own ship, along with several others of the division, in endeavouring to sail out of the narrow channel, had taken the ground, and remained stranded. Lord Nelson, it is recorded, was in depressed spirits, notwithstanding his brilliant success. He appeared to have been shocked by the explosion on board of the *Dannebrog* and the frightful slaughter of that five hours' conflict. "Well," was his remark, "I have fought contrary to orders, and may be hanged: never mind, let them."

The *Elephant* floated again at about eight o'clock in the evening; but Nelson, in ignorance of this, remained for the night on board of the *St. George*. He returned at dawn on the 3rd of April, and finding his own ship was afloat, he made a tour of inspection of the prizes that had been taken. One of the enemy's ships, the *Holstein*, a Danish line-of-battle ship, which lay under the guns of the Trekroner batteries, refused to acknowledge herself captured, although in reality she had struck to the British. Her crew quibbled that they had never hauled down their colours. Two British captains had been on board to demand her, and both had been refused possession. Nelson entreated Sir Hyde Parker to send Captain Otway on this mission, and his request was complied with. As this gallant officer went alongside the *Holstein*, he ordered his coxswain—a bold, impudent fellow—to go into the maintop and bring away the ship's pennant whilst he himself engaged the commander in conversation. The man executed this order, and returned to his place in the gig with the colour hidden in his bosom. Captain Otway's demand of surrender having been refused, he insisted that a ship which had struck her colours must be a prize, and it was agreed to refer the question to the Danish commodore, who was in the arsenal hard by. The commodore replied that the vessel had not struck her colours, adding that the pennant was still flying, and begged Captain Otway to look at it. The British officer gravely replied that he did not see it, and the mortified Danes were compelled to concede the ship. Otway hastily cut her cables and towed her clear of the batteries. This anecdote is related by Captain Brenton.

On the 4th of April Lord Nelson went on shore to visit the Prince of Denmark. Some accounts say the British admiral was received by the populace with marks of admiration and respect: in actual fact, he was accompanied by a strong guard to assure his safety. Negotiations began and continued until the 9th April, the British fleet meanwhile refitting, and preparing to bombard Copenhagen should hostilities be renewed. There was much hesitation on the part of the Danes, and they honestly avowed their fear of the Russians. Nelson answered that his reason in demanding a long armistice was in order to demolish the Russian fleet. There was a great deal of procrastination, and one of the members of the Commission, speaking in French, suggested the possibility of a renewal of hostilities. Nelson caught the words, and rounding upon the commissioner, cried: "Renew hostilities! Oh, certainly, we are ready in a moment: ready to bombard this very night!" The commissioner hastily apologised.

A banquet had been prepared in the palace, to which Nelson was invited; and as he passed through the corridors and up the staircases, he noticed that most of the apartments had been denuded of their furniture, in anticipation of a bombardment. Glancing about him as he proceeded, Nelson exclaimed to a friend, sufficiently loud to be overheard, "Though I've only one eye, I see all this will burn very well."

After this banquet Nelson and the crown prince were closeted together, and a fourteen weeks' armistice was agreed upon. The Danes had no alternative: most of their defences had been taken or destroyed. Nearly all the floating hulks had been cannonaded into sieves. Colonel Stewart states that the ships would have been knocked to pieces in much less time than four hours had Nelson's misgivings of the North Country pilots not prevented him from occupying a much closer position. Admiral Fischer admitted the loss on the Danish side to be about eighteen hundred men. The British had two hundred and

thirty-five men killed and six hundred and eighty-eight wounded. The hulks and block-ships of the enemy were thus accounted for: the *Wagner*, *Provesteen*, *Jutland*, *Kronenburg*, *Hajen*, and *Suersishen* were captured and burnt; the *Aggerstonz* and *Nyburg* sunk; the Zealand was burnt along with the Charlotte-Amelia and the *Indosforethen*; the *Rensburg* was driven ashore and burnt, and the *Holstein* alone was carried away by the British.

The Danes had fought magnificently; but the valour of the seamen whom Nelson led on was irresistible. That memorable day teems with instances of pluck on both sides. One of these, at least, no narrative of the Battle of Copenhagen would be complete without. A lad of about seventeen, named Welmoes, or Velmoes, had charge of a little floating battery, mounting six small cannon and manned by twenty-four men. He poled this raft from the shore to right under the very stern of the *Elephant*, and began peppering the huge liner with his little artillery. The marines of Nelson's ship poured in several volleys with terrible effect, and twenty of the tiny band fell, killed or wounded. But their boy commander stood, waist-deep amongst the corpses, and refused to quit his post until the truce was proclaimed. Such gallantry was a sure appeal to Nelson, and at the banquet he requested the crown prince to introduce him to young Welmoes. Having embraced the lad, he turned to the prince and remarked that such a hero should be made an admiral. "My lord," was the answer, "if I were to make all my brave officers admirals, I should have no captains or lieutenants in my service."

Three days after the conclusion of the armistice—that is to say, on the 12th of April—Sir Hyde Parker sailed from Copenhagen, leaving behind the *St. George* and two frigates. Peace was not formally concluded for a long while, and Nelson remained in the Baltic, watching the Russian fleet. But at length, on the 13th of June, despatches came, commanding the return of the *St. George* to England; and on his arrival, Nelson was created a Viscount for his services at the Battle of Copenhagen.

The Expedition to Egypt

Colonel W. W. Knollys

Too little is known by the general public of the expedition to Egypt in 1801. There is a vague idea that our troops forced a landing in the face of a stout resistance, and that afterwards a battle took place in which the French lost the day and we our general, Sir Ralph Abercromby.

The above is generally all that is known of an expedition which was well conceived, ably carried out, and completely successful. Moreover, it was fertile in acts of gallantry, and served to give a much-needed encouragement to the British army, which during the preceding forty years had not been intoxicated by success.

In 1800 the French were firmly established in Egypt, and the British Government, anticipating a design on India, determined to send an expedition to the land of the Pharaohs. At the same time a force from India of some 6,000 men was to co-operate.

The principal blow was, however, to be dealt by an army under Sir Ralph Abercromby. Before we come to the history of the campaign let us glance for a moment at the career of this gallant soldier. The son of a landed proprietor in Clackmannan, he was born in 1734, and was educated first at Rugby and afterwards at the Universities of Edinburgh and Leipsic. His father obtained for him, in 1756, a commission as cornet in the 3rd Dragoon Guards, and he first' saw active service in 1758, as *aide-de-camp* to General Sir William Pitt in the seven years' war in Germany. He became lieutenant in 1760 and captain in 1762. The year 1793 found him a major-general in command of a brigade in the army which, under the Duke of York, co-operated with the allies in the invasion of France. He greatly distinguished himself, and

displayed much capacity when in command of the rear-guard on the retreat through Holland in August and September, 1704, having, it is worth noting, under his orders Colonel the Hon. Arthur Wellesley. the future Duke of Wellington.

In November, 1795, he was sent at the head of 15,000 men to reduce the French sugar islands in the West Indies, a task which he accomplished with signal success; and after serving as commander of the troops in 1797 in Ireland (and having come into conflict with the Castle authorities by his determination to suppress the outrages of the Yeomanry and Militia), and afterwards in Scotland, he was promoted in 1790 to the rank of lieutenant-general, and sent to the Helder in command of 10,000 men. He acquitted himself so well in this brief campaign that the ministry wished to raise him to the peerage; but, disgusted at the inglorious ending of the expedition, he indignantly refused the proffered honour. This is but the briefest *résumé* of Abercromby's public career as a soldier previously to the expedition to Egypt. Of his private character, we learn from an article in the *Gentleman's Magazine* for 1801 that it was:

"Modest, disinterested, upright, unstained by any negligent or licentious vice. He was a good son, brother, father, husband, as well as an able and heroic general."

It was in Malta that the expedition was organised. Abercromby had been sent to the Mediterranean in 1800, and had proceeded, after an unsuccessful attempt to effect a landing at Cadiz, to Minorca with the intention of landing in Italy—a project which had been baffled by Napoleon's victory at Marengo. The object of the invasion, as has been said, was to arrest the apprehended danger of French designs on India, and it was arranged that the Indian contingent of 6,000 men should co-operate from the south. His army may be said to have been organised at Malta, whence it sailed on the 20th and 21st December, 1800, for Marmorice, in Anatolia, on the coast of Asia Minor.

While there, the ship which was carrying the 42nd Highlanders was visited by a venerable white-bearded old Turk, evidently a person of rank. On seeing the Highlanders in their kilts he burst into tears, and to their astonishment addressed them in Gaelic. It seemed that he was a Campbell from Kintyre, and in early youth—according to the author of *Stewart's Highlanders*, who was with the 42nd as a captain on the occasion of the visit—when playing with a schoolfellow had accidentally killed him. According to another account, the schoolfellow was converted into an adversary slain in a duel. Be that as it may, Campbell fled the country for fear of the law, and had about 1760 joined the Turkish army, in which he had risen to the position of general of artillery.

During the stay in Marmorice—which was made for the purpose

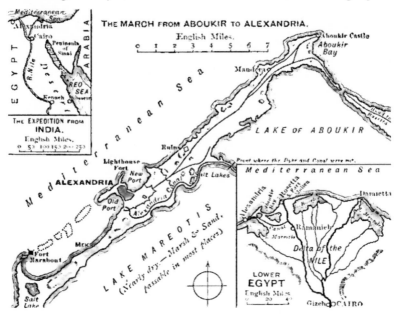

THE MARCH FROM ABOUKIR TO ALEXANDRIA.

73

of collecting gunboats and effecting arrangements with the Turks, both as to co-operation in the invasion of Egypt and a supply of horses— the troops were practised in embarking and disembarking. Only a few horses having been obtained, and there being little hope of immediate effective co-operation on the part of the Turks, the expedition sailed for its destination in February, 1801.

The expeditionary force was composed as follows:

Brigade of Guards.—Major-General Hon.' George Ludlow: eight companies 1st Battalion Coldstream Guards, the flank companies being left at home. The 1st Battalion Scots Guards, the flank companies left at home. Major-General Coote's Brigade.—1st (the Royal) Regiment; two battalions of the 54th Regiment; 92nd Highlanders. Major-General Cradock's Brigade.—8th, 13th, 19th, and 90th Regiments. Major-General Lord Cavan's Brigade.—2nd, 50th, and 79th

Highlanders. Brigadier-General John Doyle's Brigade.—18th, 30th, 44th, 89th. Major-General John Stuart's Brigade.—The Minorca, De Rolles', and Dillon's regiments. Reserve (commanded by Major-General Moore, with Brigadier-General Oakes in command).—Flank companies of the 40th Regiment, and the 23rd, 28th, 42nd Highlanders, 58th, Corsican Rangers, and detachments of the 11th and Hompesch's Dragoons. Cavalry Brigade under Brigadier-General Finch.—12th and 26th Dragoons. Artillery and Pioneers, under Brigadier-General Lawson.

The total strength was 12,864, including about 300 sick, according to Stewart; according to Walsh, 14,967, 300 sick. Wilson gives the force at 15,330 men, excluding officers but including 900 sick; 500 may be perhaps accounted for by Stewart's excluding our Maltese Pioneers and followers. He estimates the effective force at probably not above 12,000. Alison gives the following figures—16,513 infantry, artillery, and cavalry, and 999 sick. On the whole, I prefer to accept Wilson's estimate of 12,000 efficient fighting-men.

The French numbered, according to Alison, 26,520 and 994 sick; but these were distributed at different points—chiefly Alexandria and Cairo. The commander of the French army was Menou, who, from a vain belief in conciliating the Egyptians, had married the rich daughter of the Master of the Baths at Rosetta, embraced the Mahommedan faith, and assumed the name of Abdallah Jacques Francois Menou—singular conduct in one who, under Louis XVI., had been a baron and a *maréchal-de-camp*. A gallant soldier, he displayed little ability as a commander-in-chief, and was not much respected by his officers and men. It may be mentioned that at Marmorice, Abercromby received information which led him to believe that the French army was three times as numerous as the British force. This information was incorrect, as has been shown, but still the numerical superiority of the French was substantial. As will be shown, moreover, fortune gave Menou an opportunity of concentrating of which he failed to take advantage.

On the 1st March the British fleet anchored in the Bay of Aboukir, twelve and a half miles east of Alexandria. It was intended to disembark at once, but owing to bad weather the landing was not effected till the 8th March.

Though the British fleet had appeared in sight on the afternoon of the 1st March, the preparations for resisting a landing were insufficient and comparatively feeble. The total number of French troops in the Bay of Aboukir numbered only 2,000 men, including 200 dragoons with twelve guns. These were formed on the top of a concave arc of sand hills about one mile in length, and rising in the centre to about fifty or sixty feet above the beach. The slope was very steep and the sand loose, so that ascent was extremely difficult.

The arrangements for the landing were as follows:—About 5,230 men were to be put on shore first, to be supported as soon as possible by another body of troops. The men were to be conveyed from the ships in boats of the Royal Navy and of transports. The right flank of the boats was to be protected by the fire of a cutter and two gun-vessels, the left by that of a cutter, a schooner, and a gun-vessel. On each flank also were two armed launches. Two bomb-vessels and three other ships also assisted to cover the landing by their fire. Sir Sidney Smith was in charge of the launches carrying the field-artillery.

The regiments were drawn up in the following order, from right to left:—The four flank companies of the 40th; the 23rd, 28th, 42nd Highlanders, and the 58th from the reserve; the brigade of Guards, the Royal regiment, and the two battalions of the 54th on the left of all. There is no special mention of the Corsican Rangers, but they must have landed, for they lost twenty-nine killed and wounded. Thus, it will be seen that the force first disembarked consisted of the whole of the reserve, with the exception of some cavalry detachments, the Guards, and a portion

Battle
of
ALEXANDRIA
21st. March 1801.

■ English ■ French
□ English before the battle
□ French before and after the battle.

of the 1st Brigade, and ten field-pieces. Of the 2nd battalion of the 54th Regiment, only 200 landed with the first party. General Eyre Coote commanded the whole, but the commander-in-chief was close in rear of the centre. It was reported that Lord Keith, knowing the impetuosity and indifference to danger of Sir Ralph Abercromby, had given a hint to the naval officer commanding the boat which carried the commander-in-chief to keep as far back as possible; nevertheless. Sir Ralph was on shore shortly after the landing of the troops.

The troops who were first to land—about 5,320 in number—were placed in boats at 2 a.m. of the 8th March, but as there was found not to be room for all, some 1,600 were left behind to come ashore in the second trip. The remainder of the 1st and 2nd brigades were removed to the most advanced ships in order to be able to give prompt support. The boats carrying the first instalment were ordered to rendezvous in rear of H.M.S. *Mondovi*, which was out of reach of the enemy's guns. Owing to the great distances which some of the boats had to row, all did not reach the *Mondovi* before 8 a.m., and it was 9 a.m. before the order to advance was given.

The sea was as smooth as glass, and for a short time there was no sign of an enemy. Soon, however, the castle of Aboukir (which from a promontory on the British right was able to take the boats in flank), and the field-pieces on the sand hills, opened a heavy fire with shot and shell, and afterwards grape, which dashed the spray into the boats. Captain Walsh, 93rd Highlanders, *aide-de-camp* to General Coote, who was present on the occasion, and wrote a history of the campaign, declares that the effect was that of a violent hailstorm upon the water. Two boats were sunk, one of them carrying a part of the Coldstream

Guards, and most of those not slain by the fragments of the shell were drowned. The covering fire of our gun-vessels, launches, etc., produced little damage to the enemy, and as the boats approached the shore, to the shot, shell, and grape was added a destructive fire of musketry from the French infantry posted on the sand hills. Our boats, however, never faltered, and the beach was quickly reached. It had been arranged that they should all take the ground together, but owing either to the configuration of the coast or to the fact that some delay was caused in the centre owing to a momentary stopping to pick up men from the two boats that were sunk, the right wing reached the beach first;

then came with a short interval the centre, and finally the left, which consisted of hired transport boats, last of all.

As soon as we got under the fire of the enemy's artillery some of their infantry rushed down to the water's edge and bayoneted men in the act of landing. The four flank companies of the 40th, on the extreme right, are believed to have been first on shore, the first, or among the first, of them being their commander, Colonel, afterwards General, Sir Brent-Spencer. The records of the 40th Regiment state, regarding this officer:

"As he leaped on the beach a French soldier instantly ran out from behind the sand hills, and, advancing to within a short distance from him, took a deliberate aim at Colonel Spencer, and seemingly deprived him of any chance of escape. The colonel, however, was not in the least dismayed, but immediately raised his cane, for he had not drawn his sword, and shaking it at the soldier, his eyes flashing ferociously at the same time, called out, 'Oh, you scoundrel!' Spencer's extraordinary composure under such desperate circumstances seems to have paralysed the Frenchman's intentions, for without firing he shouldered his musket with all possible expedition, and darted off to his comrades behind the sand hills."

General Moore, afraid that the landing would fail unless a post of the enemy situated on a high sand hill—probably that which we have mentioned as being the highest peak—from which the fire was very destructive, ordered Colonel Spencer to take it. At the head of his four companies, aided by the 23rd on his left, he stormed that part of the position with the bayonet, broke two French battalions, pursued them, and captured three

French guns. The 42nd Highlanders landed, and formed up as steadily as if on parade, and with the 28th carried and charged up the sand hills in their front, in spite of the fire of a battalion and two guns. The French infantry were drawn off, and Captain Brown, with the Grenadiers of the 28th, captured two guns with their horses, limber, and waggons, after a desperate resistance, which cost their defenders a loss of twenty-one men. No sooner had this event taken place, when 200 French dragoons attempted a charge, which, however, was promptly repulsed. This body of cavalry, however, soon rallying, swooped down

on the Guards, who had just landed, and had not yet formed up. There was a momentary confusion, but the 58th, on the right, checked the onslaught with their fire, which gave the Guards time to get into line. This done, the Guards soon put the French horsemen to flight. The 54th and the Royal Regiment, being the last to land, appeared very opportunely on the scene, for at that moment they descried 600 French infantry, who had emerged through a hollow in the sand hills, and were advancing with fixed bayonets against the left flank of the Guards. The French, on seeing this fresh body of troops, fired a volley and retreated.

The struggle had now lasted about twenty minutes, and the French had been driven back everywhere. In fact, the action was virtually over. The French and the British, however, kept up a desultory fire of artillery for about an hour and a half, Sir Sidney Smith and the sailors having, with superhuman exertions, dragged up to the top of the sand hills several field-pieces. A little after 11 a.m. the French fell back, and our troops advanced to a position about three miles from the shore. Thus ended this hazardous enterprise, carried out under great difficulties of every description. Nor was our victory dearly purchased, our casualties being only 98 killed, 515 wounded, and 35 missing, the latter having been, no doubt, drowned. The loss of the French was computed at 400 killed and wounded, while eight guns and many horses were captured. So excellent were the arrangements that by nightfall the whole of the army was landed.

The ground which was the scene of subsequent operations was a narrow spit of land with the sea to the north and Lake Aboukir on the south; it is about a mile and a half broad and twelve miles long, on the western extremity being Alexandria. Immediately after the battle some men-of-war boats entered Lake Aboukir by an open cut. This lake was of great value to us in respect to protection to our left flank and also for the transport of stores. Thus a serious difficulty was overcome, as we were almost destitute of transport animals. Sir Ralph Abercromby was at first anxious about the water supply, but his fears were soon dispelled by Sir Sidney Smith, who pointed out to him that wherever date trees grew water was to be found. Explorations were at once made, and proved successful. The castle of Aboukir on our right rear was blocked by the Queen's and the 26th Dragoons, who were dismounted.

On the 9th, the wind being fresh, no stores could be landed. On the 10th the disembarkation was completed, and the day was spent in reconnoitring. Some skirmishing between the advanced posts took place, a surgeon and twenty men of the Corsican Rangers being captured by a sudden advance of French cavalry.

On the 12th the army advanced about four miles to Mandora Tower. Beyond a little skirmishing between the cavalry and advanced posts no fighting took place on that day. On the 13th the advance was continued, with a view of turning the right flank of the enemy, who had taken up a strong position across the peninsula, chiefly on an elevated ridge. The French having been reinforced by two regiments of infantry and one of cavalry from Cairo, and by a portion of the garrison of Rosetta, were able to put about 6,000 men and between twenty and thirty guns into line; their cavalry numbered 600 well-mounted men. Menou arrived that day from Cairo, but does not seem to have directed the operations. The advance was commenced in a line of three columns, with intervals. Each column was in mass of open column. The right column consisted of the reserve under Sir John Moore in two brigades, one in rear of the other. It skirted the sea, and was a little in rear of the alignment of the rest of the army. In the centre was Craddock's brigade with the 90th Light Infantry, under Colonel Hill as advanced guard. Craddock's brigade was followed by Coote's brigade, the Guards, under Ludlow. The left consisted of Cavan's brigade, with the 92nd Highlanders as advanced guard, Stewart's foreign brigade and Doyle's brigade following in succession.

It may here be mentioned that there had been a little redistribution of regiments, and that a battalion of marines had been added to the force. Our small body of cavalry, badly mounted and only numbering 250, were on the right of the rear of brigade of the centre column. During part of the advance Lake Aboukir was on the left, and that flank was covered by a flotilla of armed boats under Captain Hillyar, R.N.

The army marched off at 6.30 a.m., and when it came within range the enemy opened fire from their artillery, which, searching out the columns from front to rear, caused heavy loss. Sir Ralph Abercromby, therefore, ordered a deployment of the left and centre columns. They formed two lines—Doyle's brigade remaining in column in rear of the left, while the Guards formed a third deployed line in rear of Coote's brigade in the centre. The reserve, under General Moore, remained in column on the right, with their leading company on a level with the second line of the deployed troops.

Whilst the troops were deploying the French descended from their position to attack us. The 90th, which were forming the advanced guard of the centre column, were charged with impetuosity by the

26th Chasseurs-à-Cheval. It is said that the 90th, as a light infantry corps, wore helmets, which fact induced the French to mistake them for dismounted cavalry. Hence they were attacked with great confidence. It is not expressly so stated, but it would appear that the 90th received their opponents in line, receiving them with a steady fire which emptied many saddles. Some of the more daring of the *chasseurs* persevered, however, charging right up to the regiment, but were quickly bayoneted. Colonel Hill on this day owed his life to his helmet, which resisted a bullet which would otherwise have penetrated his head. In the *mêlée* Sir Ralph Abercromby, whose personal intrepidity amounted to a fault, was surrounded, his horse was shot, and he was nearly captured, when he was rescued by a party of the 90th. At about the same time the 92nd Highlanders were attacked by the 61st Demi brigade, named "The Invincibles," and were also exposed to the fire with grape of two field-pieces. Nothing daunted, however, the gallant Highlanders sprang to meet them, and poured in so heavy and effective a fire that the 61st Demi brigade were forced to retire, abandoning the two guns. For their brilliant conduct on this occasion both the 90th and 92nd were authorised to bear "Mandor" on their colours. About this period of the action Dillon's regiment attacked with the bayonet a bridge over the canal and captured it and two guns. The French fell back, halting from time to time to open on us with their well-horsed batteries. Our progress was, on the contrary, slow, for our guns had to be drawn by hand and the sand was heavy. About 2.30 p.m. the French having abandoned the crest which they had originally occupied, took up a fresh position on another crest close in front of the forts and works of Alexandria.

About this time the 44th captured in splendid style a bridge over the Alexandria Canal, which skirted the southern border of the field of battle; the bridge was defended by a body of infantry and cavalry, and a howitzer. The bridge was taken, but so heavy an artillery fire was opened upon them by the French, who had brought up some heavy guns from the fortification in their rear, that the regiment was obliged to fall back Almost simultaneously the commander-in-chief ordered General Hutchinson, with Stewart's and Doyle's brigades, to attack the enemy's right. Hutchinson was, however, met with a destructive fire, and Abercromby, fearing that even if he carried the enemy's position the fire of the forts in rear would prevent him from retaining it, ordered a retreat to the position which the French had held before the action. Our force was about 12,000 combatants, that of the French about 6,000. The respective losses were: English, 1,300; French, 700 and 4 guns.

On the 15th we commenced to fortify our position, and the day was also remarkable as being that on which tents were brought up. So few, however, could be issued, that though intended only for fifteen, it was found impossible in some cases to serve out more than one tent to every thirty-nine men. Up to that date all ranks, from the commander-in-chief downwards, had slept in the open air. On the

17th the Castle of Aboukir, having endured a very severe bombardment, surrendered. On the 18th a portion of our cavalry had an affair which, though at first in our favour, ended disastrously.

On the 19th 500 Turks joined the army. On the 20th nothing occurred, but on the following day took place the Battle of Alexandria, the most severe action of the campaign.

Before entering on an account of this glorious combat, we must describe the position of the British army on that eventful day.

The reserve, under General Moore, was on a height close to the sea, on the right and in advance of the rest of the army. On the right of the heights were some extensive ruins, evidently of palatial origin. These were occupied by the 58th. On the left of the ruins was a rock spoken of as a redoubt, but really it had no rear face. The garrison consisted of the 28th. In rear of the above-mentioned troops were the flank companies of the 40th, the 23rd, the Corsican Rangers, and the 42nd Highlanders. On the left of the height occupied by the reserve was a valley some 300 yards broad, in which was placed the cavalry attached to the reserve. To the left, or south, of this valley, on some rising ground, were the Guards, with a redoubt on the right, a battery on the left, and a trench and parapet connecting these two along the front. In echelon to the left rear was Coote's brigade, next to him stood Craddock's brigade. On the extreme left, and with part of his brigade thrown back *en potence*, so as to face the shore of Lake Mareotis, stood Cavan. In second line were Doyle's brigade, Stewart's Foreign brigade, and the dismounted cavalry of the 12th and 26th Dragoons.

It must be mentioned that Lake Mareotis was dry, and almost everywhere passable by troops. On the morning of the 21st March the army was under arms, as usual, at 3 a.m. Half an hour later a musket shot rang out in front of the left of the line. Several cannon shot followed, and the enemy advancing temporarily obtained possession of a small *flèche*, occupied as a picket post. The enemy were, however, soon driven back, and a profound stillness ensued. General Moore, who happened to be general of the day, had, on hearing the first shot, hurried to the left. He soon, however, became convinced that the real attack would be on the right, and he therefore galloped back through the dark, close, cloudy, and now silent night, to the reserve. Scarcely had he returned when cheers, followed by a roar of musketry, proved that his military instinct had not misled him.

The 28th, which had been drawn upon the left of the redoubt, were ordered into it, and the left wing of the 42nd, under Major Stirling, were directed to take up the ground left vacant by the 28th; while the right wing, under Lieutenant-Colonel Alexander Stewart, remained 200 yards in rear. The enemy attacking the redoubt were received with so heavy a fire that they fell back precipitately to a hollow a little in rear, but soon recommenced fire. In the meantime, taking advantage of the darkness, which was so great that an object two yards off could not be distinguished, a French column, consisting of the "Invincible Legion" and a six-pounder gun, advanced by a shallow valley intervening between the 42nd and the Guards, and, wheeling to their left, were marching in profound silence between the parallel lines of the wings of the Highlanders.

It was, as we have said, still pitch dark, and the Frenchmen were further shrouded by the heavy smoke which hung about in the still night air. Their feet made no noise as they fell on the sand, and it is probable that they might in another two or three minutes have reached the ruins unperceived. Providentially, a soldier of the right wing, blessed with exceptionally sharp sight, perceived them, and stepping out of the ranks said to his captain—Stewart of Garth—whose account we follow:

"'I see a strong column of the enemy marching past in our front:

I know them by their large hats and white frocks; tell the general, and allow us to charge them.' I told him to go back to his place, that the thing was impossible, as Major Stirling, with the left wing of the regiment, was in our immediate front, at a distance of only 200 yards. However, as the man still insisted on the accuracy of his statement, I ran out to the front, and soon perceived through the darkness a large moving body; and though I could not distinguish any particular object, the sound of feet and clank of arms convinced me of the soldier's correctness. In a few minutes Colonel Stewart and Major Stirling's wings charged the column in the ruins. But it is proper to explain that it was only the rear rank of the left wing that faced about and charged to their rear; the front rank kept their ground to oppose the enemy in their immediate front."

When the column saw that it was discovered it rushed towards the ruins. As the Frenchmen passed the so-called redoubt, but which was open at the gorge, the rear rank of the 28th faced about and fired into them, the front rank of the regiment, unmoved, keeping up a fire on the enemy in their immediate front. Weakened in number and in some confusion, the "Invincibles" dashed onwards to the ruins, chased by the fleet-footed Highlanders, and penetrated through the openings. The 58th and 40th, however, coolly faced about and fired into the French, When surrounded by foes and corpses the gallant survivors—two hundred in number—surrendered. The standard was given up by the officer who bore it to Major Stirling, of the 42nd, who handed it over to Sergeant Sinclair, with orders to remain with the trophy by the captured six-pounder. Subsequently he was overthrown and stunned by some French cavalry. When he came to himself the standard was gone. Sometime after, Lutz, a soldier of the Minorca regiment, came to Colonel Abercromby, and presenting him with the standard, said that he had taken it from a French officer. Lutz obtained a receipt and twenty-four dollars. This incident caused some ill-feeling. Generals Moore and Oakes were wounded about this time, but remained at their posts.

As the enemy made a renewed attack on the left of the redoubt, Moore ordered the 42nd out of the ruins to bar their progress. As the French drew close, Sir Ralph Abercromby, ever at the point of danger, rode up and called out: "My brave Highlanders, remember your country; remember your forefathers." Responsive to the appeal, the gallant Black Watch, with a true Highland rush, dashed at the foe and sent them back in disorder and hotly pursued. Moore, who had a keen vision,

differing in that respect from Abercromby, who was very short-sighted, saw through the smoke and dust some fresh French columns drawn up on the plain, and three squadrons of cavalry about to charge through the intervals of the retreating infantry. Consequently, he ordered the regiment back to its old ground. Owing to the noise of the firing the order was only heard by some. Those companies who did hear it fell back, the others hesitated, and the next

instant the French cavalry were upon them, with a fair prospect of success, for the advanced companies of the 42nd were broken and scattered. The men, however, stood firm, in groups, or even individually maintained a stout fight with the dragoons. The companies which had been withdrawn in time, and were in comparatively regular formation, repulsed the cavalry, some of whom galloped through intervals, and were almost all cut off. After penetrating our line, some wheeling to the left were shot by the 28th, who faced to the rear. They were thrown into great disorder by their horses falling over the tents and holes for camp kettles, dug by the 28th.

It must have been about this time that Sir Ralph Abercromby was nearly slain on the spot by a French dragoon. He had sent off all his staff with orders when some French cavalry reached the spot where he was watching the fight. Two of the number rode at the general, and were about to cut him down, when the gallant veteran succeeded in wresting the sword from his adversary', who was immediately shot by a corporal of the 42nd, the other, seeking to ride away, was bayoneted by a private of the same regiment. According to Sir Robert Wilson, he was unhorsed in the struggle, and it is probable that he was, for we read of him as having afterwards walked to the redoubt on the right of the Guards, and as continuing to walk about. It was only known that he was wounded by the sight of blood trickling down his leg, for he never mentioned the fact that a bullet had lodged in his hip-bone, though he complained of a contusion in the chest, caused by a blow from the sword which he had eventually wrenched from the French officer. When the battle was over he found himself utterly spent, and after having his wound attended to by a surgeon of the Guards, he was carried on board ship. While being carried to the beach he asked what had been put under his head. His *aide-de-camp* replied, "Only a soldier's blanket."

"Only a soldier's blanket!" was the rejoinder; "make haste, and return it to him at once."

A little after the attack on the right the French assailed the Guards, driving in their skirmishers. The enemy advanced in echelon from the right, with a view to turning the left flank of the Guards. Several companies, however, of the 3rd Guards being thrown back, this manoeuvre was foiled, and the steady fire of the brigade, coupled with the advance of Coote's brigade on the left, caused the French to retire.

Scarcely had this first charge of cavalry by two regiments of dragoons failed than the second line of three regiments made another bid for success. There was a good deal of hand-to-hand fighting. According to Captain Walsh, the 42nd opened and let the enemy's horsemen through, and then faced about and fired on them. The survivors strove to force their way back, but few succeeded, their commander, General Roize, falling about this time. At the end of the charge General Stewart's brigade came up on the left of the 42nd. This was about 8.30 a.m., and till 9.30 a.m., when the battle virtually ceased, nothing but a combat of artillery and an interchange of musket-shots between the skirmishers took place on this part of the field. About 9.30 a.m. the French began to retreat, and by 10 a.m. all firing ceased.

It may here be mentioned that the 92nd Highlanders had marched very early that morning towards Aboukir, where it was to go into garrison, being much weakened by casualties in action and from disease. When the firing began it was two miles from camp, but under Major Napier immediately countermarched, and arrived to take part in the battle. It is noteworthy that the steady conduct of the 42nd stood them in such good stead that, though twice engaged hand-to-hand with the enemy's cavalry, only thirteen men received sabre wounds.

The French of all arms behaved with the utmost gallantry, but it is with regret that we mention that many of them when captured were found to be drunk, and among these was an officer of high rank.

The brave and chivalrous Sir Sidney Smith was, as usual, to be found wherever the danger was greatest. In the heat of the action Major Hall, *aide-de-camp* to General Craddock, while carrying orders, had his horse killed under him close to where Sir Sidney was watching the fight. Disengaging himself from his fallen steed he went up to Sir Sidney and begged that officer to hand over to him his orderly's horse. Sir Sidney at once consented, and told the man to hand over his horse. While he was speaking a cannon ball took off the dragoon's head, on which Sir Sidney calmly remarked, "This is destiny. The horse. Major Hall, is yours."

A period of inactivity followed the battle, due, probably, to the wound of the commander-in-chief. The problem, moreover, was one that it was difficult to solve. Evidently the garrison of Alexandria would not soon surrender, and their position was strong, their resources considerable. A French force, moreover, occupied Cairo, and the capture of that city would produce a great moral and material effect. The distance, however, was great, and owing to the want of transport it would be necessary to advance on the capital by the Nile. The co-operation of the Turkish army was needed, and it was not yet certain to what extent it might be depended on. The attitude of the Mamelukes had also to be taken into consideration.

Finally, General Baird was expected from India, and some regard to his movements had to be paid. At length, however, General Hutchinson, who had succeeded to the command of the army on the death of Sir Ralph Abercromby—who expired on board ship on the 28th—decided on a plan of operations, the main feature of which was an advance by a portion of the army under his personal command, while maintaining the investment of Alexandria by the remainder, under General Coote. He was the more readily enabled to arrive at a determination because, on the 26th March, the Capitan Pasha with 6,000 Turks had disembarked in the Bay of Aboukir.

On April 2nd Colonel Spencer, with the 58th Regiment, the flank company of the 40th, and thirty of Hompesch's Hussars, was sent to take possession of Rosetta and obtain command of the Nile, for the fleet wanted water and the troops fresh meat. Besides, the capture of Rosetta was the first step in an advance on Cairo. Spencer, was accompanied by 4,000 Turks. On the 6th, Hutchinson, learning that the garrison of Rosetta had been strengthened, reinforced Spencer with the Queen's

Regiment. On the morning of the 8th, Spencer, after a trying march across the desert, reached the neighbourhood of Rosetta, and found the passage of the river opposed. It was, however, soon forced, and a portion of the French marched to El Hamed, on the left bank of the Nile. Detaching the Queen's and 500 Arnauts, under Lord Dalhousie, to blockade Fort St. Julien, with the remainder of his force Spencer marched south, and established himself in front of the enemy's strong position at El Hamed. There he remained for several days, sending out reconnoitring patrols and receiving reinforcements. Gradually during the following twelve days his command was brought up to—exclusive of Turks—about 300 cavalry, 4,000 infantry, with, however, only 100 horses and camels for the guns, water, and provisions.

Returning to Alexandria, Hutchinson had, with some misgiving and reluctance on account of the devastation which the measure would cause, cut the embankment of the canal and let in the waters of Lake Mareotis. By this means he almost isolated the town from external supplies, and succoured and secured his left flank, which was now protected by a flotilla on the lake. He was thus enabled to leave with confidence Coote, with about 6,000 men, in front of the town, while employing about 5,310 of his troops and some 9,510 Turks in the advance along the banks of the Nile towards Cairo. He himself proceeded to Rosetta, where he arrived on the 26th April. Lord Dalhousie and the Capitan Pasha had established batteries against Fort St. Julien, and on the 16th a bombardment was begun from these, aided by the fire from the men-of-war and boats. On the 19th, after a sturdy resistance, the garrison—having lost 40 killed and wounded and being without any prospect of succour—surrendered, with 15 guns and 268 men.

On the 4th May a detachment, consisting of two 6-pounders, two 12-pounders, two howitzers, twenty of the 12th Dragoons, the 89th Regiment, and a body of Arnauts with four horsed Turkish guns, under Colonel Stewart, was sent across the Nile, with instructions to conform with the movements of the main body on the left, or eastern, bank of the Nile. On the following day the main body advanced in two columns, one with its left on the Nile, the other with its right on Lake Edki, the whole preceded by about 4,000 Turks. At the same time a flotilla of Turkish gun-vessels and some armed *djerms*, or native boats, manned by British sailors, sailed up the Nile. On the 6th the allies halted in front of the canal of Deroute, which falls into the Nile on its left, or western, bank. To the south of the canal the French occupied a fortified position. On the 7th May our cavalry reported that the

French had fallen back, and by a return picked up in their abandoned camp it was found that they numbered 3,031 men, including 600 cavalry. On this day the army was joined by 600 Syrian cavalry—badly mounted, undisciplined, half-naked, and many without weapons. On the 9th the army marched towards Rahmanieh, where the canal of Alexandria falls into the river.

Some skirmishing took place on both banks of the river, and Stewart constructed batteries with which to fire on the fort and an entrenched camp situated on the left bank. The next morning, when Stewart was in readiness to open fire, the fort capitulated and the entrenched camp was found to be evacuated. On the 11th the army resumed its advance, and on that day a very daring capture of a French convoy was effected.

The Arabs reported that a considerable body of French were advancing with a convoy, but perceiving signs of the proximity of the British army they retired into the desert. General Doyle was ordered to pursue with 250 cavalry, two guns, and his own brigade. Colonel Abercromby, son of the deceased Sir Ralph, and Major—afterwards Sir—Robert Wilson, officers on the staff, galloped ahead of the force only accompanied by a few Arab horsemen. After a seven-miles' ride they came up with the enemy, whom they found drawn up in square, surrounding the convoy. A little desultory interchange of shots between the French and the Arabs ensued. Major Wilson thought that audacity might prevail, and obtained leave from Colonel Abercrombie to try what he could do. Riding up, waving a white handkerchief, he announced that he had been sent by the commander-in-chief to demand surrender on condition that the officers and men composing the party should be sent at once to France. Colonel Cavalier, commanding the convoy, peremptorily ordered him to withdraw. Major Wilson, however, persisted, saying that the offer was merely dictated by humanity, and that Colonel Cavalier would incur a heavy responsibility if he refused it. To this harangue the French colonel paid no apparent attention, and again ordered him to retire. Major Wilson, fearing that his attempt had failed, was riding towards General Doyle, who in the meantime had come up with his cavalry and was within musket shot of the convoy. Suddenly a French officer galloped up to Major Wilson with a request that he would return to Colonel Cavalier, who requested time for consultation with his officers. After some haggling it was agreed that the convoy should surrender, being allowed to lay down their arms in the British camp and not in the desert before the

Bedouins. The convoy consisted of 500 men—cavalry, infantry, and artillery (including 120 of the Dromedary Corps, who were picked men)—one four-pounder gun, and 550 camels. The captors and captured then marched off to camp, not meeting the infantry till they had gone about a league. It appeared afterwards that the mention of "France" by Major Wilson had produced so great an effect on officers and men that Colonel Cavalier had little choice about surrendering.

General Belliard, commanding at Cairo, marched with 5,500 men and twenty-four guns to attack the Grand Vizier. Meantime the advance of the British continued up the Nile, with occasionally great sufferings. On the 23rd .May, for instance, there was a sirocco, the thermometer rising to 120°. So oppressive was the heat that several horses and camels died, and the troops were almost suffocated. On the 1 6th June the British army arrived in front of Gizeh, opposite to Cairo, on the other side of the river. Preparations being made to attack Gizeh, and the Grand Vizier being in position on the east bank of the Nile, threatening an assault on Cairo, General Belliard on the 22nd sent an officer to propose a capitulation on terms. The negotiations came to an end on the 26th, and it was agreed that the garrison should surrender on the following conditions—that General Belliard and his troops, numbering upwards of 10,000 effective men, with fifty guns, were to retain their arms and personal property and be escorted to the coast. On arrival at the coast they were to be embarked on ships provided by the British and transported to France. By a secret article it was agreed that the French should give up their arms as soon as they were on board ship. By the embarkation return given by Belliard, it would appear that exclusive of native auxiliaries and civil employees, the total number amounted to 12,862.

On the 15th July the march to the coast began, in the following order: A body of Turks, the British army, the French, the British cavalry, with some Mamelukes. On the 9th, 10th, and 11th August, the British troops from Cairo marched into camp before Alexandria, having arranged for the embarkation of Belliard and his men. This reinforcement was needed, for though Coote had been joined by several battalions and some drafts, sickness had reduced his force to 3,200 men fit for duty. Now the army in front of Alexandria was raised to a strength of 16,000 effective men. On the 16th, at nightfall, Coote with the Guards, under Ludlow, Lord Cavan's and General Finch's brigades, a few field-pieces, and 100 of the 26th Dragoons—4,000 men in all—were transported in boats by Lake Mareotis to the west of Alexandria. In order to cover the

movement, on the morning of the 17th, Doyle with his brigade was ordered to carry the green hill on the French right, while Moore was directed to send some light troops to seize the knoll about a quarter of a mile in front of the French lines, in order to reconnoitre. Little opposition was made to Doyle, the French abandoning the open work on the green hill, the artillery on which had been previously removed. Moore having accomplished his object, and the knoll being too far advanced to be maintained, returned to our lines. About 7 a.m. the enemy made a furious sortie with 600 men, and attempted to recapture the green hill. The 30th, being somewhat scattered to avoid the heavy cannonade, were taken by surprise, but rallied and charged, driving back the French, who suffered some loss.

Returning to Coote: he, seeing at daybreak that the French occupied a strong position about three miles to the west of Alexandria, left Finch to make a demonstration, whilst he himself went on a few miles further, where he disembarked, without meeting with any opposition, at a spot nine miles from Alexandria. The isthmus between the sea and Lake Mareotis was about half a mile broad. On the night of the 17th-18th there was a causeless alarm in camp, with much shouting and confusion. Coote issued a severe animadversion, but a brigade order stated that his remarks did not apply to the Guards. On the 18th, batteries were begun against Fort Marabout, which was situated on a rocky islet guarding the western entrance to the harbour of Alexandria, and 1 50 yards from the shore. The batteries were begun on the night of the 17th-18th, and aided by the fire of some small Turkish and British ships and a body of sharpshooters. On the 20th the tower fell, and on the 21st the commandant surrendered, with ten guns. The garrison had originally consisted of 200 men, of whom fourteen were killed. Our loss was *nil.*

On the 18th the army advanced about one and a half miles towards Alexandria. On the 22nd the army advanced some four or five miles under a heavy cannonade, which caused us a loss of sixty killed and wounded.

The French suffered heavily, and abandoned a strong fortified position, with several guns, their camp, and baggage. On the 23rd, Coote was reinforced by a brigade under Colonel Spencer. The enemy threw many shells into our camp, causing, however, but few casualties. Soon after dark on the 24th the 20th, 54th, and a detachment of the 20th Dragoons proceeded to drive in the French outposts. Our men used only the bayonet, and were completely successful after a struggle of about three-quarters of an hour. About 11 p.m. the French made a determined counter-attack, but after another three-quarters of an hour's fighting were again driven back, their loss on both occasions being heavy, seventy Frenchmen having been captured and thirty bayoneted, besides the casualties caused by our handful of cavalry. It was in one of these actions that a most singular event occurred. Coote was advancing with a company of the Guards when a discharge of grape smote them taking off several hats but hurting no one. On another occasion a detachment of the 26th Light Dragoons were ordered to charge a halted body of French cavalry. The latter retired slowly on a battalion of infantry, who were not perceived by the 26th till they were within thirty yards. The French then fired a volley which marvellous to relate, hit neither man nor horse.

Coote on the 23rd had opened a fire from three 24-pounders and five mortars, and the French had retaliated with a heavy artillery fire. The crisis was evidently at hand, and in order to create a diversion for Coote the troops in the east, and the British batteries on that side, opened fire, and in the evening an *aide-de-camp* of Menou came in under a flag of truce with a proposal for an armistice preparatory to capitulation. After some disputing and a prolongation of the armistice, the capitulation was signed on the terms that the French Army was to be transported to France, with ten guns and private property. The embarkation return of General Menou was 11,780, exclusive of 350 sick to be left behind. Our force in front of Alexandria at that time was about 16,000 men. When General Menou signed the capitulation, he wrote his name "Abdallah Ali y Menou." Turning to General Hope, who represented General Hutchinson, he said that he was no doubt surprised

at his signature;
that he had tried most
religions, but found the Mahom-
medan the best. After the capitulation Menou entertained Hope at
dinner, horseflesh being one of the dishes. Probably this was a little *tour
de théâtre*, but there can be no doubt that the French had been reduced
to great straits for animal food, though they had plenty of rice left.

It was thought in the British camp that Menou was somewhat
hurried into a surrender by fear of possible atrocities by the Turks in
case Alexandria was carried by assault. It is undoubtedly true that, as
soon as the armistice was signed, he begged Coote to withdraw all
Turks and Mamelukes from the outposts. He had good reason to fear
the cruelty of the Turks, for when Madame Menou was captured at
Rosetta the *capitan pasha* wanted to send her as a slave to the *sultan*.
The British authorities, however, insisted on despatching her to join
her husband at Alexandria.

It now only remains to say that General Baird, with a force of
5,500 European and native troops, had proceeded from India, landed
at Cosseir, in the Gulf of Suez, marched 120 miles across the desert to
Keneh, on the Nile, and thence descended in boats to Rosetta, which
he reached on 31st August. He was thus too late to take part in the
campaign. Towards the end of September the army was broken up,
most of the regiments belonging to it quitting the country.

The loss of the British army during this campaign was 23 officers,
20 sergeants, 2 drummers, and 505 rank-and-file killed; 108 officers,
1 quartermaster, 140 sergeants, 17 drummers, and 2,723 rank-and-
file wounded; 7 officers, 1 quartermaster, 2 sergeants, 1 drummer,
and 73 rank-and-file missing.

As usual, however, disease was responsible for more casualties than the enemy. Ophthalmia and dysentery caused much loss. From ophthalmia 200 men became blind of one eye and 160 of two eyes. At one time there were no fewer than 700 men out of the two battalions of the Guards in hospital from ophthalmia, and Ensign Dalrymple, 3rd Guards, records in his unpublished journal that 3,500 men had died in the hospitals.

It will be seen from a perusal of the preceding pages that this was by no means, as so many believe, one sharp fight at landing and another in the battle before Alexandria; but a campaign in which, besides these two actions, there were many skirmishes, including some severely-contested engagements. Altogether, it was a creditable and glorious expedition, doing much to re-establish our military reputation, which, owing to our bad fortune in Flanders, had fallen very low in the estimation of Europe.

The value set upon it by the British nation was shown by the rewards conferred on the army and navy: a peerage to Abercrombie's widow, with a pension of £2,000 a year; the same to General Hutchinson, with the Bath; Lord Keith created a British peer; thanks of parliament to the army and navy employed. In addition, the *sultan* granted the Order of the Crescent to the generals, and to other officers gold medals.

The Janissary Rebellion at Widdin

William V. Herbert

When I was in the quaint old city of Widdin, on the Danube, in the year of war, 1877, I used to ask, with the triple curiosity of a stranger, a soldier, and a youngster, many such questions as these: Who built this bazaar? Who laid down that street? Who erected this formidable bastion or planned that gun-spiked quay? Whose work is this handsome mosque or yonder fine drinking-fountain? Who endowed the college of law and divinity and founded the public library? Who created that—in a hot summer—thrice-blessed institution the free ice-factory? A hundred more such questions might I quote without once varying the answer, which was, in each case, without exception: "Pasvan Oglu," until I was tempted—after the analogy of Mark Twain's *Innocent Abroad*—to cry out: "*Cut it short, and say, once for all: Who created the world*"— "Pasvan Oglu." And, sooth to say, popular sentiment in that ancient and storm-buffeted city had hallowed the very name to such an extent that many a good Mohammedan verily believed that it was he, the dead man, who commanded the nightingales to sing so divinely in the leafy shadows of that lonely graveyard, the broad blue Danube to yield its unfathomable wealth of silver-sheen fish, the flowers to bloom luxuriantly in the fertile marshes beyond the weather-beaten city wall.

"Who was Pasvan Oglu?" is the reader's pertinent question. He was many things: a good citizen, an able governor, a great warrior, the protector of the poor and the oppressed, a man with a big heart and a full purse, a loyal friend to cherish and a terrible foe to contend against, for seven years *pasha* of Widdin, and the hero of the Janissary

Rebellion of 1801, the central episode of which—the great Battle of Widdin—constitutes the earliest noteworthy bellicose action of the present century, and the subject of this humble memoir.

Pasvan Oglu was the scion of a family of *grandees* of purest Tartar blood. His ancestors had "*come over with the Conqueror*," to apply this well-worn phrase to Turkey—that is, they had been among the first Ottoman invaders of the Balkan Peninsula, and his grandsire in the twelfth generation had helped the Sultan, Bayazid I., to conquer Widdin in 1398. Since that sanguinary event the family had lived in the city, and had acquired great wealth, local influence, and a reputation extending far beyond the boundaries of the *pashalik*. Pasvan Oglu (Oglu means son) was the son of Pasvan, who had been, about the year 1770, *pasha* of Widdin, and at that period our hero saw the light of day. He fought, as a youngster, with distinction in the war of 1788 to 1791 between Turkey on the one hand and Russia and Austria on the other. When peace was made he returned to his native city and "waited for something to turn up," the something fervently expected being the chance to employ once more his arms, and with a better personal result to his ambitious nature.

Now, there reigned in Stamboul at that time Sultan Selim III., who, like his predecessors on the tottering Turkish throne, had the ardent desire to abolish the corps of *Janissaries*, but differed from them in so far as he lacked not the courage to carry his intention into execution. Consequently, he decreed (about 1795) that the *Janissaries* be for ever done away with, by Imperial will and command. But this did not at all suit the other party interested, the *Janissaries*, who were almighty in the empire, were the real masters of the situation, and had ever been in the habit of making and unmaking *pashas*, princes, commanders, and even sultans, according to their own sweet will and pleasure.

The *Janissaries*, the professional soldiers of Turkey, formed at that time the country's standing army, and numbered some two hundred thousand men, all trained, disciplined, equipped, with a magnificent *esprit de corps*, renowned and feared throughout Europe for their bravery and their dash in attack, hated for their cruelty, execrated even by their own compatriots for their unscrupulousness and lawlessness. The two centres of this powerful body of men were Constantinople and Belgrade. The latter was the capital of the Western *Janissaries*, who numbered about eighty thousand, and were distributed over Servia, Herzegovina, Bosnia, and the Western portions of Bulgaria, Eastern Roumelia, and Macedonia.

Pasvan Oglu saw his chance. He identified himself with the *Janissary* movement, and from all parts of the country the proscribed soldiers flocked to Widdin. The *sultan* declared Pasvan and his followers to be outlaws; Pasvan responded by having his own name enrolled among the Janissaries. He collected an army of fifty thousand men, and, backed by the feeling of force, addressed a demand to the *sultan* to the effect that henceforth the *pashalik* of Widdin be semi-independent, like Morocco, Fez, Algiers, Tripolis, and Tunis, and that he, Pasvan Oglu, be acknowledged as Pasha of Widdin, with the distinction—the highest in the empire—of three horsetails. Needless to say, the sovereign declined peremptorily and contemptuously, and Pasvan Oglu, in the year 1797, announced the independence of Widdin from Stamboul, called himself *kral* (king), and actually had the audacity to declare war upon his lawful liege and master. The latter collected an army of a hundred thousand men to subdue the rebellious vassal, and entrusted its command to the Fanariot, Michael Sutsos, Hospodar of the Danube Principalities (Moldavia and Wallachia, the present Roumania). The Sutsos are a renowned and ancient family of Greek nobles, which has produced many distinguished men.

The Fanariots, the Christian Greeks of Stamboul, were thus named after the Turkish word *Fenar*, meaning lighthouse, from the fact that at one time they had been the Turkish equivalent of the Trinity Brethren of England. Originally slaves, they had risen in the empire to enormous wealth and influence, the latter equalled only by that of the *Janissaries*. Indeed, it may be justly said that at that period, and until Mahmoud II. exterminated that all-powerful Praetorian Guard by sword and fire in the streets of Stamboul (1826) and, simultaneously, the Hellenic war of liberation proved disastrous to the influence of the Greek subjects of the Porte, the *Sultanic* crown was suffered to be only by reason of the rivalry and the jealousy that existed between the two dominant factors of the empire—the *Janissaries* and the Fanariots—either of which was strong enough to kick the quaking throne of the Ottoman *sultans* into eternity, but was debarred and prevented therefrom by the other. And this is not by any means the only occasion in modern history that a monarchy has been kept alive by the rivalry of opposing factions. But whereas the power of the *Janissaries* lay in terror and physical force, that of the Fanariots consisted of the subtle but far more dangerous influence of cunning courtiership, intrigue, and diplomacy.

The third mighty factor in Oriental affairs—the *harem*, with its

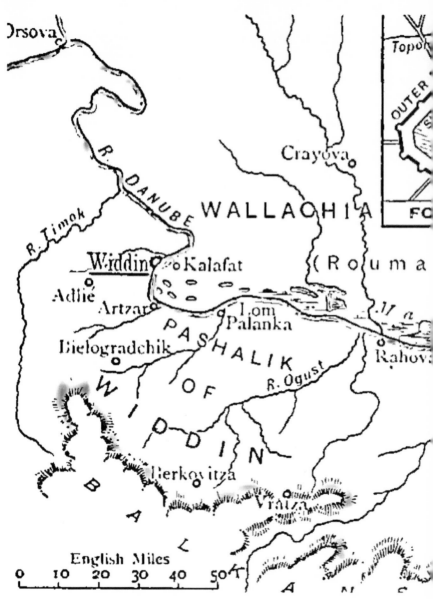

concomitants of eunuchs and petticoat *pashas*—had not acquired, at that time of blood and iron, the sly but tremendous influence which it exercises in these latter degenerate days of jabber and "soft soap."

At about the beginning of the present century the Fanariots were at the zenith of their power. Certain high offices were always filled from among their ranks, one of these being the post of Hospodar (or Vice-

YARDS
0   500   1000

ESS OF WIDDIN.

Nikopoli

Sistova

Plevna

Regent) of the Danube principalities. Michael Sutsos, the newly-appointed commander-in-chief of the Imperial army, held this dignity. His troops consisted for the most part of the native soldiers of his domain. He had also some battalions of the Stamboul *Janissaries*, who had remained faithful to their sovereign, and a large number of levies among the loyal Turkish populace. Both sides had in their ranks many adventurous vagabonds and outcasts— Austrians, Italians, Germans, Englishmen—for the French Revolution had fired the world; the First Consul was full to repletion of military projects and enterprise; Europe formed coalitions against the impertinent upstart; France, Austria, Russia, Italy, Portugal, Turkey, Sweden, England were all busily engaged in warfare: in short, this whole miserable little globe of ours wallowed in blood.

Michael Sutsos and his great army marched slowly Danube upwards, the bulk on the right, a small detachment on the left bank, and as they proceeded they ate the country bare, behaving like enemies in a conquered land, and leaving desolation and famine in their wake.

Pasvan Oglu did not wait to be attacked in Widdin. He had a fine and well-entrenched position some fifteen miles below his capital, on the right bank, near the spot where the Danube turns westward, whilst on the opposite shore Calafat was occupied and fortified. The collision took place in March, 1801, and resulted in the crushing defeat of the Imperial army.

By a lucky chance, the present author has obtained an interesting document, which for nearly a hundred years had lain dormant between lavender and rosemary, among letters, the paper of which has darkened to a deep yellow and the ink faded to a like hue with age, and with many other sentimental mementoes of the past, in an oaken box belonging to some good housewife in a German city. The document—an epistle written by a young German of the international vagabond type to his mother—describes fully the Battle of Widdin of 1801, in which he, the writer, took part on the Imperial side.

The quaint and shrewd observations in this letter fill much of what was hitherto a complete blank in the records of history; and for most of the following details the author has drawn upon the contents of the said epistle.

In the early morning Pasvan Oglu's mounted outposts, who for weeks had scoured the country, brought the news of the approach of the long-expected Imperial army. Pasvan rightly conjectured that his best chance lay in attacking the enemy before he had recovered from the fatigues of the march and formed for battle; consequently, he left his camp in charge of a small detachment, and sallied forth with the bulk of his force, among which were many thousands of irregular horsemen, the peasantry of the province.

The first encounter took place near Artzar. The vanguard of the Imperials, attacked both in front and in the left flank, was "rolled up." The *Janissaries*, true to their traditions, disdained to wait for the orthodox "preparation by artillery," but rushed to the attack at full speed and with fixed bayonets, uttering their well-worn battle-cries: "*Bismillah!*" (In the name of God), "*Allah Akbar!*" (God is great), "*Inshallah!*" (Please God), and other phrases from sacred writings. In accordance with an old custom, they carried their cooking vessels into combat the big company-copper being the most sacred of their emblems—like the standard of our modern regiments—to defend which whole *ortas* (the tactical units of the *Janissary*, of five hundred men each) would lay down their lives cheerfully. Before such a wild-cat rush the raw levies of the Imperial army were as banks of sand to the swell of the incoming tide, and crumbled away. The vanguard was almost annihilated, and the front portion of the main body was routed, battalion by battalion, as they came up in marching order, whilst the Janissaries were in battle formation, which gave them a tremendous advantage. But toward the centre of the column the assailants encountered the best troops of which the Hospodar disposed—the Stamboul *Janissaries* and the Imperial Guards—who made so brave a stand that Pasvan Oglu's forces received a decided check, which almost threatened to become fatal.

The rebels were thrust back as far as their camp, and whilst behind their trenches they restored the lines and formations, the Imperial army had leisure—the first during the day—to deploy and shape itself into solid battle array.

This happened about noon. So far, the combat had been between infantry: the cavalry had done little, whilst the cannon on both sides had hardly fired a shot, for the rebels had left the greater part of their ordnance behind in their camp, and the Imperial artillery, forming the central portion of the march-column, had never had the chance to deploy and enter into action. But now, as the slowly approaching imperials came within range, both parties let loose a hailstorm of bombs and shells, and when this had lasted for an hour or so the two forces, each forming a compact mass, a solid whole, came into awful collision. There was no pretence of tactical science, no display of cunning and skill; it was simply a furious rivalry for mastership. The rebels struggled for their existence; the Imperials fought—or imagined that they did, which is much the same thing—for the integrity of the empire. For many hours the combat swayed to and fro from one part of the vast battlefield to another; now forward, now backward went the lines; now to the left, now to the right spread the tumultuous devilry: now this side, now the other had the best of it. Finally, towards dusk, a last and desperate rush of Pasvan Oglu's best *ortas* spread disorder among the *Sultanic* ranks, and the battle—which had lasted from dawn to sunset with only one brief interruption—ended not only in the defeat but practically in the annihilation of Michael Sutsos's army.

Meanwhile, a battle of its own, equally furious and sanguinary though on a smaller scale, had been fought on the other side of the river, near Calafat. Here the positions of assailant and defender were reversed: the right flank column of the Imperial army had the offence, and Pasvan Oglu's detachment in charge of Calafat had enough to do to hold the place. Again and again the Roumanian levies charged, but the stolid tenacity of the rebels was not to be denied.

When toward the close of the day, messengers in swift boats brought tidings from the other bank, the Janissaries sallied forth, and here, too, the majority of the Imperial troops perished, the rest dispersed. Many hundreds were drowned when trying to cross the river in order to gain the fancied protection of the larger body on the other side.

I have confined myself to the broad outlines of the battle, and even these I cannot affirm to be positively accurate, since these events are treated with scant attention in the records of history. My most diligent search has revealed the deplorable fact that five volumes out of ten—good, standard works—make the barest mention of Pasvan Oglu and his rebellion, while the rest ignore both man and incident completely. What I have stated above is gathered from that German letter, preserved for nearly a century in sweet-smelling dried herbs, and from tradition, such as I ascertained by intercourse with the natives of Widdin in 1877, when it was fresh and strong among them.

The Turkish records are quite silent. "The Turks write inflated bombast and call it history," says Moltke. Civil war and defeat do not lend themselves to the enunciation of cheap sentiment and pothouse valour; therefore, *conticuere omnes*. Moreover, the words *"Yeni Seri"* ("new troops," corrupted by European writers into *"Janissaries"* and the like) were cursed in 1826 by the Sultan Mahmoud II. with a solemn and awful anathema, and are banished for ever from all Turkish books, records, and prints.

For campaigning purposes, the Imperial army was wiped out. On either side no quarter had been asked or given. Thirty thousand Imperials and 20,000 rebels are said to have been slain, which would mean a loss of exactly one-third of the fighting forces—an occurrence almost without a precedent in the whole history of warfare; and granted even that these figures are somewhat exaggerated, we cannot doubt but that the battle was of the most sanguinary description. The whole immense train of the Imperial army and almost its entire artillery—over a hundred pieces—fell to the victors. The ordnance Pasvan Oglu utilised for placing Widdin—already a formidable stronghold—into a thorough state of defence.

What was the result of this terrible civil strife? Simply that Selim III. was left without an army, and that Pasvan Oglu was master of the situation. This he proceeded to demonstrate *ad oculos*.

Tainted as he was with the predominant malady of his time—love of bloodshed—and imbued still with the good old Turkish notion as to the rights and privileges of victors and conquerors, he made it terribly manifest to the country at large that he had the upper hand. First he crossed the Danube with a large following, and devastated Wallachia as far as, and including, Crayova in the most thorough-paced and ultra-Turkish fashion. Then he returned to his own side, and did the same kind office to Bulgaria. Downstream his troops marched, with death and ruin in their train. Rahova, Plevna, Sistova, and many

other towns were conquered and sacked, and finally Pasvan actually besieged, stormed, and destroyed the Danube fortress, Nikopoli, one of Turkey's finest and most renowned strongholds.

The whole country was literally aflame; everywhere anarchy, murder, and arson reigned supreme, and Stamboul was totally helpless. At last Selim III. offered peace (end of 1801), consenting to the continuance of the *Janissaries*, granting his enemy the *pashalik* of Widdin for life, with the coveted three horsetails, and promising complete oblivion of all that had happened and unconditional amnesty to all who had participated in the revolt, entreating, as sole counter-claim, that Pasvan Oglu should nominally acknowledge his (the *sultan's*) *suzerainty*. The rebel acquiesced, returned quietly to Widdin, dismissed his troops, laid down his battered arms for ever, and henceforth devoted himself exclusively to the welfare of his native city, to which he was attached with the most tender and—in such a man—quite incomprehensible affection. The *Janissaries* withdrew to Belgrade and their other homes, and the Widdin citizens, who had all along been in complete sympathy with the rebels, acclaimed Pasvan Oglu, with much pride, pomp, and circumstance, as their leader and governor.

Both parties to the contract kept their bargain honourably: Pasvan Oglu never again rebelled against or quarrelled with Stamboul, and was at all times quite willing to acknowledge freely the sovereignty of the *sultan*, although he was shrewd enough to take care that in practice he was independent; while Selim III. forgave everybody and everything. The destroyed homesteads and hamlets, towns and villages, were rebuilt, and the fugitive survivors of the Imperial army returned to their homes and their occupations. Thus ended this singular revolution, the total cost of which in human life must have been close upon a hundred thousand beings, whilst the material loss to the commonwealth of the nation is simply inestimable.

For six years Pasvan Oglu reigned as Pasha of Widdin, wisely and well, respected and beloved by his subjects, feared by his enemies, almost worshipped by the poor. His *pashalik* extended from the Ogust in the east to the Timok in the west, and from the Danube in the north to the Balkans in the south. He kept a regal court, dispensed a sumptuous hospitality, and lavished his great wealth with a free hand. He made many important concessions to the oppressed Rayahs, who in return served and obeyed him with a never-failing loyalty; he was, *persona grata* with the Jews, because of the tremendous increase in the trade and the prosperity of Widdin, brought about by his wise measures; and that his co-religionists venerated him goes without saying. He had a perfect mania for building, introducing many Western innovations; and, unlike British speculators of these latter days, he did not attempt to shift the responsibility on the shoulders of poor deluded dupes, but paid for his passion out of his own pocket in solid coin. Although the most orthodox of Turks and a bigoted Moslem, he was quick to see and ready to adopt the advantages of European culture and civilisation. He never lost sight of what is due to one's native land,

and made Widdin so formidable a fortress that in the great wars of the century (1828, 1853, 1877) the city was one of the mainstays of the empire, and proved to be impregnable.

Although in reality the last of the grand *pashas* in the old style, with their semi-autonomy and their courts of barbaric splendour, with their affection for the time-honoured turban and their hatred of the new-fangled *fez* (which two headgears were at that time the symbols of conservatism and progress in Turkey), he was also the first of the succession of the wise modern *pashas* who have governed that city so well, until, in 1878, the Turkish reign in Widdin came to a close.

With his rigid affection for the old and his lavish introduction of the new, his love and aptitude for war, and his splendid *régime* in peace; his reign of terror and devastation when a foe, and his heart that would melt, his eyes that would swim, his pockets that would open, at the appeal of the most pitiful beggar, of the most despised and abject Christian "dog"—he was made up of contrasts. The man was a living paradox, but that made him what he was: a factor that helped to shape the history of his country. The influence for good of a single man—of a single deed of such a one—will sometimes spread over empires and last through decades; and I, in Widdin, seventy years after his death, felt the influence, in every hour that I spent within the city gates, of Pasvan Oglu, the last of the great *Janissary* leaders.

Pasvan died in 1807, in the zenith of his power and popularity, worshipped throughout a province. He was buried within the city walls, in the luxuriant vegetation of a peaceful little graveyard attached to his favourite mosque. There I saw his tombstone in 1877—a simple column crowned by a turban—and thither pious Moslems used to make leisurely pilgrimages in the cool of the evening. But the old order of things changed, and the Bulgarian Government made away with that humble memento of a great man and a stormy period.

By his revolt, Pasvan Oglu had saved the time-honoured institution of the Janissaries; but only for a while. It found its end in 1826 in the streets of the capital at the hands of Sultan Mahmoud II., amid incredible horrors, the like of which modern history has, happily, not often to record.

Laswaree and Asaye

Herbert Compton

At the beginning of the present century what was known as the Marátha Dominion had reached its zenith in India, and the progress of British policy brought the two powers into conflict. The Maráthas were a Hindu people whose home was on the tablelands of the Deccan. During the middle of the seventeenth century, under the guidance of a great national leader called Sivaji, they expanded into a martial race, and ultimately became one of the main factors in the downfall of the Great Mogul, as the titular head of the Muhammadan Empire over Hindustan was called.

In 1803 the Maráthas were masters from Delhi in the north to the confines of Hyderabad and Mysore in the south, and, excluding the Ganges provinces, from Cuttack in the east to the sandy deserts of Rajputana in the west. Their territorial or tributary possessions were probably five or six times greater than those of the English. Their government was merged in a confederacy of five powerful chiefs, of whom the principal, called the *peshwa*, held his court at Poonah. Their national characteristics were strongly marked; for, although constantly warring and jarring with one another, it needed but the presence of a foreign foe to create immediate union in their ranks. Each of these great chiefs entertained an immense feudal army of predatory horsemen (not unlike the modern Cossacks, but without their discipline), and could bring literally hundreds of thousands of them into the field to carry on the system of guerilla warfare which enabled them to sustain their rule of terror. Their wild soldiery swept over Hindustan like a whirlwind; devastation

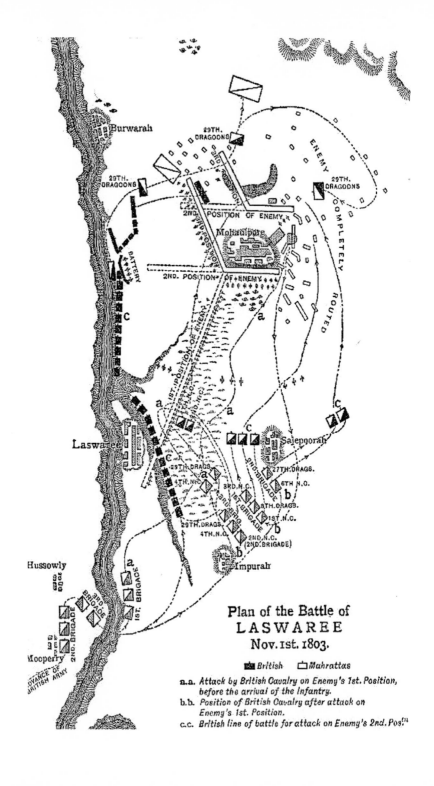

Plan of the Battle of
LASWAREE
Nov. 1st. 1803.

■ *British* □ *Mahrattas*

a.a. *Attack by British Cavalry on Enemy's 1st. Position,*
before the arrival of the Infantry.
b.b. *Position of British Cavalry after attack on*
Enemy's 1st. Position.
c.c. *British line of battle for attack on Enemy's 2nd. Pos[n]*

followed their path; they never stopped to fight, but scattered when they could not secure submission at their first appearance. They were nomads of the nomads; their saddle was their home; they slept in the open, their horses picketed to their spears stuck in the ground, and with their swords at their sides, ready at a moment's notice for foray or for flight. They were invincible vagabonds, whose invulnerability lay in the impossibility of getting a blow at them.

They would have been wise had they remained true to the system of warfare which raised them to a great martial power. But towards the end of the eighteenth century one of their chiefs—Madhagi Scindia, a shrewd statesman and an experienced soldier—observed, during a period of war with the English, the superiority in battle their disciplined ranks of infantry gave them, and how easily their small but compact bodies of foot were able to repel the attacks of the freebooting lancers, who never dared to come to close quarters. Wherefore, he began to create a regular army of his own, under the command of a very remarkable soldier of fortune named De Boigne, who entered his service as a *generalissimo* in 1784, and raised and drilled troops for him after the European fashion—an example which was soon followed in a lesser degree by other chiefs in the Marátha Confederacy.

De Boigne and his brigades became famous passwords in their day, and won many notable battles for their master in Central and Western India. The adventurer entertained friendly feelings towards the English, but when he resigned Scindia's service, in 1796, his command passed to a Frenchman named Perron, who, at a time when England and France were engaged in war, was naturally antagonistic to the British power in India. Perron increased the Marátha regular army until it amounted to 40,000 infantry, 5,000 cavalry, and 464 guns, and encouraged Dowlut Rao Scindia—a vain, worthless, dissipated chief, who had succeeded Madhaji—to regard his troops as equal to those of the English, and himself as the strongest and greatest prince in Hindustan.

Scindia's enormous standing army, large detachments of which were stationed on the British frontiers, was a menace to our power, and absolutely overawed the *peshwa*, who was constantly embroiled in troubles with his subordinate chiefs until his nominal ascendancy became a mere mockery, and it was they, not he, who directed his government and dictated his policy. At last, in 1803, matters came to such a crisis that the *peshwa* threw himself on the protection of the English; and the Marquess Wellesley, the Governor-General of India,

and one of the most far-seeing statesmen who ever ruled there–over, determined to seize the opportunity thus presented to disband these standing armies of regular troops and crush out the French interest that controlled them and, by direct intrigues with France, made them a source of grave political danger.

A treaty was entered into with the *peshwa* by which he became dependent on the English, who, in return for a large cession of territory, contracted to furnish him with troops for his protection. Scindia and the other Marátha chiefs at once took alarm, conceiving—not unreasonably—that the independence of their nation was threatened. Called on to acquiesce in the new political arrangement, they insolently refused, bade us defiance, and accepted the gage of war.

There were at this time two remarkable soldiers in India—General Gerard Lake, Commander-in Chief of the British forces, and Colonel Arthur Wellesley, a younger brother of the Marquess Wellesley, and afterwards the great Duke of Wellington. Lake had seen service in the Seven Years' War in Germany, under Lord Cornwallis in America, and in the inglorious campaign against revolutionary France in 1793.

Arthur Wellesley had recently won his spurs at the siege and storm of Seringapatam, where, "although he held only subordinate military command, his clear and commanding intellect, and his energy and skill in action, were displayed in the rapidly decisive operations with which he terminated the war." To these two great soldiers the chief conduct of affairs was now entrusted.

Scindia's influence extended from the Deccan, where he was himself, to Delhi, where General Perron governed Upper India in his name, as the nominal vice-regent of the Great Mogul—a potentate represented at this time by a poor, harmless, blind old man, kept secluded in close and cruel captivity in the citadel of Delhi. At the time of the declaration of war Scindia had about 20,000 infantry and 5,000 cavalry in the vicinity of the Mogul capital, 14,000 infantry near Poonah, and an additional 6,000 marching up from the latter place to reinforce the army of Upper India. In addition to these trained troops he had command of countless hordes of Marátha horse, contemptible as fighting material, but excellent as pure plunderers to harass an invading army and cut off its supplies. There were also several large contingents of irregular infantry belonging to the other chiefs in the confederacy, and to minor chieftains who owed them feudal obedience. The total force, disciplined and irregular, opposed to the English in what is known as the second Marátha war did not fall short of 150,000 fighting-men, of whom a third had enjoyed an almost uninterrupted career of victory for twenty years, during which they had never lost a gun, and were held to be—as indeed they subsequently proved themselves—little, if at all, inferior to our *sepoy* troops. The strength of the English amounted to about 50,000 men, distributed in five armies over the length and breadth of India, at such widely-distant spots as Cuttack, Guzerat, Cawnpore, Poonah, and the southern Marátha country. Lake, in the north, and Wellesley at Poonah, were at the head of the most considerable divisions, numbering about 11,000 men each.

War was declared in August, the height of the rainy season, and General Lake advanced against Delhi. His first exploit was the reduction of the fortress of Aligarh, where the enemy proved their valour, for they "fought like lions," and 2,000 were killed before they surrendered to the stormers. Delhi fell a week later, after an obstinate battle fought in sight of its minarets, in which 3,000 of the enemy were killed or wounded, and 68 of their guns taken; and within a month the celebrated fortress of Agra, at that time considered the key of Upper India, was captured after a thousand of the garrison had been slain.

A foe who could sacrifice 6,000 lives, or nearly a third of their fighting strength, in three consecutive actions, was not one to be despised, and the resistance offered to Lord Lake was probably the most obstinate hitherto displayed by any native army in India. The fugitives from the three places—Aligarh, Delhi, and Agra—now formed a junction at a spot equi-distant from them to the westward, where they were joined by the brigade of regular infantry that Scindia had ordered up country at the beginning of the war, and who were known as the "Deccan Invincibles."

Just previous to the outbreak of hostilities that chief had summarily dismissed from his service all his European officers whose sympathies were, or were supposed to be, with the English; and after the first reverses the French officers of the force followed Perron's example, and deserted their colours. In consequence, this army of fugitives found themselves at their most critical hour bereft of all their European leaders—a disaster sufficient to dismay the most daring. But there arose an able and gallant substitute from their own ranks in the person of a native named Surwar Khan, who assumed command, and proved himself a very capable, if unfortunate, general in the field.

Hearing of this rallying on the part of the enemy, General Lake determined to attack them, and annihilate the Marátha power in Northern India with one final blow. Leaving a force to hold Agra, he set out from that city on the 27th October, and four days later learnt that the Maráthas were encamped within a forced march of him. Ordering his infantry to follow, he pushed on at the head of his cavalry brigade of

The Marátha Confederacy.
(1802.)

The capitals of the Marátha Princes
are indicated thus — POONA
(THE PESHWA)

English Miles.
0   100 200 300 400

three regiments of British Dragoons and five of Native Horse, and at
sunrise on the morning of 1st November, 1803, came upon the enemy at the village of Laswaree.

Of all the great and gallant generals whose names adorn the roll
of British valour there is not one more distinguished for individual
prowess than Gerard Lake. He believed in personal example in the
leader, and dash and daring in the follower. As an ensign of foot he had
seen and noted, during the Seven Years' War, the tactics of Frederick
the Great, and been imbued with them. It was his creed that attacking troops enjoyed a moral superiority over a stationary enemy, and

125

although the immediate loss of life might be greater, the battle was generally to the assailants. But the assailants had to be led, and Lake conceived it was the duty of their chief to lead them. However erroneous this doctrine may be considered now, it held good a hundred years ago. Throughout his active career Lake is ever to be found at the head of his men in battle, whether cavalry or infantry, encouraging them forward. Where the danger was greatest, the assault most arduous, there was Lake surely to be seen leading the van.

So it was with him now. Notwithstanding that the Maráthas numbered over 14.000 strong, of whom 9,000 were disciplined troops and 5,000 irregular cavalry, and were advantageously posted, he determined to attack them instantly, and setting himself at the head of his little brigade, as any cavalry colonel might at the head of his regiment, he rode at the enemy's position.

He was successful in forcing their first line, but it was at a desperate cost of life. The troop; he was opposing—swarthy mercenaries though they were, and they were nothing else—had learnt the art of war under De Boigne, a general as brave and able as Lake himself. On their standards were emblazoned the names of many hard-won, but now forgotten, victories, of which they were justly proud. They had made their first reputation in restraining and repelling the wild charges of the Rhator Rajpooto, then accounted the finest horsemen in Western India, and countless squadrons of gallant Mughals and fierce Rohillas had dropped away before their withering volleys, as they stood in close serried ranks, shoulder to shoulder, reserving their fire until those who taught them discipline gave them the word of command. They were as cool and resolute now, when Lake and his dragoons dashed at them. It was the first campaign in which they had been brought face to face with the famous *Feringhee* warriors, but they were not daunted. They were prepared, for their guns had been linked together with chains, stretching from one battery to another; and these impeded Lake's cavalry, who blundered on to the unseen obstacles, for the grass of the plain was tall and rank, and before they could recover themselves were exposed to a frightful slaughter. Major Thorn, the historian of the war, writes:

" Surwar Khan's battalions reserved their fire till our cavalry came within a distance of twenty yards of the muzzles of their guns, which, being concealed by the high jungle grass, were perceptible only when a fierce discharge of grape and double-headed shot mowed down whole divisions, as the sweeping storm of hail levels the growing crops of grain to the earth. But notwithstanding this iron tempest, nothing could repress the ardour of our cavalry, whose velocity overcame every resistance. Having penetrated the enemy's line they immediately formed again, and charged backwards and forwards three times, amidst the continued roar of cannon and the incessant shower of grape und chain-shot, with surprising order and effect. The scene of horror was heightened and the work of destruction increased by the disadvantage under which our cavalry had to act; for no sooner had they charged through the artillerymen of the enemy—who to save themselves crept under their guns for shelter—than, directly our men had passed, they darted out, reloaded their pieces, and turned them on our rear."

In the face of this prodigal resistance Lake was at length compelled to retire, and drawing off his shattered brigade out of fire, he waited for his infantry and guns to come up.

They arrived about noon, after a forced march of twenty-five miles, during which the music of battle in front had quickened their footsteps and impelled them to extraordinary exertions. Their strength consisted of one regiment of European infantry and four of *sepoys*, with a few light guns, the greater part of their artillery having been unable to keep up with them in the heavy state of the roads consequent on continual rain. Two short hours were allowed them for rest and refreshment, during which Surwar Khan took up a new and stronger position, a little behind his former one, which brought a large tank, or artificial lake of water, into his front, whilst his rear was protected by the village of Mehálpur. Cutting the embankment of the tank, he flooded the space between the two armies and commanded it with his artillery. He was no common leader this, who could link his guns together, repulse a charge of British cavalry, and, on the spur of a moment, impede his enemy by transforming the ground they had to traverse into a marsh!

The Marátha army was drawn up in one long line, awaiting the attack, when, at two o'clock. Lake formed his infantry into two columns, one to support the other in turning the enemy's right flank, and ordered his cavalry to advance against their front. The renewal of the battle was ushered in with a tremendous cannonade from the Marátha guns, which had been posted with great judgment by Surwar Khan, who, directly he perceived the plan of attack, threw back his right wing with much adroitness, so as to bring it almost at right angles to his front, with the village wedged in the angle so made, and protecting both rears—seeing which the 76th Regiment, supported by

the 12th Native Infantry, wheeled and advanced against the Marátha line; but, as they closed in, the admirably-served guns of the enemy mowed down their ranks, and for a time threatened them with actual annihilation.

It was just at this urgent moment that General Lake's horse was shot under him, and his son, dismounting to offer his own, was se-

verely wounded before his father's eyes. Simultaneously a matchlock-man in the enemy's ranks aimed at the general, who fortunately happened to turn, and this accidental movement allowed the charge to pass under his arm, burning the side of his coat. But never for an instant did his cool judgment and resolute fortitude forsake him. With scarce a glance at his stricken son, he calmly remounted, watched for a moment the progress of the action, recognised it was too great a risk to wait for the reserves to come up, and determined to dare all and charge home with the bayonet.

No sooner had the command been given than, with a ringing British cheer, the 76th leapt forward, supported with praiseworthy alacrity by the Native Infantry corps. And now Surwar Khan, with consummate generalship, ordered his cavalry to charge, but even as he did so the British dragoons dashed up to the relief. Horse and foot met in one great shock of battle; sabre rang out against bayonet, and musket flashed against pistol and carbine. A short period of indescribable *mêlée* ensued, in which the fate of the day was decided.

But although defeated, the Maráthas were not disgraced. They were veteran troops, and knew how to die with a dignity seldom displayed by mercenaries. True to the traditions of "De Boigne's Brigades," they fought to the end. Their breasts met the opposing British bayonets; their gunners yielded up their lives rather than desert the pieces they worshipped with a devotion that was fanatic, if it was not actually religious. Staunch and true to the discipline they had been taught, a little remnant of the infantry retreated in good order until they were broken in column by the dragoons, who detoured and took them in rear. Then came the end. The Marátha cavalry escaped, but of their 9,000 infantry who stood in battle array that morning, only 2,000 survived to surrender as prisoners. In all the ghastly annals of war there have been few more dreadful instances of carnage, or more devoted sacrifices to the shrine of a soldier's duty, than that exhibited by this Marátha legion on the field of Laswaree.

The afternoon's battle was fought and won in less than two hours. The enemy's camp was captured, together with seventy-four guns and forty-four stands of colours. The British lost nearly nine hundred men, including forty-two officers, out of a total of about 6,000 engaged.

The credit of the victory was due to the presence of mind and cool daring of General Lake.

"His masterly plans of attack were carried into instantaneous execution by his unrivalled personal activity; and he appeared with matchless courage in front of every principal charge."

This was the tribute of the Marquess Wellesley to the conqueror, who paid one as noble to the gallantry of his foe. Lake wrote the day after the battle:

"All the *sepoys* of the enemy behaved exceeding well, the gunners standing to their guns until killed by the bayonet. If they had been commanded by their French officers the affair would, I fear, have been doubtful. For these fellows fought like devils—or rather like heroes!"

And it is recorded by one who had a share in these stirring events that on the evening of the battle, as the general was returning from the field, the Europeans, who loved him as such leaders are loved, cheered him. Whereupon, taking off his hat, he thanked them, and then pointing to the Marátha artillerymen, who lay clustered thick

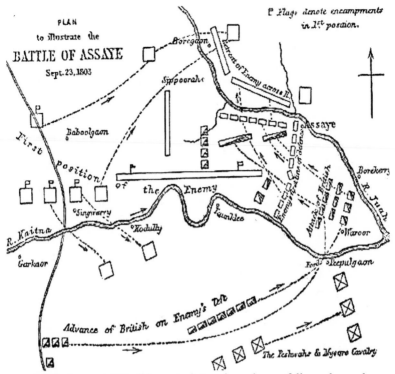

PLAN
to illustrate the
BATTLE OF ASSAYE
Sept. 23, 1803

ℙ *Flags denote encampments
in 1st position.*

around their guns, "Do," he cried, "as these brave fellows have done, and despise death!"

We must now turn our eyes to the south, where Scindia and the Rajah of Magpore, another chief of the Confederacy, took the field at the head of their united armies. General Arthur Wellesley was in command of the force sent to attack them. Crossing the Godavari River to the north-east of Poonah, he reached Aurangabad, where he learnt that Scindia had entered the territory of the Nizam, after evading Colonel Stevenson, who, with an army of 7,000 men, was watching the Ajunta Pass. In consequence of this information General Wellesley altered his route, and proceeded south, intending to intercept the enemy before they could reach Hyderabad. Whereupon Scindia, whose wild Marátha scouts kept him excellently informed, retraced his steps, and in this way managed to elude his pursuers for three weeks, in spite of several attempts to bring him to action. It was not until the 21st September that a chance occurred of doing so; and at a conference between Wellesley and Stevenson, who had formed a junction, they arranged to attack Scindia on the 24th. For this purpose the two divisions separated again, in order the more quickly to pass through some narrow and difficult defiles in the hilly country which barred their way to their objective point—a place called Bokerdun, where it was believed Scindia could be brought to bay.

In pursuance of this concerted plan of attack Wellesley, after a fatiguing march of twenty-two miles, found himself at one o'clock on the afternoon of the 23rd September at the Kaitna River, and suddenly came upon the foe drawn up on the opposite side of the stream to dispute his passage.

So shifty were the tactics of Marátha warfare, and so often had Scindia decided to fight "another day," that now the chief was within striking distance the general determined to attack him without waiting for Colonel Stevenson. India has been won for us by the boldness of our generals, who from the days of Lord Clive to those of Lord Roberts have ever seized opportunity by the forelock, no matter what the peril or how great the responsibility. But seldom has such a daring decision been arrived at as that which led to the Battle of Assaye. For Scindia's force of 17,000 foot contained 10,500 disciplined infantry. He was overpoweringly strong in artillery, being accompanied by his grand park of 115 guns; while his hordes of Marátha horse numbered not less than 30,000. Against such odds as these Wellesley prepared to lead his little force of 4,520 men, of whom 1,170 (the 74th and 78th Regiments) were British infantry, 2,000 native infantry, 1,200 cavalry, and 150 artillery. No wonder that "the Maráthas, numerous and daring as they were, stood astounded and appalled at the audacious spirit of this comparatively insignificant array that thus presumed to attack their formidable host." It was a prodigiously bold bid for fame and fortune, and laid Wellesley open to a charge of rashness. He is recorded to have said in answer:

"But had I not attacked them I must have been surrounded by their superior cavalry, my troops have starved, and I had nothing left but to hang myself to my tent pole!"

The Maráthas had taken up their position facing south, and in a triangular piece of ground formed by the junction of the rivers Kaitna and Juah, which flowed from west to east, the former intervening between them and the English, and the latter protecting their rear. Wellesley, reconnoitring the position, perceived two villages almost facing each other on opposite banks of the Kaitna, and rightly surmised that a ford communicating between them must exist. Leaving his cavalry to watch and check a demonstration on the part of the enemy's horse,

bodies of which had crossed the Kaitna towards his left, the general, turning to the right, led his infantry and guns through some ravines and broken ground, which hid their progress, until he reached the ford. Crossing it, with little or no loss, he began to form line of battle, facing westward. This necessitated a corresponding manoeuvre on the part of the Maráthas, whose line had been facing south, and with all practicable speed they changed front, until their left rested on the village of Assaye and the Juah River, whilst their right extended to the banks of the Kaitna. Thus situated they faced the British, who were hemmed in between the two rivers, whose confluence was at their rear. Round the village of Assaye, Scindia massed a great number of guns, and, while our troops were forming, their shot fell like hail, and created great slaughter in our line, and especially amongst the artillery bullocks.

At this moment one of Wellesley 's officers, who commanded on the advanced right, blundered, and, contrary to orders, attacked the

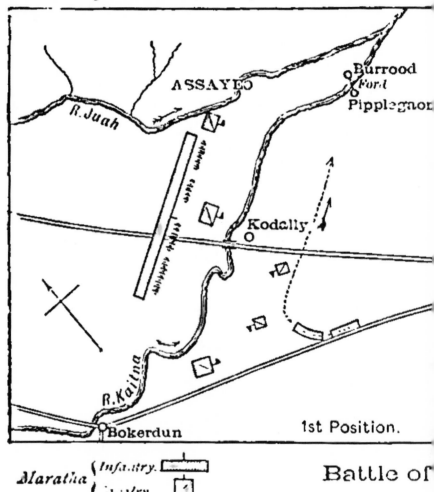

1st Position.

Maratha { Infantry. ▭
{ Cavalry.... ▢

Battle of

village of Assaye. This brought the whole fire from the guns stationed there upon the 74th Regiment, who were so dreadfully cannonaded that they lost nearly 400 of their total strength of 569 men, whilst of their nineteen officers eleven were killed and seven wounded. Taking advantage of their distressed condition, a body of Marátha horse summoned sufficient courage to charge them, and in one wild, nervous scurry broke their gaping ranks. A capable observer, who was present throughout the action writes:

"This was the critical moment of the engagement; and if the enemy's cavalry had pushed the *sepoys*, they would never have withstood that which overpowered the 74th."

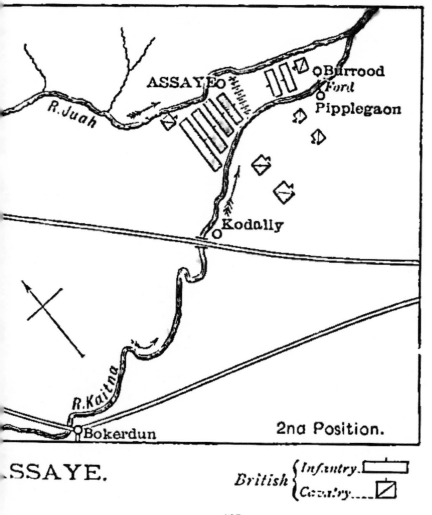

But assistance was at hand, for the general had already ordered up his cavalry, who had overawed the body of Marátha horse they were left to watch, and they were now sent to the relief of their comrades in distress. Forward dashed the 19th Dragoons, who drew 350 sabres, followed by a regiment of native cavalry. Nothing could resist their impetuous charge, and they drove the Maráthas pell-mell into the Juah River, followed them to the other side, sabred some of the enemy's infantry whom they stumbled across there, and then re-crossing, joined our main line.

Despite this serious check on our right, the British advance had not been really impeded. Pressing steadily forward in the face of a tempest-blast of shot and musketry, the troops reserved their fire until it could be given with effect, and then, delivering but a single volley, charged bayonets and stormed the enemy's line of guns. The ardour of their onslaught carried them over and past it in their determined pursuit of the Marátha infantry, who were now falling back to a second line in their rear. Whereupon—as at Laswaree—the Marátha gunners crawled out from under their pieces, where they had taken refuge, and manning them again, turned them round and poured grape and chain-shot into the rear of the victorious British advance.

This obliged our infantry to turn back and storm the guns for the second time, but from an opposite di-

rection—a movement that had so much the resemblance of a retreat that the Marátha infantry, who were still in good order, were encouraged to halt, face about, and come back to the attack.

Whilst the main tide of action was thus surging backwards and forwards, a body of the enemy's infantry, whose line in the first instance completely outflanked ours, having slipped past our flank, managed to reach some of our guns, which, owing to the destruction of the bullocks dragging them, had perforce been left behind. Observing this dangerous movement, General Wellesley—who throughout the whole battle had been riding everywhere, directing the officers and encouraging the men—placed himself at the head of the 78th foot and 7th Regiment of Native Cavalry, and led them to the spot. On the way his horse was shot under him, and himself exposed to the most imminent danger; but mounting another charger, he quickly achieved his object and drove the enemy off. This marked a phase in the battle, for the whole Marátha line now began to waver and fall back, fighting desperately notwithstanding, until they were brought to bay on the banks of the Juah River, which intercepted their natural retreat to the northwards. Here, huddled and cramped for room, they made their last stubborn stand, until they were finally defeated and scattered after a spirited and sanguinary conflict that had lasted for three hours.

Long before the end Scindia and the Rajah of Berar deserted them, flying at an early stage of the action, whilst the Marátha cavalry, after their one charge against the wrecked ranks of the 74th, never again adventured to face those "perfect war tigers" the British dragoons. Wrote one of their captains:

"These dragoons are large, powerful men, the weight of whose sabres almost annihilated us, whilst they unhorsed numbers of my troopers by merely riding against them!"

And so the Marátha horsemen contented themselves with hovering on the outskirts of the battle until they saw the day was lost, when they sought safety in flight, followed by the remnants of their infantry.

Thus ended one of the most important and, so far as British losses were concerned, most sanguinary battles ever fought in India. Our casualties amounted to 1,566 killed and wounded, of whom 600 were Europeans and 50 officers. The percentage was one in three of the total number engaged—probably the highest ever recorded amongst Europeans in a pitched battle. The enemy's loss was estimated at less than our own, but their 98 guns, 100 tumbrils, and entire camp and military stores were captured. It was a glorious victory, gloriously won by General Wellesley. Writes one who was by his side throughout the day:

"It is nothing to say of him that he exposed himself on all occasions, and behaved with perfect indifference in the hottest fire (for I did not see a European do otherwise, nor do I believe people do); but in the most anxious and important moments he gave his orders as clearly and coolly as if he had been inspecting a corps or manoeuvring at a review."

The enemy that withstood us at Assaye were no common "country" foe—to use an adjective of disparagement indigenous to India—but a trained and disciplined army; and officers present who had witnessed the power of the French artillery in the wars of Europe, declared that the Marátha guns were equally well served, and that they fought with a prowess worthy of a European nation. Nor was it to be wondered at, for "De Boigne's Brigades" had won a reputation at that time in India as great amongst the native Powers as ever did the legions of ancient Rome in the countries they conquered.

This "matchless victory" (as his brother the governor-general termed it) raised Wellesley to the first rank of British generals, and laid the basis of that great career of glory and renown which he subsequently increased on the plains of Spain and crowned on the field of Waterloo.

To the genius of Gerard Lake and Arthur Wellesley Great Britain owes the chief expansion of its empire over India. For their victories crushed out the last remnant of French influence in that country, broke down the powerful dominion of the Marátha, secured an immediate increase of territory that doubled our then-existing possessions, paved the way for future conquest, and obtained for us the mastery of the entire seaboard of India. For these advantages, which we have enjoyed for nearly a hundred years, and which have helped to raise us to our proud pre-eminence among the nations of the world, we are indebted to the British blood so freely poured out by Britain's gallant sons on the battlefields of Laswaree and Assaye.

The Action Off Pulo Aor

A. J. Butler

The present writer was once walking through the fields in the spring-time, when he became aware of a great commotion in some trees over his head. Presently a kestrel flew out, hotly pursued by a missel-thrush. It was quite clear that the "bird of prey" had been investigating too closely the opportunities afforded by the domestic arrangements of the other—thinking, no doubt, that he had to do with a peaceable member of the feathered world. Unluckily for him, he had lighted on one who, not by profession a fighter, was quite ready to defend himself if attacked. The same kind of thing now and then happens among our own species; and the following pages describe a characteristic instance. It is not so much the story of a battle as of how a battle which would probably have been disastrous to the weaker force was averted by pluck and promptitude.

In March, 1803, it was pretty clear that the short-lived peace between England and France was not going to last much longer. The Peace of Amiens had restored to France the settlement of Pondicherry, and General Decaen was sent out as governor. On March 6th he sailed in the line-of-battle ship *Marengo*, accompanied by the frigates *Atalante*, *Belle-Poule*, and *Sémillante*, as well as transports taking troops for the garrison of the place. This fleet was commanded by Rear-Admiral Linois. It was obviously stronger than was at all necessary for the service on which it was sent. Nor need we have much hesitation in assuming that Bonaparte in sending it out had ideas of inflicting injury upon English shipping in the Eastern seas, before the news of the resumption of hostilities could reach the English authorities in

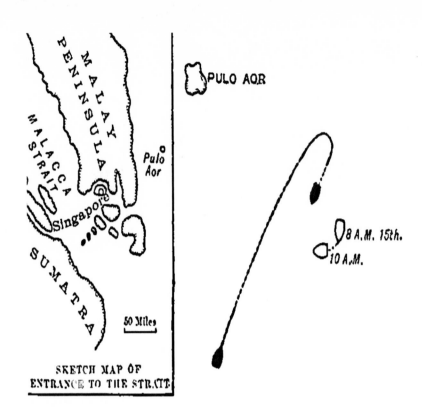

PULO AOR

MALAY PENINSULA

MALACCA STRAIT

Pulo Aor

Singapore

SUMATRA

50 Miles

SKETCH MAP OF
ENTRANCE TO THE STRAIT

8 A.M. 15th.

10 A.M.

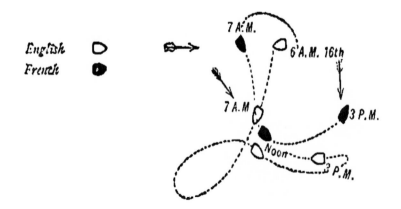

English

French

7 A.M.

6 A.M. 16th

7 A.M.

3 P.M.

Noon

3 P.M.

those parts. The *Belle-Poule*, being a fast sailer, reached Pondicherry on June 16th, Linois with the rest of his squadron following on July nth. One of the transports arrived the next day, together with another vessel, the *Bélier*, which had been despatched ten days later, when war appeared imminent.

Pondicherry had not yet been handed over, and a British squadron, under Vice-Admiral Rainier, was at anchor in the neighbourhood. Just before the *Bélier* sailed in, the captain of the French flagship had gone on board the vessel of the English admiral with a polite invitation to breakfast next morning with Admiral Linois, which was no less politely accepted. But when the morning came flag-ship, admiral, breakfast and all were gone. It could only be conjectured that the *Bélier* had brought fresh instructions, in pursuance of which the French admiral had departed. That evening the other transport, the *Côte d'Or*, turned up; and as matters looked suspicious, two of the English ships thought it as well to anchor alongside of her. The *Belle-Poule* had been on a private trip to Madras. On the 15th she returned, in company with the English *Terpsichore*; but while the latter remained, the French frigate, after signalling to the transport, stood back to sea. That same night the *Côte d'Or*, likewise moved out; but the *Terpsichore* followed, and after some demur, and even the firing of a few shots, prevailed on her to come back. It was then learnt that she had been ordered, doubtless by signals from the *Belle-Poule*, to sail for Mauritius, then a French possession, whither Linois was also gone to refit and provision in preparation for a renewal of the war. She was detained till the 24th, when she was allowed to depart, an English frigate accompanying her for some distance, to make sure that she went the right way.

The English squadron proceeded to Madras, when news of the actual declaration of war reached them early in September; but Linois lay quiet at Mauritius until October 8th. Then he sailed for Java and Sumatra, picking up some rich prizes on the way. On December 10th, he anchored off Batavia, in Java, in a convenient position for snapping up the East India Company's fleet on its way back from China. There he lay till December 28th, when he went on to look out for it. His squadron at this time consisted of the *Marengo* (74), the frigates *Belle-Poule* (40), and *Sémillante* (36), the *Berceau* corvette (22), and a 16-gun brig belonging to Batavia.

On January 31st the China fleet sailed from Canton, under the command of Commodore Nathaniel Dance. It consisted of sixteen great Indiamen, besides eleven "country ships," or vessels hailing from Indian ports, one vessel belonging to Botany Bay and one to Portugal. An armed brig, the *Ganges*, accompanied it. This fleet of thirty ships in all was a good deal better armed than a fleet of merchantmen would be in these days. The Indiamen carried from thirty to thirty-six guns each. But the guns were in many cases of a nearly obsolete class; they threw, as a rule, a much less weight of metal than those on board a man-of-war; and they were hampered by having water-butts lashed between them, and by the general lumber of the decks. But even greater was the comparative weakness of the crews. None of these exceeded 140 men, whereas we know that the complement of even the little *Berceau* was 200. The officers and crews had not been trained to fight, and among the latter were a great many Chinamen and Lascars, who could hardly be depended upon to render much service if it came to action. The "country ships" went apparently unarmed.

Such was the force at the disposal of Commodore Dance for the protection of the enormously valuable fleet under his charge. He was, as it were, the shepherd in charge of a flock of sheep; and sheep, even though they have horns, are a poor match for even a small pack of wolves. Something of this sort Dance must have felt on the morning of February 15th. The island of Pulo Aor, which lies, so to speak, just " round the corner " from the Straits of Malacca, and at no great distance from the entrance to the straits, bore about N.W., at seven or eight leagues' distance, when one of his vessels, the *Royal George*, signalled four strange sail in the southwest—that is, right in their road. Four Indiamen with the *Ganges* were sent to examine the strangers, and soon reported them to be a French squadron. Dance hove to, with head to westward, but the Frenchman, puzzled by the number of ships, which was greater than his advices had led him to expect, and preferring to approach them with the advantage of the weather-gauge, held on his course till he was well in their rear. In those latitudes the wind at that season blows from the north-westward or northward, though on this particular morning there were light airs from N.E. to S.W., finally settling into the west. Then he about went, and by nightfall the French squadron was close astern of the fleet. Linois, however, seems even by this time to have suspected that his wolves might find the sheep a somewhat tougher morsel than they had anticipated, and accordingly deferred his attack till daylight.

The morning confirmed him in his opinion. As he wrote himself:

"If the bold face assumed by the enemy had only been an artifice to conceal their weakness, they might have tried to slip away in the darkness. But I had soon to convince myself that there was no feigning about their confidence; they lay-to all night with lights burning, and in good order."

At daybreak the French fleet was seen also lying-to about three miles to the windward, the wind being light from west. Both sides hoisted their colours, but as the enemy showed no signs of advancing. Dance resumed his course, proceeding in line under easy sail upon the starboard tack. The three French ships and the brig then filled on the same tack, and bore up with the intention of cutting the long line of the merchant fleet in two. Perceiving this, Dance made at one o'clock the signal to tack in succession, the effect of which would be to bring his line on to a course more or less parallel with that of the French line, and to windward of it, and to engage on coming abreast of the enemy. The manoeuvre was correctly executed, the *Royal George*, Captain John Timmins, leading, followed by the *Ganges*. Dance, in the *Earl Camden* (he had commanded the ship for nearly twenty years), occupied the third place in the line; and so the sheep stood towards the wolves. The French were nothing loath, and in order to hasten the issue, sailed a little more away from the wind, which had now veered to N.N.W. At 1.15 Linois opened fire upon the *Royal George*, which returned it vigorously, firing eight or nine broadsides in all, the *Ganges* and *Earl Camden* taking up the ball as they came into range, respectively five and fifteen minutes later. The only other vessels engaged were the *Warley* and *Alfred*. Admiral Linois in his report to his own government relates the rest of the action. "The enemy's leading ship, having sustained some damage, put her helm up; but supported by those which followed, she again brought her broadside to bear, and with the other vessels kept up a brisk fire. The ships, as they tacked, joined the combatants, and three of those which had been the first to come into action began manoeuvring to get into our rear, while the rest of the fleet, making all sail and keeping away, showed a design of surrounding us. By this manoeuvre the enemy would have rendered my position very dangerous. I had ascertained his superior force"—Linois seems all along to have been under the impression that there were some king's ships present—"and I had no further occasion to deliberate as to the steps I should take to avoid the fatal results of an unequal contest. Taking advantage, therefore, of

the smoke which hung about me, I wore and went off on the port tack.[1] Then, shaping my course east-north-east, I drew away from the enemy, who continued to pursue the squadron till three o'clock, firing several ineffectual broadsides."

The sheep fairly made the wolves turn tail after a fight which had lasted not quite three-quarters of an hour.

The pursuit, though well intended, and forming an appropriate finish to the game of bluff which Commodore Dance had so successfully played, could not have any results, and only took the fleet in the wrong direction. At three o'clock, therefore, after having, as a recent writer says, "enjoyed for two hours the extraordinary spectacle of a powerful squadron of ships of war flying before a number of merchantmen," Dance made the signal to go about, and by eight the ships anchored in a convenient situation for entering the straits next morning. The losses had been very trifling. The *Royal George*, which had been longest in action, was a good deal knocked about in hull and rigging, and had one man killed and another wounded. The other ships had scarcely suffered at all, while on the French side not a man seems to have been injured.

---

1. James, following Dance's log, says, " hauled his wind on the port tack," but the word employed by the French admiral seems only to mean "wore." Before the action began both fleets were on the starboard tack. The wind, however, shifted, and had drawn more towards the norm after the action began, so as to bring him on to the port tack without any material change in his direction; and it must have been then that he wore.

A long "butcher's bill" is, however, not necessary as evidence of courage and resource in action, and so Dance's countrymen felt. The news of his exploit was received with enthusiasm in England. He was knighted by the king, and well rewarded by those whose property he had so pluckily and effectually defended. His words in returning thanks are worth quoting. Taken in connection with his conduct in command of the fleet, they show that the combination of courage with modesty, which was so characteristic of the best seamen of those days, was not confined to those employed more directly in the service of the nation, and that England has no less reason to be proud of her merchant skippers than of her post-captains.

"Placed by the adventitious circumstances of seniority of service and absence of convoy in the chief command of the fleet entrusted to my care, it has been my good fortune to have been enabled, by the firmness of those by whom I was supported, to perform my trust not only with fidelity, but without loss to my employers. Public opinion and public rewards have already far outrun my deserts, and I cannot but be sensible that the liberal spirit of my generous countrymen has measured what they are pleased to term their grateful sense of my conduct rather by the particular ability of the exploit than by any individual merit I can claim."

Sir Nathaniel Dance survived till 1827.

Austerlitz

C. Stein

On the 21st of November, 1805, a striking and warlike cavalcade was traversing at a slow pace a wide and elevated plateau in Moravia. In front, on a grey barb, rode a short, sallow-faced man with dark hair and a quick, eager glance, whose notice nothing seemed to escape. His dress was covered by a grey overcoat, which met a pair of long riding-boots, and on his head was a low, weather-stained cocked hat. He was followed by a crowd of officers, evidently of high rank, for their uniforms, saddle-cloths, and plumed hats were heavily laced, and they had the bold, dignified bearing of leaders of men. In front and in the flanks of the party were scattered watchful vedettes, and behind followed a strong squadron of picked cavalry in dark green dolmans with furred pelisses slung over their shoulders, and huge fur caps surmounted by tall red plumes. The leading horseman rode in silence over the plateau, first to one point then to another, examining with anxious care every feature of the ground. He marked carefully the little village from which the expanse took its name, and the steep declivity which sloped to a muddy stream below. No one addressed him, for he was a man whose train of thought was not to be lightly interrupted. Suddenly, at length, he drew rein, and, turning to the body of officers, said: "Gentlemen, examine this ground carefully. It will be a field of battle, upon which you will all have a part to play." The speaker was Napoleon. His hearers were his generals and staff. He had been reconnoitring, surrounded and guarded by his devoted Chasseurs of the Guard, the plateau of Pratzen, the main part of the arena where was to be fought in a few days the mighty conflict of Austerlitz.

Napoleon's headquarters were then at Brunn. The French host, then for the first time called the " Grand Army," had, at the command of its great chief, in the beginning of September broken up the camps long occupied on the coasts of France in preparation for a contemplated invasion of England, and had directed its march to the Rhine. It was formed in seven corps under Bernadotte, Marmont, Davoust,

Soult, Lannes, Ney, and Augereau, with its cavalry under Prince Murat, and the Imperial Guard as a reserve.

The Rhine was crossed at different points, and the tide of invasion swept upon the valley of the Danube. From the beginning the
movements had been made with a swiftness unprecedented in war.
Guns and cavalry had moved in ceaseless and unhalting stream along

every road. Infantry had pressed forward by forced marches, and had been aided in its onward way by wheeled transport at every available opportunity. The emperor had resolved to strike a blow by land against his foes which should counterbalance the several checks which the indomitable navy of England had inflicted on his fleets at sea. Austria and Russia were in arms against France, and he was straining every nerve to encounter and shatter their separate forces before they would unite in overwhelming power. The campaign had opened for him with a series of brilliant successes. The veterans of the revolutionary wars, of Italy and of Egypt, directed by his mighty genius, had proved themselves irresistible. The Austrians had been the first to meet the shock, and had been defeated at every point— Guntzberg, Haslach, Albeck, Elchingen, Memmingen—and the first phase of the struggle had closed with the capitulation at Ulm of General Mack with 30,000 men.

But there had been no stay in the rush of the victorious French. The first defeats of the Austrian army had been rapidly followed up. The corps which had escaped from the disaster at Ulm were pursued and, one after another, annihilated. The Tyrol was overrun, and its strong positions occupied by Marshal Ney. From Italy came the news of Massena's successes against the celebrated Archduke Charles, and at Dirnstein Marshal Mortier had defeated the first Russian army under Kutusow. The Imperial headquarters had been established at Schönbrunn, the home of the Emperor of Austria. Vienna had been occupied and the bridge across the Danube secured by Lannes and Murat. Kutusow, after his defeat at Dirnstein, had been driven back through Hollabrunn on Brunn by the same marshals at the head of the French advanced guard, and had now joined the second Russian army, with which was its Emperor Alexander in person, and an Austrian force under Prince Lichtenstein, accompanied by the Emperor of Austria.

The main body of the "Grand Army" had, under Napoleon, followed its advanced guard into the heart of Moravia. Its headquarters and immediate base were now at Brunn, but its position was sufficiently critical, at the extremity of a long line of operations, numbering less than 70,000 disposable men, while the Russo-Austrian army in front amounted to 92,000. So rapid had been the movements since the camp at Boulogne was left, that the common saying passed in the ranks that "Our emperor does not make use of our arms in this war so much as of our legs;" and the grave result of this constant swiftness had been that many soldiers had fallen to the rear from indisposition

or fatigue, and even the nominal strength of corps was thus for the time seriously diminished. It is recorded that in the *Chasseurs à Cheval* of the Guard alone there was a deficiency of more than four hundred men from this cause. But all these laggards were doing their best to rejoin the army before the great battle took place which all knew to be inevitable, and in which all were eager to bear their part.

Napoleon had himself arrived at Brunn on the 20th of November, and during the following days till the 27th he allowed his army a measure of repose to enable it to recover its strength after its long toils—to repair its arms, its boots and worn material, and to rally every man under its eagles. His advanced guard had been pushed forward under Murat towards Wischau on the Olmutz road, Soult's corps on his right had pressed Kutusow's retreat towards Austerlitz, and the remainder were disposed in various positions to watch Hungary and Bohemia and to maintain his hold upon Vienna.

On the 27th the French advanced guard was attacked and driven back by the Russians at Wischau, and certain information arrived that this had been done by a portion of the main Russian army under the Emperor Alexander. It had been thought possible by Napoleon that peaceful negotiations might be opened, but this confident advance of his enemies seemed to show that they had by no means lost heart, and when on the 28th he had a personal interview with Prince Dolgorouki, the favourite of Alexander, he found the Russian proposals so insulting and presumptuous that he broke off abruptly any further communication.

We have seen Napoleon reconnoitring on the 21st of November, and we have marked the marvellous *coup d'œil* and prescience with which he foresaw the exact spot where the great battle, then looming before him, must take place. Every succeeding day saw the reconnaissances renewed, and never was a battlefield more thoroughly examined, never was forecast by a general of the actual turn of events to be expected more completely justified by fulfilment.

It had become certain that the united army of two mighty empires was close at hand. From the tone of Dolgorouki's communication it was evident that both the Russian and Austrian monarchs had resolved to trust their fortunes to the ordeal of battle, and that they, with their generals and soldiery, were eager to retrieve their previous misfortunes, and full of confidence that they would do so. That confidence had been increased by the repulse of the French advanced guard at Wischau; and they now longed to complete their work by pouring their superior numbers on the comparatively weak French main body. With this knowledge before him, Napoleon proceeded to carry out the plan of action which he had carefully matured. To the astonishment of many veterans in his army, a general retreat of his advanced troops was ordered. Murat fell back from Posoritz and Soult from near Austerlitz. But this retrograde movement was short, and they were halted on the ground chosen by Napoleon for his battle-line. The outlying corps of Bernadotte and Davoust were summoned to complete his array. Munitions, food, ambulances were hurried to their appointed posts, and it was announced that the battle would be fought on the 1st or 2nd of December.

The line of a muddy stream, called the Goldbach, marked the front of the French army. This stream takes its source across the Olmutz road, and flowing through a dell, of which the sides are steep, discharges itself into the Menitz Lake. At the top of its high left bank stretches the wide Pratzen plateau, and it appeared to Napoleon's staff that he had made an error in relinquishing such a vantage ground to his enemy; but he told them that he had done so of set purpose, saving:

"If I remained master of this fine plateau, I could here check the Russians, but then I should only have an ordinary victory; whereas by giving it up to them and refusing my right, if they dare to descend from these heights in order to outflank me, I secure that they shall be lost beyond redemption."

Let us examine the positions occupied by the French and the Austro-Russian armies at the close of November, and we shall the better understand the general strategy of the two combatant forces and the tactics which each made use of when they came into collision. The Emperor Napoleon rested his left, under Lannes and Murat, on a rugged eminence, which those of his soldiers who had served in Egypt called the "Santon," because its crest was crowned by a little chapel, of which the roof had a fancied resemblance to a minaret. This eminence he had strengthened with field works, armed and provisioned like a fortress. He had, by repeated visits, satisfied himself that his orders were properly carried out, and he had committed its defence to special defenders under the command of General Claparède, impressing upon them that they must be prepared to fire their last cartridge at their post and, if necessary, there to die to the last man.

His centre was on the right bank of the Goldbach. There were the corps of Soult and Bernadotte, the grenadiers of Duroc and Oudinot, and the Imperial Guard with forty guns. Their doubled lines were concealed by the windings of the stream, by scattered clumps of wood, and by the features of the ground.

His right was entrusted to Davoust's corps, summoned in haste to the battlefield, and of which only a division of infantry and one of dragoons had been able to come into line. They were posted at Menitz, and held the defiles passing the Menitz Lake and the two other lakes of Telnitz and Satschau. Napoleon's line of battle was thus an oblique one, with its right thrown back. It had the appearance of being only defensive, if not actually timid, its centre not more than sufficiently occupied, its right extremely weak, and only its left formidable and guaranteed against any but the most powerful attack.

But the great strategist had weighed well his methods. He trusted that the foe would be tempted to commit themselves to an attack on his right, essaying to cut his communications and line of retreat on Vienna. If they could be led into this trap, the difficulty or movement in the ground cut up by lake, stream, and marsh would give to Davoust the power to hold them in check until circumstances allowed of aid being given to him. Meantime, with his left impregnable and his centre ready to deal a crushing blow, he expected to be able to operate against the Russo-Austrian flank and rear with all the advantage due to unlooked-for strength.

The right of the Russo-Austrians, commanded by the Princes Bagration and Lichtenstein, rested on a wooded hill near Posoritz across the Olmutz road. Their centre, under Kollowrath, occupied the village of Pratzen and the large surrounding plateau; while their left, under Doctorof and Kienmayer, stretched towards the Satschau Lake and the adjoining marshes.

The village of Austerlitz was some distance in rear of the Russo-Austrian position, and had no immediate connection with the movements of the troops employed on either side, but the Emperors of Russia and Austria slept in it on the night before the battle, and Napoleon afterwards accentuated the greatness of his victory by naming it after the place from which he had chased them.

The two great armies now in presence of each other were markedly unequal in strength—92,000 men were opposed to 70,000, and the advantage of 22,000 was to the allies. But this inequality was to a great extent compensated by the tactical dispositions of the leader of the weaker force. Of the two antagonist lines, one was wholly exposed to view, the other to a great extent concealed—first advantage to the latter. They formed, as it were, two parallel arcs of a circle, but that of the French was the more compact and uninterrupted—second advantage; and this last was soon to be increased by the imprudent Russian manoeuvres. The two armies, barely at a distance of two cannon-shot from each other, had by mutual tacit consent formed their bivouacs, piled arms, fed and reposed peaceably round their fires, the one covered by a thick cloud of Cossacks, the other by a sparse line of vedettes.

Napoleon quitted Brunn early in the morning of the 1st December, and employed the whole of that day in examining the positions which the different portions of his army occupied. His headquarters were established in rear of the centre of his line at a high point, from

which could be seen the bivouacs of both French and allies, as well as the ground on which the morrow's issue would be fought out. The cold was intense, but there was no snow. The only shelter that could be found for the ruler of France was a dilapidated hut, in which were placed the emperor's table and maps.

The grenadiers had made up a huge fire hard by, and his travelling carriage was drawn up, in which he could take such sleep as his anxieties would permit. The divisions of Duroc and Oudinot bivouacked between him and the enemy, while the Guard lay round him and towards the rear.

In the late afternoon of the same day Napoleon was watching the allied position through his telescope. On the Pratzen plateau could be seen a general flank movement of Russian columns, in rear of their first line, from their centre to their left and towards the front of the French position at Telnitz. It was evidently supposed by the enemy that the French intended to act only on the defensive, that nothing was to be feared from them in front, and that the allies had only to throw their masses on their right, cut off their retreat upon Vienna, and thus inflict upon them a certain and disastrous defeat. It was forgotten by the Russo-Austrians that in thus moving their principal forces to the left, the centre of their position was weakened, and on the right their own line of operations and retreat was left entirely unprotected. When Napoleon detected what was being done, trembling with satisfaction and clapping his hands, he said:

"What a manoeuvre to be ashamed of! They are running into the trap! They are giving themselves up! Before tomorrow evening that army will be in my hands!"

In order still more to add to the confidence of his enemy and to encourage them in the prosecution of their mistaken plan, he ordered Murat to sally forth from his own position with some cavalry, to manoeuvre as if showing uneasiness and hesitation, and then to retire with an air of alarm. This order given, he returned immediately to his bivouac, dictated and issued the famous proclamation in which he assured his army that the Austro-Russians were exposing their flank and were offering certain glory to the soldiers of France as a reward for their valour in the coming struggle: he said that he himself would direct their battalions, but that he would not expose himself to danger unless success was doubtful, and he promised that, after their victory, they should have comfortable cantonments and peace.

The evening of the 1st of December closed in. The allied movement towards their left was still continuing, and Napoleon, after renewing his orders, again visiting his parks and ambulances and satisfying himself by his own observation that ah was in order, threw himself on a bundle of straw and slept. About eleven o'clock he was awakened and told that a sharp attack had been made on one of the villages occupied by his right, but that it had been repulsed. This further confirmed his forecast of the allied movements, but, wishing to make a last reconnaissance of his enemy's position, he again mounted, and, followed by Junot, Duroc, Berthier, and some others of his staff, he ventured between the two armies. As he closely skirted the enemy's line of outposts, in spite of several warnings that he was incurring great risk, he, in the darkness, rode into a picquet of Cossacks. These sprang to arms and attacked him so suddenly that he would certainly have been killed or taken prisoner if it had not been for the devoted courage of his escort, which engaged the Cossacks while he turned his horse and galloped back to the French lines. His escape was so narrow and precipitate that he had to pass without choosing his way the marshy Goldbach stream. His own horse and those of several of his attendants—amongst others Ywan, his surgeon, who never left his person—were for a time floundering helpless in the deep mud, and the emperor was obliged to make his way on foot to his headquarters past the fires round which his soldiery were lying. In the obscurity he stumbled over a fallen tree-trunk; and it occurred to a grenadier who saw him, to twist and use some straw as a torch, holding it over his head to light the path of his sovereign.

In the middle of the anxious night, full of disquietude and anticipation, the eve of the anniversary of the emperor's coronation, the face of Napoleon, lighted up and suddenly displayed by this flame, appeared almost as a vision to the soldiers of the nearest bivouacs. A cry was raised, "It is the anniversary of the coronation! *Vive l'Empereur!*"—an outburst of loyal ardour which Napoleon in vain attempted to check with the words, " Silence till tomorrow. Now you have only to sharpen your bayonets." But the same thought, the same cry, was taken up and flew with lightning quickness from bivouac to bivouac. All made torches of whatever material was at hand. Some pulled down the field-shelters for the purpose—some used the straw that had been collected to form their beds; and in an instant, as if by enchantment, thousands of lights flared upwards along the whole French line, and by thousands of voices the cry was repeated, "*Vive l'Empereur!*" Thus was improvised, within sight of the astonished enemy, the most striking of illuminations, the most memorable of demonstrations, by which the admiration and devotion of a whole army have ever been shown to its general. It is said that the Russians believed the French to be burning their shelters as a preliminary to retreat, and that their confidence was thereby increased. As to Napoleon, though at first annoyed at the outburst, he was soon gratified and deeply touched by the heart-felt enthusiasm displayed, and said

that "This night is the happiest of my life." For some time he continued to move from bivouac to bivouac, telling his soldiers how much
he appreciated their affection, and saying those kindly and encouraging words which no one better than he knew how to use.

The morning began to break on the 2nd of December. As he buckled on his sword, Napoleon said to the staff gathered round— "Now, gentlemen, let us commence a great day." He mounted, and from different points were seen arriving to receive his last orders the

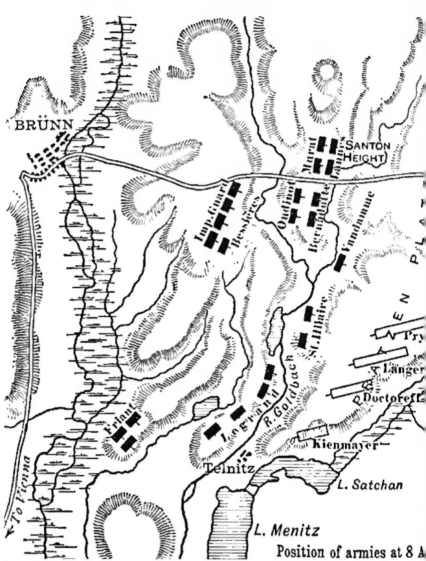

Position of armies at 8 A

renowned chiefs of his various *corps-d'armée*, each followed by a single *aide-de-camp*. There were Marshal Prince Murat, Marshal Lannes, Marshal Soult, Marshal Bernadotte, and Marshal Davoust. What a formidable circle of men, each of whom had already gathered glory on many different fields! Murat, distinctively the cavalry general of France, the intrepid *paladin* who had led his charging squadrons on all the battlefields of Italy and Egypt; Lannes, whose prowess at Montebello had made victory certain; Soult, the veteran of the

BATTLE OF
AUSTERLITZ
Dec. 2, 1805.

English Miles

0   1   2   3   4

■■■ ....*French*

▭ . *Austrians & Russians.*

long years of war on the Rhine and in Germany, the hero of Altenkitchen, and Massena's most distinguished lieutenant at the battle of Zürich; Bernadotte, not more renowned as a general in the field than as the minister of war who prepared the conquest of Holland; Davoust, the stern disciplinarian and leader, unequalled for cool gallantry and determination—all were gathered at this supreme moment round one of the greatest masters of war in ancient or modern times, to receive his inspiration and to part like thunder-clouds bearing the storm which was to shatter the united armies of two empires.

The emperor's general plan of action was already partly known, but he now repeated it to his marshals in detail. He was more than ever certain, from the last reports which he had received, that the enemy was continuing the flank movement, and would hurl the heaviest attacks on the French right near Telnitz.

To Davoust was entrusted the duty of holding the extreme right and checking, in the defiles formed by the lakes, the heads of the enemy's columns which, since the previous day, had been more and more entangling themselves in these difficult passes.

Of Soult's three divisions, one was to assist Davoust on the right, while the other two, already formed in columns of attack, were to hold themselves ready to throw their force on the Pratzen plateau.

Bernadotte's two divisions were to advance against the same position on Soult's left. This combined onslaught of four divisions on the centre of the Russo-Austrians which they had weakened by the movement to their left, would be supported by the emperor himself with the Imperial Guard and the grenadiers of Oudinot and Duroc. Lannes

163

was ordered to hold the left, particularly the "Santon" height; while Prince Murat, at the head of his horsemen, was to charge through the intervals of the infantry upon the allied cavalry which appeared to be in great strength in that part of the field.

It was thus Napoleon's intention to await and check the enemy's attacks which might be expected on both his flanks, and more especially on his right, while he himself made a determined and formi-

dable forward movement against their centre, where he hoped to cut them in two, and then, from the dominant position of the Pratzen plateau, turn an overwhelming force against the masses on their too-far-advanced left, which, entangled and cramped in its action among the lakes, would then be crushed or forced to yield as prisoners.

It was eight o'clock. The thick wintry mist hung in the valley of the Goldbach and rolled upwards to the Pratzen plateau. Its obscurity, heightened by the lingering smoke of bivouac fires, concealed the French columns of attack. The thunder of artillery and the rattle of musketry told that the allied attack on the French right had begun and was being strenuously resisted, while silence and darkness reigned over the rest of the line. Suddenly, over the heights, the sun rose, brilliantly piercing the mist and lighting the battlefield—the "Sun of Austerlitz," of which Napoleon ever after loved to recall the remembrance.

The moment of action for the French centre had come, and the corps of Soult and Bernadotte, led by the divisions of Vandamme and St. Hilaire, rushed forwards. No influence that could animate the minds of these gallant troops was wanting. They fought directly under the eye of their emperor. They were led by chiefs in whom they had implicit confidence. Their ardour was fired by the proclamation which had been issued on the previous evening, and the bands accompanied their regiments, playing the old attack march—

On va leur percer le flanc
Rataplan, tire lire en plan!

The Pratzen height was escaladed at the double, attacked in front and on the right and left, and the appearance of the assailants was so sudden and unexpected, as they issued from the curtain of mist, that the Russians were completely surprised. They had no defensive formation ready, and were still occupied in the movement towards their left. They hastily formed in three lines, however, and some of their artillery were able to come into action. Their resistance was feeble. One after another, their lines, broken by the stern bayonet charge, were driven back in hopeless confusion, and at nine o'clock Napoleon was master of the Pratzen plateau.

Meanwhile, on the left, Lannes and Murat were fighting an independent battle with the Princes Lichtenstein and Bagration. Murat, as the senior marshal and brother-in-law of the emperor, was nominally the superior; but, in real fact, Lannes directed the operations of the infantry, which Murat powerfully supplemented and aided with his cavalry. General Caffarelli's division was formed on the plain on Lannes's right, while General Suchet's division was on his left, supported by the "Santon" height, from which poured the fire of eighteen heavy guns. The light cavalry brigades of Milhaud and Treilhard were pushed forward in observation across the high road to Olmutz. The cavalry divisions of Kellermann, Walther, Nansouty, and d'Hautpoul were disposed in two massive columns of squadrons on the right of Caffarelli. Against this array were brought eighty-two squadrons of cavalry under Lichtenstein, supported by the serried divisions of Bagration's infantry and a heavy force of artillery.

The combat was commenced by the light cavalry of Kellermann, which charged and overthrew the Russo-Austrian advanced guard. Attacked in turn by the Uhlans of the Grand Duke Constantine, Kellermann retired through the intervals of Caffarelli's division, which, by a well-sustained fire in two ranks, checked the Uhlans and emptied many of their saddles. Kellermann re-formed his division and again charged, supported by Sebastiani's brigade of dragoons. Then followed a succession of charges by the chivalry of France, led by Murat with all the *élan* of his boiling courage. Kellermann, Walther, and Sebastiani were all wounded, the first two generals seriously. In the last of these charges the 5th Chasseurs, commanded by Colonel Corbineau, broke the formation of a Russian battalion and captured its standard. Caffarelli's infantry were close at hand, and, pushing forward, made an Austrian battalion lay down its arms. A regiment of Russian dragoons made a desperate advance to rescue their comrades, and, mistaking them for Bavarians in the smoke and turmoil, Murat ordered the French infantry to cease firing, The Russian dragoons, thus encountering no resistance, penetrated the French ranks and almost succeeded in taking Murat himself prisoner. But, consummate horseman and man-at-arms as he was, he cut his way to safety through the enemy, at the head of his personal escort.

The allies profited by this diversion to again assume the offensive. Then came the opportunity for the gigantic *cuirassiers* of Nansouty. which hurled the Russian cavalry back upon their infantry, and, in three successive onslaughts, scattered the infantry itself, inflicting terrible losses with their long, heavy swords and seizing eight pieces of artillery. The whole of Caffarelli's division advanced, supported by one of Bernadotte's divisions from the centre, and, changing its front to the right, cut the centre of Bagration's infantry, driving its greater part towards Pratzen, separated from those who still fought at the extremity of their line.

The Austro-Russian cavalry rallied in support of Bagration, who was now hotly pressed by Suchet. Then came a magnificently combined movement of dragoons, *cuirassiers*, and infantry. The dragoons drove back the Austro-Russia squadrons behind their infantry. Simultaneously followed the levelled bayonets of Suchet's division and the crushing shock of d'Hautpoul's mail-clad warriors. The victory was

decided—the Russian battalions were crushed, losing a standard, eleven guns, and 1,800 prisoners. The rout was completed by the rapid advance of the light cavalry brigades of Treilhard and Milhaud on the left, and of Kellermann on the right, which swept away all that encountered them, and drove the shattered allied troops towards the village of Austerlitz. The Russo-Austrian losses on this part of the field of battle amounted to 1,200 or 1,500 killed, 7,000 or 8,000 prisoners, two standards, and twenty-seven pieces of artillery.

While Napoleon had thus struck a heavy blow at the allied centre and had been completely victorious on his left, his right, under Davoust, was with difficulty holding its own against Buxhowden (who had assumed the command of the columns of Doctorof and Kienmayer), and but that the masses brought against it were unable to deploy their strength it must inevitably have been crushed. Thirty thousand foemen of all arms were pressing in assault upon 10,000 French, already wearied by a long and rapid march to their position at Raygern. But Davoust was able to concentrate what power he had, and to meet at advantage the heads only of the columns which were winding their way along the narrow passes that opened between the lakes and through the marshy ground in his front. Even so the strain was terrible, and would have been more than less hardy troops under a less able and determined leader could have stood. But Napoleon was quite alive to the necessities of the gallant soldiers who were standing their ground so staunchly. He ordered his reserve of grenadiers and the Imperial Guard to move up to the support of his right centre and to threaten the flank of the columns that were attacking Davoust, while he also directed the two divisions of Soult's corps, which had made the attack on the Pratzen plateau against Buxhowden's rear.

It was one o'clock, and at this moment, while the orders just given were being executed, the Russian infantry, supported by the Russian Imperial Guard, made a desperate effort to retrieve the fortunes of the day near Pratzen, and threw themselves in a fierce bayonet charge on the divisions of Vandamme and St. Hilaire, which offered a stout resistance. But, with the Russian Guard ready to join in the combat, the odds against the French divisions were too great. It was the crisis of the day.

Napoleon, from the commanding position where he stood, saw before him the Emperor Alexander's guard advancing in dense masses to regain their morning position and to sweep before them his men, wearied and harassed by the day's struggle. At the same time he heard on his right the redoubled fire of the advanced Russian left, which was pressing Davoust and was threatening his rear. From the continued and increasing roar of musketry and artillery it almost seemed as if success must, after all, attend the great flank movement of the allies. Small wonder if even his war-hardened nerves felt a thrill of confusion and anxiety when he saw dimly appearing through the battle smoke another black mass of moving troops.

"Ha! Can those, too, be Russians?" he exclaimed to the solitary staff-officer whom the exigencies of the day had still left at his side. Another look reassured him, however. The tall bearskins of the moving column showed him that it was his own Guard, which, under Duroc, was moving towards the lakes to the support of Soult and Davoust. His right and rear were, at any rate, so far safe.

But the Russian infantry attack had been followed by a headlong charge of the Chevalier Guards and *cuirassiers* of the Russian Guard, under the Grand Duke Constantine, brother of the Emperor Alexander, supported by numerous lines of cavalry. So well led and so impetuous was the attack, that the two battalions on the left of Vandamme's division were broken and swept away in headlong flight. One of these battalions belonged to the 4th of the line, of which Napoleon's brother Joseph was colonel, and the emperor saw it lose its eagle and abandon its position, shattered and destroyed, forming the one dark spot to sully the brilliancy of French steadfastness on that day of self-devotion. The tide of panic-stricken fugitives almost surged against the emperor himself. All efforts to rally them were in vain. Maddened with fear, they heard not the voices of generals and officers imploring them not to abandon the field of honour and their emperor. Their own response was to gasp out mechanically: "*Vive l'Empereur!*" while still hurrying their frantic pace. Napoleon smiled at them in pity; then, with a gesture of contempt, he said: "Let them go!" and, still calm in the midst of the turmoil, sent General Rapp to bring up the cavalry of his Guard.

Rapp was titular Colonel of the Mamelukes, a corps which recalled the glories of Egypt and the personal regard which Napoleon, as a man, had been able to inspire into Orientals. They, with the *Grenadiers à Cheval* and the Chasseurs of the Guard, now swooped upon the Russian squadrons. The struggle of the *mêlée* was bloody and obstinate between the picked horsemen of Western and Eastern Europe; but the Russian chivalry was at length overwhelmed and driven back with immense loss. Many standards and prisoners fell into the hands of the French, amongst others Prince Repnin, colonel of the Cheva-

lier Guards. His regiment, whose ranks were filled with men of the
noblest families in Russia, had fought with a valour worthy of their
name, and lay almost by ranks upon the field. It had been the mark of
the giant *Grenadiers à Cheval,* whose savage war-cry in the great charge
had been, as they swayed their heavy sabres, "Let us make the dames of
St. Petersburg weep today!"

When success was assured, Rapp returned to report to Napoleon—a warlike figure, as he approached, alone, at a gallop, with proud
mien, the light of battle in his eye, his sword dripping with blood and
a sabre cut on his forehead.

"Sire, we have overthrown and destroyed the Russian Guard and taken their artillery."

"It was gallantly done: I saw it." replied the emperor. "But you are wounded."

"It is nothing, sire: it is only a scratch."

"It is another quartering of nobility, and I know of none that can be more illustrious."

Immediately afterwards the young Count Apraxin, an officer of artillery who had been taken prisoner by the *chasseurs*, was brought before Napoleon. He struggled, wept, and wrung his hands in despair, crying: "I have lost my battery; I am dishonoured: would that I could die!" Napoleon tried to console and soothe him with the words, "Calm yourself, young man, and learn that there is never disgrace in being conquered by Frenchmen."

The French army was now completely successful on its centre and left. In the distance could be seen, retiring towards Austerlitz, the remains of the Russian reserves, which had relinquished hope of regaining the central plateau and abandoned Buxhowden's wing to its fate. Their retreat was harassed by the artillery of the Imperial Guard, whose fire ploughed through their long columns, carrying with it death and consternation. Napoleon left to Murat and Lannes the completion of their own victory. To Bernadotte, with the greater part of the Guard, he entrusted the final crushing of the enemies who had been driven from the Pratzen plateau; while he himself, with all of Soult's corps, the remainder of his cavalry, infantry, and reserve artillery descended from the heights and threw himself on the rear of the Austro-Russian left near Telnitz and the lakes. This unfortunate wing— nearly 30,000 men—had in vain striven since the morning to force its way through Davoust's 10,000. Now, still checked in front and entangled in the narrow roads by the Goldbach and the lakes, it found itself in hopeless confusion, attacked and ravaged with fire from three sides simultaneously by Davoust, Soult, Duroc with his grenadiers and Vandamme. It fought with a gallantry and sternness which drew forth the admiration of its enemies, but surrounded, driven, overwhelmed, it could not hope to extricate itself from its difficulties. There was no way of escape open but the Menitz lake itself, whose frozen surface seemed to present a path to safety, and in an instant the white expanse was blackened by the flying multitude. The most horribly disastrous phase of the whole battle was at hand. The shot of the French artillery which was firing on the retreat broke the ice at many points, and its frail support gave way. The water welled through the cracks and washed over the broken fragments. Thousands of Russians, with horses, artillery and train, sank into the lake and were engulfed. Few succeeded in struggling to the shore and taking advantage of the ropes and other assistance which their conquerors strove to put within their reach. About 2,000, who had been able to remain on the road between the two lakes, made good their retreat. The remainder were either dead or prisoners.

At four o'clock in the afternoon the battle was over, and there was nothing left for the French to do but to pursue and collect the spoils of their conquest. This duty was performed with energy by all the commanders except Bernadotte (even then more than suspected of disloyalty to his great chief), who allowed the whole of the Russo-Austrian right, which had been defeated by Lannes and Murat and driven from its proper line of retreat on Olmutz, to defile scatheless past his front and to seek shelter in the direction of Hungary.

After the great catastrophe on the Menitz lake which definitely sealed the issue of the conflict, Napoleon passed slowly along the whole battlefield, from the French right to their left. The ground was covered with piles of the poor remains of those who had died a soldier's death, and with vast numbers of wounded laid suffering on the frozen plain. Surgeons and ambulances were already everywhere at work, but their efforts were feeble in comparison with the shattered, groaning multitude who were in dire need of help. The emperor paused by every disabled follower and spoke words of sympathy and comfort. He himself, with his personal attendants and his staff, did all in their power to mitigate the pangs of each and to give some temporary relief till better assistance should arrive. As the shades of night fell on the scene of slaughter and destruction, the mist of the morning again rolled over the plain, bringing with it an icy rain, which increased the darkness. Napoleon ordered the strictest silence to be maintained, that no faint cry from a miserable sufferer should pass unheard; and his surgeon Ywan, with his Mameluke orderly Roustan, gave to many a one, who would otherwise have died, a chance of life by binding up their hurts and restoring their powers with a draught of brandy from the Imperial canteen.

It was nearly ten o'clock at night when the emperor arrived at the Olmutz road, having almost felt his way from one wounded man to another as they lay where each attack had been made and each stubborn defence maintained. He passed the night at the small posthouse of Posoritz, supping on a share of the soldiers' rations, which was brought from the nearest bivouac, and issuing order after order about searching for the wounded and conveying them to the field hospitals.

Though many of the most noted leaders in the French army were wounded in the great battle, comparatively few were killed. One of the most distinguished dead was General Morland, who commanded the *Chasseurs à Cheval* of the Guard. His regiment had suffered terrible losses in the charge under Rapp against the Russian Guard, and he himself had fallen, fighting amongst the foremost. Napoleon, who was always anxious to do everything to raise the spirit of his troops and

to excite their emulation, ordered that the body of General Morland
should be preserved and conveyed to Paris, there to be interred in a
specially magnificent tomb which he proposed to build on the espla-
nade of the Invalides. The doctors with the army had neither the time
nor the materials necessary to embalm the general's body, so, as a simple means of conservation, they enclosed it in a barrel of rum, which
was taken to Paris. But circumstances delayed the construction of the
tomb which the emperor intended for its reception until the fall of
the Empire in 1814. When the barrel was then opened for the private
interment of the body by General Morland's relations, they were astonished to find that the rum had made the dead general's moustaches
grow so extraordinarily that they reached below his waist.

The defeat suffered by the Russians was so crushing, and their
army had been thrown into such confusion, that all who had escaped
from the disaster of Austerlitz fled with all speed to Galicia, where

there was a hope of being beyond the reach of the conqueror. The rout was complete. The French made a large number of prisoners, and found the roads covered with abandoned guns, baggage, and material of war. The Emperor Alexander, overcome by his misfortunes, left it to his ally, Francis II., to treat with Napoleon, and authorised him to make the best terms he could for both the defeated empires.

On the very evening of the 2nd December the Emperor of Austria had asked for an interview with Napoleon, and the victor met the vanquished on the 4th. An armistice was signed on the 6th, which was shortly afterwards followed by a treaty of peace concluded at Presburg.

The total losses of the Austro-Russians at Austerlitz were about 10,000 killed, 30,000 prisoners, 46 standards, 186 cannon, 400 artillery caissons, and all their baggage. Their armies practically no longer existed, and only about 25,000 disheartened men could be rallied from the wreck.

In the joy of victory Napoleon showed himself generous to Austria and Russia in the terms which he imposed, and he at once set free Prince Repnin, with all of the Russian Imperial Guard who had fallen into his hands. To his own army he was lavish of rewards and acknowledgments of its valour, and in the famous order of the day which he published he first made use of the well-known expression—"*Soldiers, I am content with you.*" Besides a large distribution of prize-money to his troops, he decreed that liberal pensions should be granted to the widows of the fallen, and also that their orphan children should be cared for, brought up, and settled in life at the expense of the State.

The campaign of Austerlitz is probably the most striking and dramatic of all those undertaken by Napoleon, and its concluding struggle was the most complete triumph of his whole career. It was the first in which he engaged after assuming the title of emperor and becoming the sole and irresponsible ruler of France. Unlike the vast masses of men which he directed in subsequent wars, his army was then almost entirely composed of Frenchmen, and its glories belonged to France alone. Though for several years to come the great emperor's fame was to remain undimmed by the clouds of reverse, it never shone with a brighter lustre than at the close of 1805.

Trafalgar

C. J. Cutcliffe Hyne

If the electric telegraph had existed in 1805, or railways, or if there had even been roads in the great European Peninsula along which a mounted courier could make decent pace, the battle off the shoals of Cape Trafalgar might very well never have been fought, or at least have been considerably modified in its details and results. It is an historical fact that when on the 19th of October M. de Villeneuve put out from Cadiz in command of the Franco-Spanish fleet, which was fated to be so crushingly beaten, a recall from his great master. Napoleon, was hastening down the Peninsula as fast as horsemen could carry it. Admiral Rosily was to be promoted to the chief command, and the man he superseded was to return forthwith to Paris and answer a catalogue of grave charges.

De Villeneuve's chief sin was want of success, and under the first Napoleon no graver charge could have been framed against him. On the 23rd July of the same year he had fought an action with Sir Robert Calder, the commander of the blockading squadron off Ferrol, in which neither side, according to the sentiment of the time, covered itself with credit. The British with the smaller force captured two ships, and inflicted more loss than they received; but the indignant howls of his country forced the admiral to demand a court-martial, which, as it turned out, heavily censured him. They said he ought to have done far more.

The incident shows how the British prestige, bought at St. Vincent, Aboukir Bay, and countless other actions, was appreciated both in these Islands and by our then enemies on the Continent; and, in fact. Napoleon himself, though the last man to admit such a thing until

it was forced upon him, forbade his sea commanders to accept action unless they had a strong surplus of force following their flag. But presuming that the allied fleet could annihilate any squadron which the British could put on the seas to meet them, he sent De Villeneuve definite instructions as to what he wanted to be done. They were to force the Straits of Gibraltar, land troops on the Neapolitan coast, sweep the Mediterranean of all British cruisers and commerce, and enter the port of Toulon to re-victual and re-fit. And it was on this errand that—anticipating his recall—Admiral de Villeneuve led out of the harbour of Cadiz the fleet of French and Spanish battleships under his supreme command.

That day was the 19th of October, 1805; but the wind drew light, and it was not till the 20th that the entire combined fleet got into the long Atlantic swell, and showed to a pair of British reconnoitring frigates no less than thirty-three sail of the line—battleships of two, three, and in one case four gundecks—besides attendant smaller craft.

The two frigates, the *Euryalus* and the *Sirius*, had a shot or so pitched at them occasionally when they pried too close; but they contrived to hang on the skirts of the allies, and to glean news which kept the bunting on a constant dance up and down from their trucks. De Villeneuve took the frigates for scouts, and scouts they were; but he did not know that they were telegraphing detailed news of his movements to the British Mediterranean fleet under the most skilful seaman of all time—Horatio, Viscount Nelson.

The Island warships lay hove-to out of sight beyond the curve of ocean, riding laboriously over the swells, with copper glancing green and gold in the sunlight. They had waited for this moment for many a weary windy month.

Looked at from the light of our after-knowledge, they were clumsy, leewardly, ungainly hulks, with square, ponderous, wake-drawing sterns, and bows like the breasts of an apple; with narrow yards which had to be reinforced by studding-sail booms before a decent spread of cloth could be shown; with massive hempen rigging, and many a piece of uncouth gear and titling whereof the very name is lost to us in this year of grace. They had single topsails and single topgallant sails, and each carried under her rearing bowsprit a spritsail with round holes in the leaches, set on a swaying spritsail yard.

Their bellying sides towered above the sea like great black walls, as though to make the largest possible mark for hostile shot; and in these walls were doors, as many as a hundred to a ship, which could lift and show a grinning cannon- mouth framed in its proper porthole.

Their manning was typical of the time. There was the marine, a pipe-clayed, pig-tailed soldier, with garments about as suited to shipboard as an archbishop's would be. The foremast hand, though nine times out of ten the scouring of a press-gang from a crimp's house in some unlucky seaport town, was usually a seaman by education and a fighting-man by instinct; and at his best the primest exponent of his two trades which the world has ever seen. He was a tough handful, the Jack of 1805, and he required an iron discipline to keep him under full command—and he got it. It was a rare day when some six or eight of him did not appear spread-eagled on the gratings which were rigged in the gangways, to receive three or four dozen caresses of the "cat," laid with zeal upon the bare back.

His officers, too, were not what we should call refined and educated men nowadays. But they were skilful in both branches of their profession; because, without consummate seamanship, the leewardly slow-sailing craft of that day would not keep afloat; and in an era when the ocean breeze always smacked of battle, whoso was not an excellent fighting-man was quickly weeded from the ranks by captivity or death.

It is as well to understand these matters clearly, and then one can

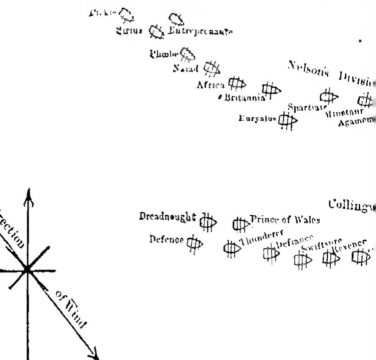

BATTLE OF TRAFALGAR.

21st Octr, 1805.

British ⸺⸺⸺⸺

French ⸺⸺⸺⸺

Spanish ⸺⸺⸺⸺

better appreciate that supreme outcome of the time, the British vice-admiral in command, who put the capstone on his glory by the sea-fight which averted the invasion of England and made the fate of the world what it is.

The fleet lay pitching clumsily over the dull green Atlantic swells, the wooden routine going on unchangeably as it had run for years before—watches, quarters, drill, meals, hammock; and then the same might be expected to follow over again. But of a sudden a change began to take place. The scene was brightened with patches of gaudy bunting. From every mast-truck in succession there broke out strings of flags, which the signalmen, book in hand, translated into words. Phrase by phrase they read out the signals, and the officers tingled with expectancy.

"The French and Spaniards are out at last; they outnumber us in ships and guns and men: we are on the eve of the greatest sea-fight in history."

The news hummed round the fleet, forward and aft; but there was neither hustle nor scene. Lord Nelson's instruction to his captains had gone round days before, and they were such a masterpiece of tactics that there was nothing to add to them They mapped out the plan of battle with all distinctness, but they did not cramp the enterprise of the inferiors. Knowing from his infinite experience that in the thick of action circumstances might well occur which called for individual judgment, the leader ended his charge thus:

"In case signals cannot be seen or clearly understood, no captain can do very wrong if he place his ship alongside of an enemy."

The men, too, after the custom of the day, did not indulge in any morbid thought of possible death or maiming.

"They were as merry at the thought of this sanguinary fight as a mob of schoolboys set loose for an unexpected holiday, and their conversation was concerning the prize-money they would take, and the jinks and jaunts they would have ashore when they put in to port to refit."

But there was more waiting yet before the battle began to burn in grim red life. The breezes were fitful, and the allies full of clumsy caution. It was not till the 21st that the fleets came together, and the British were able to force an action.

At 8.30 of that historical morning, De Villeneuve made the signal for his ships to form in close order on the port tack, thereby to bring Cadiz on his lee bow, and facilitate, if necessary, his escape into that port. The order was obeyed clumsily, and what with unskilful seamanship, light breeze, and heavy ground-swell, the resulting formation was crudely crescent-shaped, the ships clustering in knots and bunches, with great green gaps of tenantless water between them. And to this thirty-three sail of the line bore down on them in two columns from the windward twenty-seven British war-ships under every stitch of canvas that they could show, yet making a bare three knots with the catspaws that played over the swells.

The English commander-in-chief had hoisted his flag on his old 100-gun ship *Victory*, and in her led the van of the weather column. He was a little, slight, one-armed man, blind of one eye, and most shabbily dressed. The seams of his uniform frock coat were threadbare, the fabric white with sea salt, the gold lace tarnished to black, flattened rags. Amongst the folds of the left breast were four frayed, lack-lustre

stars, dull caricatures of what had once been brilliant decorations. He was a most slatternly admiral.

There might be little of Lord Nelson remaining, but of what there was, the quality was excellent. His solitary eye was as bright as a bird's. His brain was the most perfect sea-brain that ever schemed a tactic. In a ship's company where all were active, none were more active than he. As his vessel lunged over the Atlantic swells, nearing the enemy, he visited all the different decks, overseeing everything himself, and addressing the men at their quarters, and cautioning them not to fire a single shot without being certain that it would find a suitable resting-place.

He spoke in the rough sea-argot of his day, which differs from the more refined speech of ours. But what he said went home to the hearts of that rough, fighting crew, and a bubble of cheers rippled against his heels throughout all his progress along those narrow 'tween decks. They knew what a fight was, and they knew what a fight that little, shabby man would give them. The joy of battle was as meat and drink to them, and they licked their lips and made their noises of glee, like dogs held back on a chain. Their one wish was for close action. Amongst the officers on the quarter-deck a different topic was being discussed. They were men without a single thought for their own lives, but their reverence for Lord Nelson was idolatrous, and their fears for him heavy. It seemed to them that on his safety alone depended the success of the day; and as things were going, they knew that it must soon be desperately imperilled.

The *Victory*, both as van-ship of a column, and as bearing at her fore the flag of the commander-in-chief, would inevitably draw down upon herself all the concentrated force of the enemy's first fire, and the slaughter on her decks would be murderously heavy.

It was an awkward task to put this to the admiral, a man notoriously careless of his own personal safety; but when he returned from his tour of inspection, his anxious officers clustered round him, and one of them spoke the wishes of all. Would he not allow the *Téméraire*, then close astern, to slip past him, and as van-ship take off the brunt of the first fire?

Nelson laughed, and turned to Hardy, his flag-captain.

"Oh, yes," he said; "let her go ahead if she can."

Captain Hardy faced the taffrail, and hailed the *Téméraire*. His chief, still laughing, ran forward along the decks to the officers in command of the sail-trimmers, giving eager orders—a pull at a brace here, at a sheet there. The *Téméraire* might race him into action, but he would take care that the *Victory* should be first engaged.

"There, Hardy," he said, as he came back to the quarterdeck, "let the Téméraires open the ball if they can—which they most assuredly can't. I think there's nothing more to be done now, is there, till we open fire? Oh, yes; stay a minute, though. I suppose I must give the fleet something as a final fillip. Let me see. How would this do— 'Nelson expects that every man will do his duty'?"

Captain Hardy suggested that "England expects" would be better, and on Nelson rapturously consenting, the message went up flag by flag, and broke out in a dazzle of colour at the *Victory's* mizzen topgallant masthead. A hundred telescopes read the bunting, and when the message was translated to the British crews, their wild, exultant cheers spread out over the ocean's swell like the rattle of musketry.

Only one other signal was made, and that was belayed fast to the *Victory's* main truck and stayed there till it was shot away. It read: "Engage the enemy more closely." But it did not incite any special enthusiasm. It was Nelson's customary order on going into action, and was taken entirely as a matter of course. The Island seamen of that day were never chary of coming to hand-grips when they got the chance. They had entire confidence in pike and cutlass and club-butted pistol when wielded by their own lusty selves, and a superb contempt for the physical powers of Don and Frenchman, both of which matters were very serviceable to their success.

It was just before noon that the French *Fougeux* opened fire upon Vice-Admiral Collingwood in the *Royal Sovereign*, and, as though it had been a signal, the two admirals' flags broke out at their foremastheads, and the ships of both fleets hoisted their ensigns. The wind was very light, the sea oil-smooth, with a great ground-swell setting in from the westward. A glaring sun from out a cobalt sky blazed down on the freshly- painted flanks of the French and Spanish ships, and for a moment the fluttering national flags lit the scene with brilliant splashes of red and blue and white and gold. Then the grey powder-smoke filled the air in thicker volumes, and the flags and the ships themselves disappeared in its mist, and only the lurid crimson flashes of the guns shone out to tell that the fight had begun from every battery that had drawn into range.

To the first salute of iron and lead the *Royal Sovereign* made no response in kind. She held grimly on in silence, with her sail-trimmers working as though they were at a peace review; but when she drew astern of the great three-decker *Santa Anna*, the gun-captains of the port batteries drew the lanyards as their pieces bore. The guns were double-shotted, and so great was the precision of their murderous, raking fire that no less than fourteen of the Spaniard's guns were disabled and four hundred of her crew either killed or wounded.

At the same time, in passing, she let fly her starboard broadside into the *Fougueux* in the endeavour to pay her the somewhat similar compliment of raking her from forward aft; but, owing to the distance and the smoke, that discharge did but comparatively little damage.

"Ah!" said Collingwood to his flag-captain; "they've got off this time, but we'll give them gruel later on. By Jove, Rotheram, this is a sweet place, isn't it? What would Nelson give to be here just now?"

James says in his history:

"And, by a singular coincidence Lord Nelson, the moment he saw his friend in his enviable position, exclaimed, 'See how that noble fellow Collingwood carries his ship into action!'"

Having in this way played the overture to the great opera which was to follow, Admiral Collingwood put his helm a-starboard, and ranged so close alongside the *Santa Anna* that their guns were nearly muzzle to muzzle. The cannonade between the two three-deckers was something terrific, but the *Royal Sovereign* soon had more than one opponent battering at her. The *Fougueux* bore up and raked her astern; ahead the *San Leandro* wore and raked her in the other direction; whilst upon the Island ship's starboard bow and quarter were the *San Juste* and *Indomptable*, completing the ring of fire.

Under such a murderous attack, any other crew might well have been driven below; but the Royal Sovereigns stuck to their guns, and, stripped to the waist, fought them like fiends. So incessant was the fire that they frequently saw the cannon-shot clash against one another in mid-air; and, moreover, they could congratulate themselves that the ships which ringed them in quite as often hit friend as foe.

Aware at length of this injury which they were receiving from their own fire, and observing that four more British ships were already looming through the battle mist as they bore down to the support of their leader, the four two-deckers, one by one, drew off to attend to other affairs, and the *Royal Sovereign* took up position upon her big opponent's lee bow. The British *Belleisle* threw in a broadside as she passed to the thick of the fight beyond, and then Admiral Collingwood had the Spanish admiral all to himself. Though mounting 112 guns to her opponent's 100, the *Santa Anna's* crew were beginning to

learn that in the practical fighting of these guns there were other men who could beat them. Splinters flew, men were cut in half by the raining shot, and spars fell clattering down from aloft, and still the fire kept up. At the end of seventy minutes the *Santa Anna's* masts were all over the side, and still her officers would not surrender; and it was not till 2.15 p.m. that she finally struck and was taken in possession.

The *Royal Sovereign* herself was in little better plight. Her mizzen-mast she had already lost, and no sooner did she drive down a little ahead of the prize, to put herself somewhat to rights, than her main-mast went over the starboard side, tearing off two of the lower deck ports in its crashing fall. With foremast shot through in ten places, and rigging in bights and streamers, the victor was almost in as unmanageable a plight as the Spanish three-decker which she had so gallantly fought and captured.

But meanwhile, the hottest centre of the action was elsewhere. Lord Nelson had, time past, in a two-decker, shown with point how little he feared coming in contact with a Spanish first-rater, and the *Santissima Trinidad*—the towering four-decker towards which he first steered—had already known what it was to dread and flee from him. But though on Trafalgar day he directed his course first towards this old opponent, it was not with the intention of attacking her. A Spanish rear-admiral was but poor game when a French vice-admiral commanded the allied fleet, and it was Pierre Charles Jean Baptiste Sylvestre de Villeneuve whom he had marked out for his first quarry in that world-famous sea-fight.

The powder-mist was thickening down, and human eyes could not peer far through it. Although every glass on board the *Victory* was quartering the grey haze, not one could discover a ship with the French admiral's flag, and Nelson fumed with disappointment. The four-decker's flag at the mizzen could be made out, and some signals were occasionally seen at the main of two or three other vessels; but no French ensign flew at the fore to denote an admiral's flagship. Often did the little chieftain himself, with his remaining eye, cast a puckered glance towards the Franco-Spanish line in search of that ship which he so lusted to fight and capture; and so lightly did he value personal risk that, though urged more than once on the subject, he would not suffer the hammocks to be stowed one inch higher than usual, preferring rather to risk the pelting of grape and musketry than have his view in any way obstructed.

At last the *Bucentaure* tired a shot at the *Victory*, which then, with studding-sails set on both sides, was making scarcely a knot-and-a-half through the water. The shot fell short, but others followed, and others, until at last one plunged through the belly of a sail.

A minute or so of awful silence followed, and then, as if by signal from the French admiral, the eight weathermost vessels opened upon the *Victory* such a tornado of fire as had never before been borne by one single ship, and perhaps never will be again. The wind had died away to a mere breath, and she lifted over the swells with scarcely steerage-way on her. Not a gun could be brought to bear. Her mizzen-topmast was shot away, the wheel was smashed, and the ship had to be steered by the tiller in the gun-room. A double-headed shot killed outright eight marines on the poop and wounded some others. And meanwhile the admiral and his flag-captain continued their quarter-deck promenade as though dinner required digestion and a sea-battle was the last thing in the world to trouble their thoughts.

Presently a shot smashed through the launch as she lay on the booms, and, passing between Lord Nelson and Captain Hardy, bruised the left foot of the latter, tearing the buckle from his shoe. They both instantly stopped and looked inquiringly, each supposing the other to be wounded.

"Neither touched? Lucky!" said Nelson. "We're getting it now, aren't we? But this work is too warm to last long. Hardy. We'll give it 'em back directly, and then they'll see our lads know how to hand back punishment as well as take it. By Jove, aren't the crew behaving beautifully? I've been in one or two fights in my time, but I never saw such pluck as this ship's company is showing today."

"They're behaving splendidly," replied Hardy. "And they'll be using themselves directly, please the Lord. But the enemy are closing up their line. Look ! we can't get through without running one of them aboard."

"I can't help that," replied Nelson; "and I don't see it much matters which we tackle first. Take your choice. Go on board which you please."

By this time the *Victory* had a loss of fifty men in killed and wounded, her studding-sail booms were shot off like carrots at the iron, and her canvas was like fishing-nets; but now she began to pay back in kind what she had received. A forecastle 68-pounder carronade, loaded with a round shot and 500 musket balls was delivered through the *Bucentaure's* cabin-windows as an envoy of what was coming—to wit, a treble shotted broadside at fathom range. The effect of this terrible salute was to disable 400 men and 20 guns, and reduce the *Bucentaure* to a comparatively defenceless state. Then the British ship went on and engaged the *Neptune* and the *Redoutable*.

The *Neptune*, not liking the look of things, kept her distance; so Hardy ported his helm and laid the *Victory* alongside the *Redoutable*, where she was soon pinned by the interfouling of their gear. The French, when they saw collision inevitable, shut their lower-deck ports and fired from them no more; but whilst the ships' black flanks ground against one another to the liftings of the swell, the British fought their guns like men possessed, and dashed water after the shots lest their hoped-for prize should catch fire before she was taken.

But the *Redoutable* had by no means surrendered yet. The fire from her upper decks continued, and a still more destructive fire poured down from the brass swivels mounted in her tops. It was a ball from one of these last which has rendered the battle off Trafalgar shoals doubly memorable down through history.

As they had been doing all through the engagement. Lord Nelson and his flag-captain were continuing their parade up and down the centre of the poop-deck. With his usual disregard for personal comfort when the claims of the service came in. Nelson had caused his cabin skylight to be removed when he hoisted his flag on the *Victory*, and the gap filled in with planking. This gave an uninterrupted

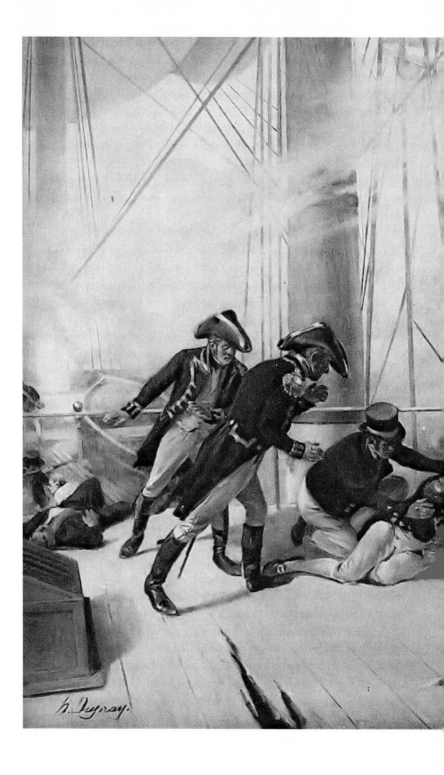

passage-way between the two lines of guns. They had arrived within one pace of the regular turning spot at the cabin ladder-way, when the admiral suddenly faced about. Hardy turned also, and saw his chief in the act of falling.

"You're never hit?" he cried.

"They have done for me at last, Hardy."

"Oh!" I hope not."

"Yes," replied the admiral quietly, "my backbone is shot through." And that, indeed, was very near the truth.

But admiral or powder-boy, in action the treatment is much the same. A marine and two seamen took the wounded man below, and the fight went on without a check. The fire from the *Redoutable's* tops as well as from her second-deck guns, which were pointed upwards, proved terribly destructive, and nearly the whole of the men and officers on the *Victory's* upper deck fell killed or wounded.

The French were not slow to perceive their chance. The bellying curve of the two ships prevented their stepping from bulwark to bulwark, but they lowered their mainyard for a bridge, and across that streamed over to the assault.

"Boarders repel boarders!"

The cry was yelled through the 'tween decks by furious panting officers, and the half-naked men, filthy with gunpowder and blood, streamed up the hatchways in answer. With axe and pike, pistol and cutlass, rammer and tearing fingers, they made their onset; and though the French fought like wolves to retain a footing, the Islanders ravened at them like bulldogs so long as one remained alive upon their sacred deck planks.

Another thirty of the *Victory's* crew were put outside the combat by repelling that gallant assault.

It was the *Redoutable's* final effort. For some time before she had been engaging the *Téméraire* on her port side, and now the British ship, getting athwart her bows, lashed her bowsprit to his gangway and raked her till she surrendered. She had only her foremast left standing, and out of a crew of 645 had 300 killed and 222 wounded, including nearly every one of her officers. But of the ships on the losing side that day, the *Redoutable* fought the best fight of all.

The *Téméraire* herself had meanwhile been getting badly mauled in the rigging, and as her gaff had been shot away, her ensign had fluttered to the deck. Observing this, the French *Fougueux*, then for the moment disengaged, and with 680 men still unhurt, fancied she saw a good opportunity for taking a prize, and bore down upon her. The *Téméraire* was quite prepared. Whilst Hervey, her captain, devoted his attention to the *Redoutable* to port. Kennedy, his first lieutenant, assembled a portion of the crew to starboard, and manned the starboard batteries. They delivered their fire at 100 yards. Crippled and confused, the *Fougeux* ran foul of the British ship and was lashed there, and then Kennedy, accompanied by two midshipmen and a couple of dozen of seamen and marines, boarded her in the port main rigging.

A madder, more reckless piece of work was, perhaps, not done in all that desperate day. The Frenchman had quite 500 men left sound and scatheless; and yet that handful of Téméraires, by sheer dash and insane valour, drove these before them with the bare steel, slaying many, and forcing the rest overboard or down the hatchways; so that in ten minutes the great French two-decker was entirely their own.

To look back now at the *Belleisle*. After throwing in, whilst passing, a broadside to the *Royal Sovereign*'s antagonist, the *Santa Anna*, this British 74 sustained for the next twenty minutes a tremendous fire from half a dozen different ships. Her rigging was terribly cut up, and she lost sixty men. Then, whilst the wreck of her mizzen mast masked her after guns, the French *Achille* engaged her with comparative impunity, whilst the *Aigle* gave it her on the starboard side, and other ships fired into her as they passed. Later, the French *Neptune* came up, and shooting away her remaining masts by the board reduced her to a helpless hulk. It seemed as though she had to choose between strike or sink.

Her hull was almost knocked to pieces; guns were unshipped, and lay on a pulp of torn carriages and men; ports, port-timbers, channels, chain-plates, anchors, boats, spars, were all reduced to splintered wood and twisted iron; but she fired with the few guns she could use, and when the *Swiftsure* came up to her rescue she hoisted a Union Jack on a pike, and sent up a thin cheer from amongst the tangled wreckage. Her loss in men was fearfully severe; but though she was totally unmanageable, her gun-crews stood by their weapons and fired at any enemy that came within range to the very end of the action.

In the meanwhile other ships which had been left behind by failure of the wind came up into the hot *mêlée*, and began by finishing off what others had begun. The English *Neptune* poured a broadside into the *Bucentaure*, Nelson's first antagonist, and knocked away the main and mizzen masts. The *Leviathan* gave her another

dose at thirty yards, smashing her stern into matchwood, and the *Conqueror* soon afterwards did the same, bringing down her one remaining stick, and with it her flag. A marine officer and five men went off in a boat to take possession, and he found that Nelson

had guessed right the *Bucentaure* was indeed the ship of the allies' commander-in-chief

De Villeneuve and his two captains offered their swords to the marine, but he, thinking it more properly belonged to his captain to disarm officers of their rank, declined the honour of receiving them. Having secured the magazine and put the key in his pocket, and placed one of his men as sentry at each cabin door, the marine clapped the admiral and captains in his boat, and with his three remaining hands pulled away. The *Conqueror*, however, had proceeded elsewhere in chase, but at length the boat load was picked up by the *Mars*, her sister ship. Lieutenant Hennah, however, the acting commander of the *Mars*, had no nice scruples about illustrious prisoners. He curtly ordered De Villeneuve and his friends below, and went on fighting.

The *Leviathan* meanwhile, meeting with the Spanish 74 *San Augustino*, had another set-to at a hundred-yards range. The Spaniard attempted a raking fire, but by sheer seamanship the British two-decker avoided this and poured one in herself at pistol range. Down went like a falling tree the *San Augustino's* mizzenmast, and with it her colours; and then to make certain that she should strike in fact, as she had done in accident, the *Leviathan* laid her on board. A smart and well-directed fire cleared the upper decks, and then the British third lieutenant and a party of seamen and marines followed it up and took her without further opposition.

Scarcely had the *Leviathan* lashed this prize to herself than the *Intrépide*, a fresh ship from the allied fleet, came surging up; and after raking the *Leviathan* ahead, ranged up along her starboard side and prepared for close action. Here, however, she got more than she wanted, for the *Africa*, another late-comer of the Island fleet, dropped in to share her fire and return it with compound interest. The *Africa*, which was only a 64-gun ship, got a tremendous mauling, but she half knocked her big antagonist into her primitive staves, put two hundred of her crew *hors de combat*, and in the end forced her to strike.

Thus, one after another, of the nineteen ships composing the rear of the allies, eleven had been captured and one burnt, while seven quitted the line and ran to leeward. The burnt ship was the French 74 *Achille*, which, in passing encounters with other craft, had lost her mizzenmast, main-topmast, and foreyard, and was also on fire in her foretop. Her fire-engine had been wrecked by a gunshot, and as the flames could not be extinguished, the only alternative was to cut away the mast in its entirety, so that it might fall clear of the ship. The crew were about to do this when a furious broadside from the *Prince* cut the mast in two about its centre, and the wreck with its spouting flames fell directly upon the boats in the waist. These soon caught fire also, and the blaze bit into the wooden fabric of the ship itself and crept hungrily down to the decks below.

The *Prince*, seeing what had befallen her antagonist, ceased fire and hove-to, and then, with the *Swiftsure*, hoisted out all the boats left that would float, to save the *Achille's* crew. It was a dangerous service, because the guns of the blazing ship fired of their own accord when the fire reached them, and the *Swiftsure's* boats had three men killed by the shot. That the *Achille* had already suffered heavy loss may be judged from the fact that her senior surviving officer was a midshipman. He, however—poor fellow!—perished with most of his crew when the ship exploded. But to his credit be it said that the *Achille* went down with her colours flying, an untaken ship.

And now let us return for a minute and look at the British commander-in-chief. Though conscious of having been smitten by his death-wound, and being in the most excruciating agony of body, his thoughts were still for the fleet's success rather than for himself. As the three bearers were carrying him down the steep ladders to the lower deck, he observed that at least a dozen men were trying to control the jumpings of the tiller, by which the *Victory* had been steered since her wheel was shot away. He sharply bade one of those with him to get relieving tackles rigged without delay; and then another thought struck him. At any moment any of the men who were fighting the guns might recognise him; might pass the word along; and the crew, on hearing that the chief whom they so worshipped had fallen, would be damped and disheartened. In another man this might have been egotism—in Nelson it was a just recognition of the facts; and when with his one remaining hand he spread a handkerchief over his face, so that the features might not be recognised, he proved how truly he had at heart the interests of the day.

The scene in the cockpit to which the dying man was carried was a thing which we can, happily, never reproduce again in real life nowadays. Picture a small wooden den, alive with the writhings of the wounded, and cumbered with dismembered limbs; the warm, sour air thick with dust and powder-smoke; foul cockroaches shambling along the beams, and frightened rats scuttling behind the ceiling. And in the thick of it all, by the light of three miserable "purser's dips" in dull horn-windowed lanterns, which barely made darkness visible with their smoky yellow gleam, were the surgeon and his mates sweating, swearing, slashing, all splashed with horrid red, "*turning out Greenwich pensioners*" (as the phrase ran then) of every poor wretch who came alive into their hands. There was little conservative surgery in 1805. If a limb was wounded, off it came. There was no reducing a fracture; and—there were no anaesthetics. The surgeon was like the times, rough-and-ready; and whilst he plied saw and amputating-knife, his lusty mates pinned down the shrieking victim like an ox in the shambles.

The admiral received all the attention this poor place could give. He was laid on a spread- out hammock bed, which rested on the deck planks, stripped of his clothes, and examined by Beatty, the surgeon. The diagnosis was only too certain: there was not a vestige of hope; and his life would be hours of anguish and torment till death gave him lasting ease.

The deck beams above him buckled and creaked to the working of the guns; the deck planks on which he rested swung to the kick of furious broadsides; and the din of the fight drowned the moanings of the maimed around him. Between the maddening spasms of torture, the battle's outcome was his sole thought during that terrible lingering in the gateway of Death. Again and again he sent anxious messages to his flag-captain, but it was not till more than an hour after the admiral had received his wound that Captain Hardy could find a moment's respite from his duties in order to visit the cockpit.

They shook hands affectionately, and Nelson said—

"Well, Hardy, how goes the battle? How goes the day with us?"

"Very well, my lord. We have got twelve or fourteen of the enemies' ships in our possession. But five of their van have tacked, and show an intention of bearing down on the *Victory*. I have therefore called two or three of our fresh ships round us, and have no doubt of giving them a drubbing."

"I hope none of our ships have struck. Hardy?"

"No, my lord. There is small fear of that."

"Well, I am a dead man. Hardy, but I am glad of what you say. Oh, whip them now you've got 'em; whip them as they've never been whipped before."

Another fifty minutes passed before the flag-captain could come below again, but this time he was able to report that the number of captures was fourteen or fifteen.

"That's better," replied the dying man, "though I bargained for twenty. And now, anchor, Hardy— anchor."

"I suppose, my lord, that Admiral Collingwood will now take upon himself the direction of affairs?"

"Not while I live," said Nelson, raising himself on his elbow and then falling back. "No; I command here—yet. No. Do *you* anchor, Hardy."

"Then shall *we* make the signal, my lord? "

"Yes," said Nelson, "for, if I live, I'll anchor." There was a silence for a minute, broken only by the dull booming of guns, and then, in a faint voice, "I say. Hardy," whispered the admiral.

"Yes."

"Don't have my poor carcase hove overboard. Get what's left of me sent to England, if you can manage it. Goodbye, Hardy. I've done my duty, and I thank God for it."

The flag-captain could not speak. He squeezed his chieftain's hand, and left the cockpit; and ten minutes later Horatio, Viscount Nelson, stepped in rank with the world's greatest warriors who are dead.

The news was taken to the *Royal Sovereign*, and Vice-Admiral Collingwood assumed the command. Hardy carried it himself, and at the same time delivered Lord Nelson's dying request that both the fleet and prizes should come to an anchor as soon as practicable. An on-shore gale was imminent, the shoals of Cape Trafalgar were under their lee, and scarcely a ship was left fully rigged. Many, indeed, were entirely dismasted, and in tow either of the frigates or of their less-mauled fellows. But, bosom friends though they had always been, Nelson and Collingwood were diametrically opposed in their plans of proceeding. "What!" the new admiral exclaimed when he heard the message, "anchor the fleet? Why, it is the last thing I should have thought of."

The fleet was not anchored, and the British ships and their prizes were ordered to stand out to sea. But the rising gale moaned round them as though singing a dirge for the dead, and the power of the elements was more than a match for the most superb seamanship on all the oceans. Out of eighteen prizes captured, four were retaken by the allied ships, which swooped down on their worn-out prize crews; some were driven ashore and wrecked; some foundered at sea with all hands; one was scuttled; and of the total only four were brought safely to the British naval station in Gibraltar Bay.

There have been other actions between French and British ships since 1805, but never one of any magnitude. The sea power of France and her ally was broken for good, and with it was made the first real move towards the overthrow of Napoleon. The victory was due to the prestige and genius of one man, and he died in the moment of his

triumph. His death has been regretted, but who shall say that he could have gained any worldly advantage by remaining on? He died at the zenith of his fame, and he could not have added to it, because no great battle had afterwards to be fought. Had he survived, he would have had a triumphal entry into London, with honours and riches showered on him. And after that? Would his old age have been without reproach? It is open to doubt.

As it befell, he was accorded a magnificent national funeral, a niche in Westminster Abbey, and statues all over the islands whose safety he so gallantly preserved. His failings are forgotten; his name is a household word—*sans peur, sans reproche.*

How different a fate was that of the man who fought against him! De Villeneuve lay a prisoner in England till 1806, and then obtained his freedom. On his journey to Paris he stopped at Rennes to learn how the emperor would receive him. On the morning of April 22nd he was found dead in bed, with six knife-wounds in his heart.

October 14, 1806

Jéna

D. H. Parry

To the Prussian people 1806 was an *année terrible*, and their subsequent reprisals of 1814, 1815, and even of 1870, have not effaced the memory of Jéna, as the French elect to call the little Saxon town.

Whatever difference of opinion may exist as to the *bona fides* of Napoleon and the Prussian Government respectively in their diplomatic relations, all are agreed that the military spirit of that country hastened on the war; and never did nation undertake hostilities at a more un- fortunate moment or in clumsier fashion.

The French army, returning slowly from its glorious campaign of Austerlitz, was close at hand, and flushed with victory; and although in rags, with its pay held advisedly in arrears, it was in high moral feather, and looking forward to the fetes that were promised it when it should arrive in France.

The Prussian army, on the other hand, while full of undoubted courage, was precisely in that condition one would expect as the result of its ruling system.

Its regiments, like our own in the last century, were farmed by their colonels; class distinction was rife among the officers, and the men were ruled by "Corporal Schlague"—in other words, flogged unmercifully into shape.

Their drill and traditions went back to the days of Frederick the Great, and the only pension granted to the discharged veteran was *a licence to beg publicly!*

So wretched was the condition of the soldier, even when serving, that Marbot was solicited for alms by the grenadiers at the king's gates

SKETCH MAP

English Miles

0   6   12   18   ·24

both at Potsdam and in Berlin; and yet it was this army, with little or no sympathy between its officers and men, strapped up in tight uniforms, hampered with absurd regulations, and in every respect half a century behind the times, that sharpened its sabres on the doorsteps of the French ambassador, and clamoured wildly to engage the invincible legions of the emperor.

It had its wish, against the better judgment of its sovereign, and met with perhaps the most crushing defeat recorded in history, being sacrificed to the crass stupidity of its leaders, of whom a word must be said here in justice to the army itself.

The Duke of Brunswick, its actual commander-in-chief, the father of our unfortunate Queen Caroline, was seventy years old, and credited with a great military reputation, though authentic proofs of it may be searched for in vain. He had fought under the celebrated Frederick, who disliked him, and had been beaten by the *sans-culottes* in the wars of the Revolution.

One review-day at Magdeburg, when a field-marshal, he sprang from the saddle, allowed his charger to run loose, and caned a non-commissioned officer for some mistake in a manoeuvre; but nevertheless it was into the hands of this egregious old ass that the Prussian fortunes were entrusted.

Associated with Brunswick—and in truth they seem to have been unable to do anything without previously holding a long *pow-wow* when they ought to have been marching—were Marshal Möllendorf, a worn-out old man of eighty-two; Prince Frederick Louis of Hohenlohe-Ingelfingen, an infantry general, whose sixty years had afforded him little opportunity of distinction in the field; Colonel Massenbach, Hohenlohe's quartermaster-general, whose practical advice was not listened to, probably because it was practical; and several other officers, some of whom distinguished themselves later on in the War of Liberty, but the majority men of no account, who squabbled at the councils, disobeyed orders, and had nothing but personal bravery to commend them.

At the head of the younger branch of officers was Prince Louis Ferdinand, a dashing, hare-brained young fellow, whose passion was pretty equally divided between the worship of Venus and Mars, and whose early death was much deplored.

Between the two factions, ancient and modern, there was perpetual strife, and between these two stools, which the energetic French kicked over in an incredibly short time, the Prussian army came heavily to the ground.

******

"The insolent braggarts shall soon learn that *our* weapons need no sharpening!" said Napoleon, when Marbot told him of the affront to his ambassador; and again, when he read the foolish demand that his troops should cross the Rhine and abandon German territory by a given date, he exclaimed to Berthier, "Prince, we will be punctually at the rendezvous; but instead of being in France on the 8th, we will be in Saxony."

The October of 1806 was a splendid month—a slight frost during the nights, but the days magnificent, with white *cumuli* rolling across the blue, when the blue was not entirely unclouded; and on the 8th day of that eventful month the French advanced in three great columns into the rocky valleys that led from Franconia to Saxony: an army—when the cavalry and artillery of the Guard joined it—of 186,000 men, led by masters in the art of war.

The emperor accompanied the centre column, composed of the infantry of the Guard, under Lefebvre, husband of the well-known

"*Madame Sans-Gêne*," Bernadotte's 1st Corps, Davout's 3rd Corps, and Murat's Cavalry Reserve; the whole marching by Kronach on the road to Schleitz and Jéna.

The right column, consisting of Soult's 4th and Ney's 6th Corps, with a Bavarian division, set out for Hoff by forced marches, and the left, made up of Lannes with the 5th Corps and Augereau with the 7th, turned its face towards Coburg, Gräfenthal, and Saalfeld.

The Prussians, to the number of 125,000, which did not include garrisons and sundry detached forces, were also divided into three bodies: General Rüchel with the right, 30,000, being on the Hessian frontier about Eisenach; the main army of 55,000, under Brunswick and the king in person, around Magdeburg; and the left wing, under Hohenlohe, 40,000 strong, being advanced towards the enemy round and about the fortified places of Schleitz, Saalfeld, Saalburg, and Hoff, in defiance of Brunswick's orders, which desired Hohenlohe to recross the Saale and take post behind the mountains that rise above that river.

Their motive was to cut off Napoleon from his base in the Maine valley; but directly they heard that his march was directed towards their left and centre, they changed their plans and attempted a concentration about Weimar, which exposed their magazines, threw their flank invitingly open to the enemy, and necessitated marches by cross roads and byways in a country of which, extraordinary fact, their staff possessed no reliable map!

While this movement was in progress the French came upon them, and struck the first blow at the little town of Saalburg, where

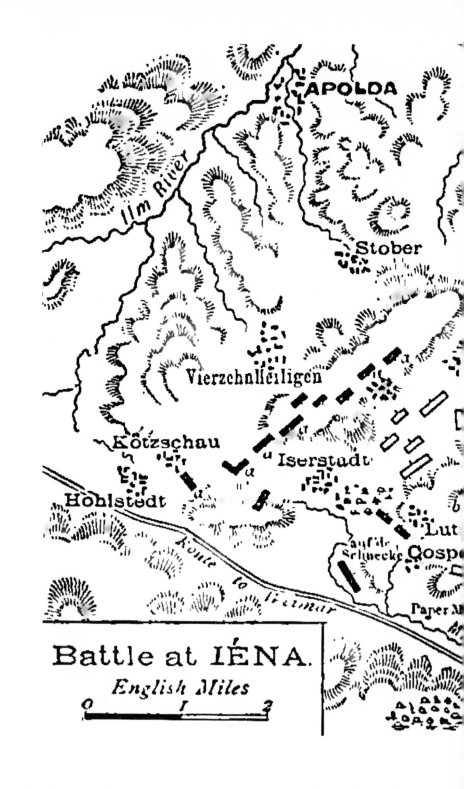

Battle at IÉNA.

English Miles

0   1   2

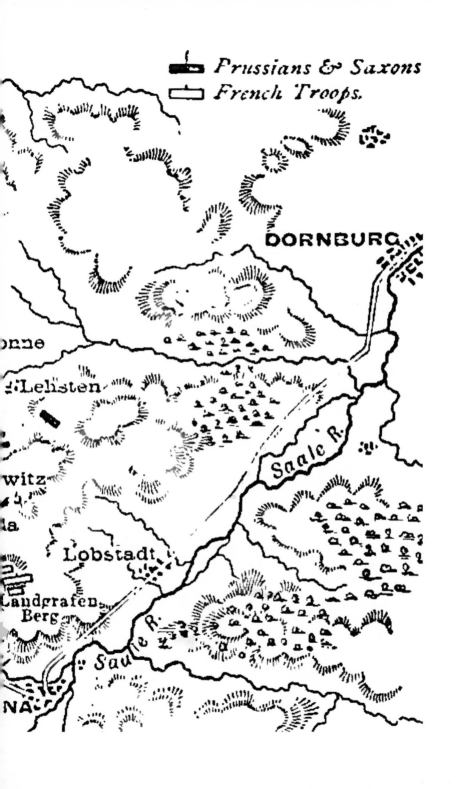

a portion of Hohenlohe's men under General Tauenzien were entrenched behind the river.

It was the first day of the advance, and Murat, with some light cavalry and the famous 27th Light Infantry, lost no time in falling to. Some cannon-shots, an advance of the 27th Léger, and Tauenzien melted away in the direction of Schleitz, where on the 9th, about noon, the centre found him drawn up beyond the Wisenthal in order of battle with his back against a height. While Bernadotte, who commanded, was reconnoitring, Napoleon arrived, and ordered the attack.

Bernadotte sent the 27th Léger forward under General Maisons, and the regiment quickly debouched from the town upon the enemy; but finding himself in the presence of a superior force, Tauenzien again ordered a retreat.

The 94th and 95th of the Line under Drouet followed close on their heels, mounted the height, and hastened down the other slope; while Murat, riding at the head of the 4th Hussars—the regiment in which Marshal Ney had made his *début* as a private—charged the cavalry that turned upon him. At the first shock the 4th overthrew the Prussians; but they were reinforced by several fresh squadrons, and Murat sent for the 5th Chasseurs post haste, who coming up at the gallop flung their green and yellow ranks into the *mêlée*.

Tauenzien hurled his hussars and the red Saxon Dragoons against the two regiments, and matters looked serious for Murat, although Captain Razout of the 94th opened from an ambuscade and killed fifty of them; but Maisons arriving with five companies of the 27th Léger poured in such a terrible fire that 200 red troopers went down in a mass and the rest bolted.

These dragoons were antiquated looking fellows, with cocked hats and pigtails, their officers riding with huge canes significantly dangling from wrist or saddle; and as they went about to the rear the 4th Hussars and 5th Chasseurs re-formed and spurred in pursuit, driving them into the woods among their disorganised infantry.

It was short and sharp, but the effect upon the Prussians—who left 2,000 muskets behind them in their flight, nearly 500 prisoners, and 300 killed and wounded—was serious.

Murat still pushed on, and next day, the 10th, Lasalle captured the enemy's baggage, and a pontoon train, Napoleon writing that the cavalry "was saddled in gold;" but on the same day a much more important engagement took place at Saalfeld between the French left, under Marshal Lannes, and Prince Louis, who commanded Hohenlohe's rear-guard.

Saalfeld was a little walled town of about 5,000 inhabitants, and partly to allow time for the evacuation of the magazines in its rear, partly from a burning desire to fight. Prince Louis obtained Hohenlohe's permission to remain there. He was then thirty-four, brave as a lion, but insubordinate, and of very loose morals.

In Prussia he is regarded as a hero, and there is something in his oval face as it hangs in the Hohenzollern Museum with the hair tied in a ribbon, that reminds one of our own "Prince Charlie."

He had eighteen guns, eighteen squadrons of hussars, and eleven battalions of infantry; and with that force he rashly engaged the experienced Lannes, who was advancing with 25,000 troops, although in effect only the artillery, two regiments of cavalry, and the division of Suchet came into action.

The division of Suchet, which comprised the 17th Léger, and the 34th, 40th, 64th, and 88th of the Line, with the 9th and 10th Hussars, found themselves before the enemy at 7 o'clock in the morning.

Instantly ranging his guns on the heights that commanded the Prussians, Lannes opened fire, and sent part of Suchet's skirmishers through the woods to gall Prince Louis' right.

Until nearly 1 o'clock the Prussians stood their ground, but Suchet working round in their rear and Lannes pouring down upon them in front, they broke and fled, leaving fifteen guns behind them.

Louis charged gallantly with two cavalry regiments flanked by the white-uniformed Saxon Hussars, but Claparède's and Vedel's brigades routed them, and they also retreated.

Rallying them with difficulty, he charged again at the head of the Saxon Hussars, whose tall flowerpot *shakoes* and bright blue *pelisses* were soon jumbled together in a confused mass among the willow-fringed marshes by the river bank, where the scarlet and blue 9th, and the light blue 10th Hussars made short work of them.

Then came the crowning catastrophe of the day; for as the prince's charger got into difficulties with a hedge, Quartermaster Guindé of the 10th rode up sabre in hand. Covered with glittering orders and in general's uniform, he replied to the word "Surrender!" with a slash that laid Guindé's face open; but the *maréchal des logis* ran him clean through the chest, and he fell dying on to the grass under his horse.

Marbot, to whom he had been very courteous not long before in Berlin, saw his body on a marble table, naked to the waist, next day, and his death sent a thrill of consternation through the Prussian army.

Guindé, ignorant at first of the man he had slain, was awarded the

Legion of Honour, and appointed soon after to the Horse Grenadiers of the Guard, in whose ranks he was killed, when a captain, at Hanau in 1813.

The spirit of prophecy would seem to have been present with the men of that age, for Jomini foretold the exact movements that Napoleon would make, Massenbach the Prussian defeats, and Napoleon himself, speaking of Prince Louis, said, "As for him, I foretell that he will be killed in this campaign."

So far the French advance had been a succession of triumphs, destined to continue without rebuff for the rest of the war; and as the Prussian spirit sank at the news of each defeat, that of the invaders rose. Reviewing the 2nd Chasseurs-à-cheval at Lobenstein on the 12th of

October, Napoleon asked Colonel Bousson how many men he had present. "Five hundred, sire," said the colonel; "but there are many raw troops among them."

"What does that signify? Are they not all Frenchmen?" was the angry reply; and turning to the regiment, he cried, "My lads, you must not fear death: when soldiers defy death they drive him into the enemy's ranks," with a motion of his arm which called forth a sudden convulsive movement among the squadrons and a wild shout of enthusiasm.

The losses of the Prussians at Saalfeld, which are variously stated, seem to have been about thirty guns, a thousand prisoners, and a similar number of killed and wounded, together with a quantity of baggage; but these were only the shadows of coming events, and the French columns moved on swiftly, learning by the capture of the post-bag that the enemy were moving on Weimar from Erfurt.

Hohenlohe's troops were ordered to place the hills and forests of Thuringia between them and the victorious foe, and, worn out by marching, were struggling on in the midst of waggon-trains and bad roads, when fugitives from Saalfeld spread terror among them, and they fled in disorder across the Saale into Jéna.

Napoleon likewise concentrated his troops, and the map must be studied to understand their movements in and among towns and villages unknown outside the history of this campaign.

Lannes was directed upon Auma, where the headquarters were, by way of Pösneck and Neustadt, with Augereau on his left; Soult was to proceed by Weida to Gera along the Elster; and Ney was to occupy Auma when the *grand quartier général* should have left it.

ut was sent north to Naumburg, with Bernadotte to follow as Murat's cavalry scoured the country towards Leipsic, which rs afterwards took with true French audacity; and on the ., .apoleon set out for Gera, escorted by the brilliant 1st Hussars with their sky-blue white-laced uniforms and scarlet pantaloons, his cavalry of the Guard not having then arrived at the front.

A strong barrier now intervened between the two armies, French and Prussian, the river Saale flowing, roughly, northward to the Elbe through hilly country, and only passable to an army at five points where there were bridges—*viz.* at Jéna, Löbstadt, Dornburg, Camburg, and Köser, the latter place opposite Naumburg.

The Prussians having gone helter-skelter across that river at Jéna, they were virtually hemmed in an angle, formed by the Thuringian Mountains to the south and the Saale to the west, so that as their fortresses, their remaining magazines, and their very capital lay open to the enemy, they had but two alternatives—either to make another long flank march to the line of the Elbe or to stay where they were and defend the Saale and its fringe of hills.

The Duke of Brunswick, however, seems to have had a genius for keeping himself out of harm's way; and leaving Hohenlohe to defend the heights of Jéna, though with strict orders not to attack, and Rüchel to collect the outlying forces at Weimar, he set off with his five divisions, bag and baggage, to pass the Saale at Naumburg and reach the line of the Elbe, hastened in this fatal decision by the news

of Davout's advance on Naumburg—in other words, he ran away with 65,000 men and left others to do the fighting.

On the 13th of October the army started—ominous date for the superstitiously inclined; and on the same day Napoleon, expecting to find the entire enemy before him, set out from Gera for Jéna, having despatched Montesquiou, one of his *officiers d'ordonnance*, to the King of Prussia with proposals of peace—in reality to gain time for his troops to come up.

It was, to a great extent, a game of cross-purposes; for Brunswick, anticipating a free passage at Naumburg, found Davout and *death*; Napoleon, expecting the whole Prussian army beyond Jéna, found only its rear-guard; and Hohenlohe, looking for Lannes and Augereau, received the full weight of the emperor himself with the bulk of his forces.

Lannes preceded the emperor, and had a sharp skirmish with Tauenzien beyond the little university town of Jéna (or Jena), and when Napoleon arrived some of the quaint gabled houses were burning—ignited, it is said, by the Prussian batteries.

Jéna nestles under the lea of a range of hills, the most important being the Landgrafenberg; and the high road to Weimar runs through a difficult valley named the Mühlthal from the paper-mill which stood there.

Having no mind to force that defile, which determined men might have rendered a veritable Thermopylæ, the emperor made a reconnaissance with Lannes under fire to find some means of carrying the army over the hills on to the plateau beyond, where he should find the Prussians and a natural battle-ground.

Lannes's *tirailleurs* had captured a pass, but it was useless for artillery; and it was a Saxon parson, exasperated at the sight of the burning town, who pointed out a path on the Landgrafenberg itself, by which, with the help of the sappers, the French could get up their guns.

For this action the worthy man endured such after persecution that he was obliged to leave the country and reside in Paris.

How they cut away the rock and hauled each cannon to the summit with teams of twelve horses apiece, how the battery that was to open fire next morning stuck fast in the dark and was assisted by Napoleon with a lantern in his hand, is well known, and nowhere is it better told than in the pages of "Tom Burke of Ours," which, in spite of its numerous errors, remains one of the most magnificent pictures of Napoleonic times ever penned.

During the long, cold night the Prussian bivouac fires lit up the

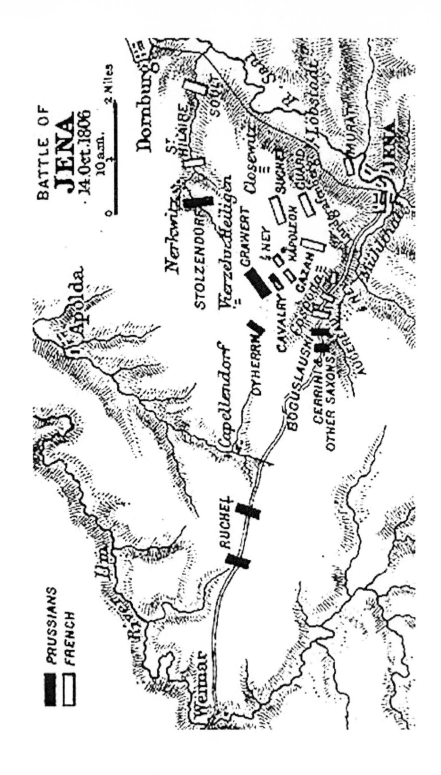

BATTLE OF
JENA
14 Oct. 1806
10 a.m.

PRUSSIANS
FRENCH

horizon beyond the hill-tops, but those of the *Grande Armée* made only a faint gleam high up on the crest of the mountain, and the enemy saw nothing to warn them that 40,000 men were tightly packed there, the crossbelts of one almost touching the cowskin pack of his front rank.

Suchet's division lay waiting for dawn with its right on the Rauh-thal ravine; Gazan lurked on the left before the village of Cospoda, 4,000 of the Guard formed a huge square, in the centre of which the Emperor snatched a short repose, and the engineers were busy widening the Steiger path for the passage of the guns.

The Capitaine Cogniet, then a private in the Grenadiers of the Guard, has told us how twenty men per company were allowed to descend into the narrow streets of the deserted town below them to search for food; how they found it in plenty, together with good wine in the cellars of the hotels, each grenadier bringing back three bottles, two in his fur cap, and one in his pocket, with which they drank to the health of the King of Prussia; how they imbibed hot wine all night, carrying it to the artillery, who were half-dead with fatigue; and—ingenuous Cogniet!—confessing that the Guard up on the mountain side were all more or less elevated in a double sense.

At last the morning came, but with it a fog so thick that the enemy were invisible.

Napoleon had been astir at four o'clock, and having sent his final orders to his marshals, issued from the curtains of his blue and white striped tent, and passed before Lannes's corps by torchlight.

"Soldiers," said he, "the Prussian army is turned as the Austrian was a year ago at Ulm. . . . Fear not its renowned cavalry; oppose to their charges firm squares and the bayonet."

The cheers of the soldiers still carried no warning to the Prussian lines. Their hussars had intercepted Montesquiou during the night, and arguing from his message of peace that there would be no fighting on the 14th, the army had made no provision even for the day's rations, and lay in the fog in fancied security.

Then, about six, when the mist lightened, came a rude awakening. The 17th Leger and a chosen battalion, under Claparède, crept forward in single line, flanked by the 34th and 40th in close column, commanded by Reille, with the 64th and 88th, under Vedel, in their rear—in short, Suchet's division making silently for Closwitz, while Gazan felt his way towards Cospoda on Suchet's left.

With Gazan were the 21st Leger, and the 28th, 100th, and 103rd of the Line, and the two divisions enveloped in the fog drew nearer and

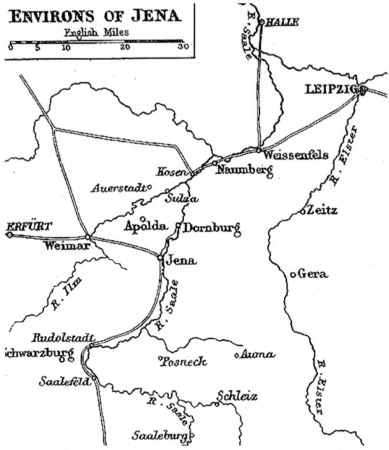

ENVIRONS OF JENA

English Miles

nearer to the unsuspecting foe until, after they had groped their way for nearly an hour, Claparède suddenly received the fire of Zweifel's Prussian battalion and the Saxon ones of Frederick Augustus and Rechten, seeing only the flash of musketry from the wood that surrounded Closwitz.

The 17th returned the fire warmly, firing into the vapour before them, but when they saw the trees looming up in front, Claparède charged and bayoneted them out of wood and village.

Gazan was also successful in his attack on Cospoda, and, advancing farther, took the hamlet of Lutzenrode from the enemy's fusiliers; but a withering fire was soon opened on both divisions by Cerrini's Saxons, which they sustained for some time until the 34th, which had relieved the 17th, went at them with the bayonet and put them to flight, a disorder which carried the rest of Tauenzien's corps away, leaving twenty cannon and a host of fugitives in the hands of Lannes, who followed at a swinging pace downhill after the cowards.

In less than two hours they had cleared their front for the army on the heights to deploy. A lull came about nine o'clock, and before the action was resumed Ney had arrived at speed; Soult with one division took post behind Closwitz; and Augereau, who was then lamenting the loss of his amiable wife, after pushing Heudelet, his guns, and cavalry along the Mühlthal towards Weimar, left the Gibbet Hill with Desjardin and placed himself on Gazan's left among the fine fir woods that clothed the plateau.

The mist was rising and promised to break, but it was yet some time before the sun shone brightly.

Prince Hohenlohe, whom disaster seemed to pursue, galloped to his troops, who were encamped on the Weimar road awaiting the French left wing as they thought, where Tauenzien's fugitives soon alarmed him, and called forth his better qualities to prepare for a general action.

Hurrying the Prussian infantry under Grawert to occupy Tauenzien's lost positions, he posted two Saxon brigades under Burgsdorf and Nehroff, Boguslauski's Prussian battalion, and a strong force of artillery to hold the Weimar road to the death, with Cerrini, who had rallied and been reinforced by four Saxon battalions, in support.

Dyherrn, with five battalions, acted as reserve to Grawert. Tauen-

zien was rallied a long way to the rear, and Holzendorf, who formed Hohenlohe's left, was ordered to attack the French right, while he himself should fall on their centre with cavalry and guns, pending the arrival of Rüchel from Weimar.

The heights above Jéna, the ravines, and the dense woods were capable of the most stubborn defence, and the French would have had to *fight climbing*; but the passage of the Landgrafenberg had altered everything, and as the sun shone out about ten o'clock Hohenlohe saw an astonishing spectacle.

The enemy stretched in dark masses along the high ground on *his own* side of the mountain, outnumbering him in the proportion of two to one, outflanking him to left and right, and prepared to foam down the slope and sweep him off the face of the earth.

Nor did the foe allow him much time to digest the surprise; for the impetuous Ney, who had hurried forward with 3,000 men and deployed in the mist between Lannes and Augereau, flung himself upon the village of Vierzehn-Heiligen in the very centre of the battlefield, and anticipated the emperor's orders for a renewal of the fight.

Soult with St. Hilaire's division advanced from Löbstadt and constituted the French right; Lannes, with Suchet and Gazan, formed the centre, and Augereau having scrambled out of the Mühlthal, menaced Iserstädt on the left; the Guard and the artillery being in rear, and Murat's cavalry marching to join the army.

Indignant at the firing in his front. Napoleon sent to learn from which corps it proceeded, and was greatly astonished to find that Ney, whom he supposed to be still in the rear, was engaging on his own account. Ney's troops were the 25th Léger under Colonel Morel, two battalions formed of the *compagnies d'élite* of several regiments, and Colbert's light cavalry brigade, formed of the 3rd Hussars and 10th Chasseurs-à-cheval; and with these the marshal attacked Hohenlohe with his usual bravery, leading them, as his *aide-de-camp* tells us, " like a corporal of *voltigeurs*."

Hohenlohe's horse-artillery was in position. and the 10th Chasseurs, forming under cover of a little wood, darted out upon it, and took seven guns at one swoop under a fearful fire; but while they were sabring away, the Prussian cuirassiers of Holzendorf and Prittzwitz's dragoons came down with a thunderous rush, and the 10th went about.

The 3rd Hussars, forming behind the same trees, spurred on the Prussian flank and checked the cuirassiers for a moment, but had to retreat in their turn; and Ney, throwing his infantry into two squares, found himself in a bad case at the moment when Napoleon reached a height overlooking the conflict.

Sending Bertrand to Ney's assistance with two light cavalry regiments, probably the 9th and 10th Hussars, he ordered up Lannes; and the gallant Ney made an heroic struggle to hold his own, pushing his grenadiers to the clump of trees that had sheltered his horsemen, and flinging his *voltigeurs* at Vierzehn-Heiligen itself

Up came Lannes at the head of the 21st Léger, and as Grawert deployed before the village in magnificent order, opening a terrible fire, Lannes led five of Claparède's and Gazan's regiments to outflank him.

In every part of the field the crash of musketry and the boom of heavy cannon resounded. Napoleon still believed he had the entire Prussian army before him, and the stubborn resistance justified that opinion.

The Prussian regiments of Zathow and Lanitz covered themselves with glory before Vierzehn-Heiligen. The *cuirassiers* were true to their traditions of Seidlitz and the Seven Years' War; but inch by inch the French gained ground, although it was an hour after midday before they obtained a permanent advantage.

Hares fled terrified about the stubble fields, the soldiers cheering them as they fought. The October woods were strewn with dead men among the fallen leaves, and the hollow ways were full of smoke.

Thanks to the Prussian horse, Hohenlohe took some guns, and his hopes were so far raised that he wrote to Rüchel, "At this moment we beat the enemy at all points."

He soon learned, however, that Soult had almost annihilated his left wing, and Augereau and Lannes under his own eyes drove back his right more than half a mile. The brave man appeared everywhere at once: now heading his *cuirassiers*, now encouraging the infantry, again peering through the clouds that hung before the batteries; but it was all to no purpose. Grawert was badly wounded, Dyherrn's five battalions fled before Augereau, and with a tremendous rolling of drums the whole French army advanced down the slope, the Guard included, about two in the afternoon.

Hohenlohe's next letter to Rüchel was significant:

"Lose not a moment in advancing with your as yet unbroken troops. Arrange your columns so that through your openings there may pass the broken bands of the battle."

In vain Rüchel arrived at last with 20,000 men; Soult fell upon him and they made poor stand, the growing rout already communicating itself to the newcomers.

The French musicians played under the heavy fire; Rüchel was seriously hurt; Hohenlohe's own regiment and the grenadiers of Hahn gave way; and, most terrible of all, Murat and his cavalry came on the scene and overwhelmed everything in a whirlwind of slaughter.

No battle can show a carnage more merciless and horrible than that surge of heavy horsemen among the flying Prussians after Jéna.

They spared nothing in their path, and every one of those fifteen thousand long swords was red with blood from point to hilt.

Rüchel's men had the double misfortune to meet both the victorious French and their flying countrymen in a disorganised mass rolling down hill, and though here and there individual battalions fought bravely to the last, panic seized the whole army and it tore madly to the rear.

Brown-and-gold hussars of Anhalt Pless; light infantry in green jackets piped with red; white Saxon hussars and grim dragoons with the bristle taken out of their moustaches, all mingled in a shocking, terror-stricken mob, covering the roads and fields for miles; Murat's cuirassiers and dragoons slashing and slaying until compelled to halt from very weariness. Many colours were taken in that pursuit, and two curious incidents are worthy of record: Quartermaster Humbert of the 2nd Dragoons captured a standard, but was killed by three musketballs, seeing which, the dragoon Fauveau leaped to the ground, rescued the prize, and carrying it to his colonel under a hail of shot, said modestly, "It was the Quartermaster Humbert who took this flag," for which he received the Cross the same day.

The other instance was that of Colonel Doullembourg of the 1st Dragoons, who was unhorsed and momentarily captured, in the confusion his name appearing in the bulletin as killed.

"It is not worth the trouble of alteration," said Berthier when he protested; and, oddly enough, the mistake was still further perpetuated after the Polish campaign; for certain squares and streets of Paris being named after the officers who fell at Jéna, a Rue Doullembourg came into existence, and again the colonel protested.

"What!" said Berthier, "would you have me give back to the emperor an order so honourable to you? No; live in the Rue Doullembourg and establish your family there."

That night Soult bivouacked round Schwabsdorf; Ney at Weimar, where the rest of his corps joined him, the 59th, as an instance of the fatigue they had endured in their efforts to arrive, lying exhausted for half an hour before they recovered energy sufficient to light a fire;

Lannes halted between Umpferstädt and Ober Weimar; and Marshal Augereau took up his quarters in the house of the Prince of Weimar's head-gardener, where, after twenty-four hours of fasting and fighting, they found nothing to eat but pineapples and hothouse plums.

Napoleon returned to Jéna for the night, where he received the professors of the university, and rewarded the Saxon clergyman to whom he owed so much; and there he composed the Fifth Bulletin, one of the most mendacious of his productions.

It is also recorded that he crossed the battlefield and administered brandy with his own hands to many of the wounded.

But Jéna, sanguinary as it was, was not *the* battle of the campaign. Another action had been fought near Auerstädt at the same moment, which broke up the main body of the enemy, and covered Davout with a glory for which he was not allowed his full mead of praise.

The Prussian army of the centre marched leisurely towards the Saale, taking no heed to the whereabouts of Davout and Bernadotte, flattering itself that it was out of danger, and bivouacking about Auerstädt on the night of the 13th with empty stomachs.

The Prussian patrols gave warning of their approach to a battalion of the 25th of the Line, which Davout had posted where the great high road winds down the defile of Köser to the bridge across the Saale; and Davout, whose extreme short-sight made him remarkably minute in his reconnaissances, rode up with his staff in the evening to investigate how matters stood.

Learning from some prisoners that the Prussian centre was before him, he ordered his corps to march at midnight and occupy the heights between the enemy and the river over which he must pass, and went to Bernadotte to concert measures with him.

Then one of those strange things happened which often sully the page of history and the fame of great men. Bernadotte chose to interpret certain orders of Napoleon's to his own liking, an old quarrel existing between the two marshals.

In the belief that a force of 80,000 men (for Brunswick's army was magnified to that number) menaced a post to be held at all hazards, the future King of Sweden carried off his corps of over 20,000 to Dornburg, and left Davout with 28,756 to bear the entire brunt of the battle.

Brunswick's army not having been as yet engaged may be justly estimated at close upon 66,000. Consequently Davout's task was heroic, and he set about it with that methodical care which distinguished all his actions, and earned his title of Duke of Auerstädt nobly.

Between the bridge of Köser and the village of Auerstädt, which lies ten miles south-west of Naumburg and about twelve due north of Jéna, there is a natural hollow intersected by a rivulet, through which the high road runs, and after passing through Hassenhausen on the Naumburg side of the hollow, descends by the defile of Köser to the Saale.

To this position Davout marched in the darkness of the early morning, and formed Friant's division on the edge of the dip at six o'clock as Blücher's advance-guard of cavalry reached the other ridge.

The fog was so dense that the combatants could not see each other,

and Blücher's troopers, after crossing the basin and pushing up the opposite slope, fell in with Davout's light horse, and exchanged pistol-shots, losing a few prisoners.

As both sides paused and the French *chasseurs* fell back behind their infantry, the 25th of the Line unlimbered some guns and fired grape into the valley below.

Blücher's party retreated, leaving a battery in Davout's hands, and the Prussian staff held an anxious council near the rivulet which they had passed with Schmettau's division forming their van.

Brunswick, as usual, advised caution and to wait, but was overruled by the King and Marshal Möllendorf.

Meanwhile, Davout had posted Gudin about Hassenhausen, especially to the French right of that village, and filled a fir plantation with *tirailleurs*, who gave Schmettau a warm welcome as he deployed and advanced.

When the fog lifted and they saw Gudin on the ridge, Blücher made a detour and charged his flank with a cloud of cavalry; but the 25th, 21st, and 12th of the Line formed square, a general in each, Davout himself hovering about them to direct their efforts, and Blücher led four desperate rushes in vain, getting his horse shot under him and retreating in disorder.

The 25th was one of those regiments which Napoleon had recently clothed in white as an experiment, abandoned after Eylau in consequence of the fearful spectacle the blood-bedabbled field presented. Its facings were bright orange, as were also its towering plumes.

While his cavalry hastened the retreat of Blücher, Davout concentrated Gudin in Hassenhausen, placed Friant on its right and Morand, when he arrived, on the left, an arrangement hardly completed when the Prussians, reinforced by the divisions of Wartensleben and Orange, attacked with great fury.

Wartensleben, in particular, attempted to rush the village, and there was some ghastly work with the bayonet in the street and gardens, but the 85th, 25th, and 21st held it well.

From nine o'clock until ten the attack lasted, both sides displaying magnificent bravery.

Gudin lost half his men, all the divisions suffered severely, but the Prussians had also to lament several of their chiefs.

Schmettau, wounded, refused to leave the field, and was hit a second time, mortally; Brunswick, brave in action if timid in council, received a mortal wound, some say in the mouth, others in the chest, while fighting in the thick of it; and poor old Möllendorf, who had been page to Frederick the Great, was struck down and afterwards captured in Erfurt.

The King of Prussia had his horse killed, and a piece of shell that entered Davout's hat at the cockade tore away some of the marshal's hair. When Morand came up, leaving one battalion at the bridge of Köser, he dislodged Wartensleben, and was gaining ground on the left when he was charged by the cavalry under Prince William. Morand formed his men into squares, and, shattered as they were by the terrific fire. Prince William's ten thousand horse could make no impression upon them.

Morand took his place in one square, Davout in another, and so deadly were the volleys from them that they created "around them a rampart of corpses."

The 17th of the Line in particular was noticed for its coolness; it was another of the "white" regiments, with scarlet facings, and as the enemy approached it raised its *shakoes* on the bayonet-points, and shouted "*Vive l'Empereur!*"

"Why not fire, then?" cried Colonel Lanusse.

"Time enough for that: at fifteen paces you will see!" was the answer. Then they fired!

At length, when the mangled squadrons retired behind the shelter of their infantry, Morand formed his squares into columns of attack, and forced Wartensleben back to the stream as Friant advanced on his side and drove Schmettau's division and the Prince of Orange's first brigade down the slope, clearing Hassenhausen of all but the fallen.

The fighting was now abandoned on the slope, and was transferred to the marshes in the hollow and to the villages in front of Auerstadt, both sides exhausted with the six hours of combat.

The Prussian reserve under Kalkreuth still remained intact, and the king, backed up by brave Blücher, was disposed to make a final effort; but, overwhelmed by the many opinions which were allowed expression, a retreat was decided upon—a retreat on Weimar, where Hohenlohe and Rüchel would join them—for nothing was known yet of the Battle of Jéna.

Kalkreuth protected the wreck nobly with his two divisions, and the broken army, encumbered with baggage, set off on its road while Morand's cannon and the other divisions under Davout pressed the rear-guard hotly. Kalkreuth was obliged to fall back, and the French took 115 guns and 3,000 prisoners; but Davout having only the 1st, 2nd, and 12th Chasseurs in the field, was unable to produce the same disorder that Murat's horse had effected. He sent to Bernadotte, whose men were quietly cooking at Apolda, but that marshal gave him no aid, and even retained Beaumont's dragoons who had been detached to assist Davout in common with himself.

Unfortunately, there has been but little authentic incident preserved of personal valour at Auerstadt, but the losses on both sides were enormous.

The Prussians had about 10,000 killed and wounded, and the

French 270 officers and 7,200 men; 134 officers and 3,500 privates belonging to Gudin's division alone.

Morand, Gudin, and half the superior officers were wounded, and Davout had kept the bridge as heroically as Horatius of old. Nor was that all; for Hohenlohe's fugitives began to mingle with the retreating Prussians, and the defeated army broke and fled, their king, who had had two horses killed, escaping under Blücher's escort. After that there

was an end to cohesion, and the pitiful remnants of the great fighting machine of Prussia were disposed of in detail by the conquerors.

The whole country was covered with fugitives, waggons, guns, and independent parties; the Prussians plundered their own baggage; Bernadotte, or more properly General Dupont, destroyed Eugene of Würtemberg at Halle on the 17th.

Erfurt, Magdeburg, all the fortified places, fell one after the other into French hands, and in twenty days from passing the frontier Napoleon made his triumphal entry into Berlin.

His treatment of the conquered country is unhappily too well known to need much comment here; barbarous, insulting, and mean as it was, it proved the ultimate making of Prussia, for it roused a spirit of national independence, which has borne fruit in our own day, and may do again, unless their Rosbach of 1870 finds another Jéna in the future!

Napoleon's bulletin announcing the double victories of the 14th October is curious as showing the man; for he blends the two battles under the name of Jéna, merely saying of Davout, "On our right the corps of Marshal Davout performed prodigies," etc. And yet Napoleon himself had only overthrown the corps of Hohenlohe and Rüchel with the bulk of the *Grande Armée*, while Davout with only three divisions, 44 guns, and three regiments of light cavalry, had put the Prussian centre to flight!

Between Naumburg and Merseburg on the road to Halle the emperor sent General Savary into the stubble-fields to look for a monument of former French defeat, and at the waving of Savary's handkerchief he rode over to him and gazed upon a little stone pillar not above four feet high with an almost illegible inscription commemorating Frederick's victory of Rosbach in 1757, which Suchet's pioneers were ordered to pack in their waggons for transmission to France.

Later on the sword and orders of the Great Frederick, taken from his coffin-lid, shared the same fate, a proceeding decidedly in the *then* French taste, but not easy to reconcile with our own ideas of what should be the attitude of a successful general towards the feelings of the people he has conquered under Providence.

Jéna and Auerstädt, but the former especially, were soldiers' battles: both armies were full of spirit, and on the fields themselves were nobly led. Only to these causes, then, can one ascribe the remarkable breaking down of Prussia in so short a time: the folly of an overdrilled system that refused to move with the times, having no unity in its plan of campaign or harmony at headquarters; the whole machine covered with a fine green mould of ancient tradition which got into the wheels and prevented its keeping pace with modern needs.

The Battle of the Maida

A. J. Butler

When the year 1806 opened, it is probably not too much to say that the state of affairs on the continent of Europe was the most momentous which the world has ever seen. The victory of Austerlitz had, for the time at all events, laid all the lands from the North Sea to the Pyrenees, and from the Atlantic to the Adriatic, at the feet of one man. Half the old monarchies of Europe had gone down, and on their ruins new dynasties were being set up, new boundaries traced at the pleasure of a soldier of fortune whose name a dozen years before was unknown beyond the limited circle of his comrades and kinsfolk. In no part of Europe was the pressure more acutely felt than in Italy. In the closing years of the eighteenth century, not for the first or second time in history, French armies had overrun and pillaged that unlucky country. Compelled to withdraw for a time, they had soon returned in stronger force; and in 1805 Buonaparte assumed the title of King of Italy. For a while the Kingdom of Naples, which had always been regarded as a separate State, was allowed to remain under its former sovereign of the Bourbon family, Ferdinand IV., but in the early days of 1806 he, too, was expelled and forced to take refuge in Sicily. The kingdom was given en by Napoleon to his own brother Joseph, and French armies were sent to overcome any objections which the inhabitants might have to being transferred without their own consent from one sovereign to another. The Bourbon Government had indeed been about as bad as it well could be; but this fact did not make the task of the French appreciably easier. Under the lax and corrupt rule of their old kings the wild mountainous country of Calabria swarmed with brigands, with

whose aid the partisans of the expelled monarch had no difficulty in keeping up a guerilla warfare. A clever French man of letters, who by one of the odd turns of chance not unusual in troubled times was then serving as an officer of artillery in Calabria, gives the following picture of the kind of opposition which the French had to face, and of the way in which they met it.

"Imagine on the slope of some hill a detachment of our people, a hundred strong or so, marching carelessly along beneath rocks covered with myrtle bushes and aloes. Why take any precautions? We have not had a soldier murdered in this neighbourhood for the last week. At the foot of the slope runs a swift torrent which has to be crossed; part of the line is in the water, some have got across, some are still on this side. Suddenly a thousand men jump up in every direction; peasants, brigands, escaped convicts, deserters, all under the command of a sub-deacon. Well-armed, good shots, they open fire on our men before they are themselves seen. The officers are the first to fall; those who die on the spot are the lucky ones; the others serve for the next few days to furnish sport for their captors. Then the general or whoever he may be, who has sent the detachment without taking the trouble to ascertain the state of the country, takes it out of the nearest villages. He sends an *aide-de-camp* with five hundred men; they pillage the place, ill-use the women, cut the men's throats; and whoever escapes goes to swell the sub-deacon's forces."

In this fashion General Reynier's army made its way to the city of

Reggio, which stands at the tip of the " toe" of Italy. Sicily, of which Ferdinand was still king, lay on the other side of the narrow strait, only a mile or two away. But for Reynier that strait was as impassable as if the blue Mediterranean water had been a stream of fire. Here, as at Boulogne, the effect of Trafalgar was felt, and the Straits of Messina marked no less surely than the Straits of Dover the limit of Napoleon's power. Sir Sidney Smith, the brilliant yet wary admiral, whom Napoleon feared and hated perhaps more than any other man on earth at that time, held the Tyrrhenian Sea with his squadron small indeed, but sufficient to prevent any French transport from putting out so long as he was within striking distance. Moreover, not very far up the coast, just where the "toe" passes into the "instep," the fortress of Amantea still held out for Ferdinand. Presently, too, Reggio itself was recaptured, and Reynier thought it better to turn back.

Some English troops, under Sir James Craig, had been sent to co-operate with a Russian army in aiding the Neapolitans to resist the first entry of the French upon their territory; but the news of Auster-litz showed the hopelessness of checking their advance at this point, the Russians withdrew, and Craig saw that the stand could best be made in Sicily. Thither he accordingly transferred his force; but, being himself invalided, he was in the course of the spring of 1806 replaced by Major-General Sir John Stuart, a gallant and able officer who had distinguished himself in the Egyptian campaign of 1801.

Before the end of June, Stuart was in command of about 5,000 men, including a certain number of Corsicans, Sicilians, and others. Of English troops he had the 20th, 27th, 58th, 78th, and 81st Regiments. The flank companies of these regiments, after the fashion of the time, were detached and formed into a grenadier battalion and a light bat-talion respectively, the latter with the Corsican Rangers forming the light brigade under Colonel Kempt. Stuart's total force amounted to 4,795 men, with a strength of artillery consisting of ten 4-pounders, four 6-pounders, and two howitzers. Of cavalry he had none, unless some of Sir Sidney Smith's "young gentlemen"—who are said to have accompanied the army after its landing, on donkey-back—may be reckoned under that head.

On June 30th, the 20th Regiment was sent off from Messina, in some large open boats, to cruise along the coast to the south of Reggio, in order to draw off the attention of the French com-mander while the main body was preparing to land in the Bay of St. Eufemia, some fifty miles further to the north, and close to the still uncaptured fortress of Amantea. With a view of still further deceiving the enemy, the regiment was distributed among a much larger number of boats than would have sufficed to carry the whole number; a ruse which may possibly have contributed to the exaggerated estimates of Stuart's strength which French writers have chosen to put forth.

The general himself, with his main body, reached St. Eufemia Bay. on the evening of July 1st, and began at once to disembark his troops. No opposition was offered. A sand-bag redoubt (afterwards magnified by French reports into an entrenched camp) was thrown up to protect his stores and supplies, of which a considerable quantity had been brought, with the intention of equipping the Calabrian insurgents. Four companies of the light, and an equal number of the grenadier battalion, covered the landing; and by daylight, or soon after, on the 2nd, the whole force was on shore, the stores being landed in the course of the day. On the same day the advance-guard pushed forward, dispersing a detachment of French and Poles, clearing the wooded hills on the British left, and establishing outposts as far as the village of San Biaggio.

The army was now encamped near the north-west angle of a horseshoe-shaped plain facing westward, and about six miles across in either direction. Mountains covered with forest and brushwood rise all round, sending down on the south side two considerable spurs into the plain The plain itself is intersected longitudinally by two streams, the Sant' Ippolito and the Amato, which flow nearly parallel from the upper end of the horseshoe in a W.S.W. direction, and fall into the sea about a mile apart; the Amato, which is much the larger stream, skirting the foot of the southern hills. Besides these there are a number of smaller watercourses, and the whole plain is marshy and covered with thickets of myrtle and scarlet geranium. Behind the more easterly of the two spurs abovementioned lies the town of Maida, through which a road runs to Cotrone, at the south-west corner of the Gulf of Tarantum; while another and more direct road to Naples crosses the plain diagonally, and leaves it at Nicastro. In the other direction both roads unite a little south of the point where the River Amato falls into the sea, and runs near the coast toward Reggio. By this road Reynier was retreating, as already stated; and he had got as far as Monteleone, just south of the Bay of St. Eufemia, when he heard that the British force had landed. Hastening his march, the French commander took up a strong position on the more westerly and larger of the two spurs. Below him and on his flanks were woods, and the Amato flowed through marshy ground at the foot of the hill. He could hardly have posted himself better.

Towards evening on the 3rd, General Stuart, while making a reconnaissance, discovered his enemy in this strong position. It was hardly to be expected that Reynier, who seemed to hold nearly all the cards in the game, would deliberately choose to meet his adversary on even terms. The French commander had only to stay where he was, and allow the Calabrian sun and the exhalations from the marshes to produce their inevitable effect on the English army. Moreover, though at that moment his force was probably not superior to Stuart's—that is, between 4,000 and 5,000 men, including cavalry—his second division, numbering 3,000 more, was on the way from Monteleone, and might join him at any moment. It was, therefore, his interest to stay where he was, while Stuart's object was rather to force a battle as soon as possible.

At dawn on the 4th, accordingly, the British troops were under arms and starting to march along the coast in close column of subdivisions: Sir Sidney Smith, in the *Apollo* frigate, with two smaller vessels, sailing abreast of them, ready to give any assistance that might be in his power. As a matter of fact, however, the action was fought nearly three miles inland, quite out of the longest range of any gun that went to sea in those days.

On reaching the mouth of the Sant Ippolito the troops halted for a while on the long spit of land lying between the river and the shore. At this point they were in full view of the opposing army, and they were at once surprised and delighted, one may suppose, to see that it was moving. It is not easy to conjecture Reynier's motive in having thus thrown away the immense advantage that his initial position had given him. He may have feared that Stuart would turn his flank, and get him between the English army and the ships. The French writer above quoted thinks that the presence of Lebrun, the Imperial Commissioner, had a good deal to do with Reynier's decision to fight. He says:

"Reynier found himself in presence of an overlooker, with directions to report. If he had won the battle, it would have been the emperor's genius, the emperor's idea, the emperor's orders. As he lost it, it is all our fault."

Another French writer, writing some years later, mentions a belief

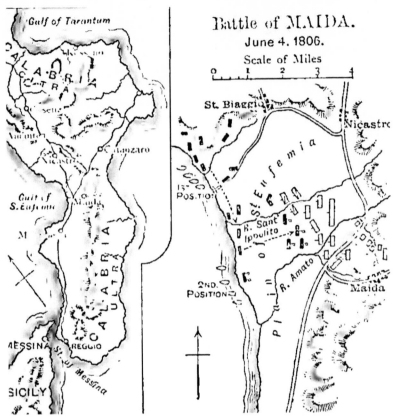

current at the time that Reynier was decided by personal motives. He and Stuart had been opposed to each other during the Egyptian campaign in 1801, and Reynier had got the worst of it. Possibly all these reasons, combined with a sort of chivalrous feeling that so pointed a challenge ought not to be declined, may have urged him to take what proved so disastrous a step.

Crossing the stream, which is everywhere fordable, the English force deployed, and proceeded across the plain in echelon, the right wing in advance. The formation was as follows:—On the right was the light brigade, made up, as has been said, of the light companies of the various regiments, with the Corsican Rangers, under Colonel Kempt. To the left of them, and in rear of all the other brigades, came the 3rd, commanded by Colonel Oswald, and consisting of the 58th Regiment, and the foreign auxiliaries under Sir Louis de Watteville. In the centre, at the regular echelon distance to the left rear of the light brigade, was the 2nd brigade, comprising the 81st and 78th, under Brigadier-General Acland; while the left wing—that is, the 1st brigade—under Brigadier-General Lowry Cole, was made up of the 27th Inniskillings and the grenadier battalion.[1]

While Stuart's men are advancing through the myrtle-scrub, it may be worthwhile to call attention to a point which is apt to be overlooked. The long subsequent series of battles between British and French troops which culminated at Waterloo, proved to the world that our soldiers could, as a rule, hold their own against Napoleon's veterans. But in 1806 this was far from being the case. It was, indeed, five years since an English and a French army had met in the Alexandrian campaign; and though on that occasion our arms had been successful, their success was hardly enough to cancel the impression produced by the disasters which mismanagement had brought upon our forces in Holland and on the northern frontier of France during the early part of the war. The enormous "prestige" which the collapse of the great military monarchies of Europe had conferred on the French armies must also be taken into consideration. Sir Sidney Smith, writing about this time, had spoken of the idea—which, though he calls it mistaken, he admits was much too prevalent—"that the progress of the French armies is irresistible." It will be seen, then, that Stuart's little force had no reason to think, lightly of the task that lay before it.

By half-past eight the French had descended into the plain, and formed line on their right; and it was then seen that the expected reinforcements had come up, and that Reynier had little short of 8,000 men at his disposal. His force was as follows:—(It must be remembered that a French regiment contains many more men than one of ours, and in those days the difference was even greater.) On the right was the 23rd Regiment, then the 42nd, next to them a brigade of Poles and Swiss, while the left was held by one of the crack regiments of the French service—the 1st Léger. The cavalry, 300 in number, was at the beginning of the action posted on the left wing. Thousands of Calabrian peasantry thronged the surrounding hills, and anxiously awaited the result of the struggle.

Some skirmishing seems to have taken place before the main armies were fully engaged, between the light company of the 20th Regiment— which, as has been explained, formed with other light companies a part

---

1. This account of the disposition of the force is taken from an admirable plan of the battle, published in the following April, a copy of which is preserved in the library of the Royal United Service Institute. I must here express my thanks to the Secretary and Librarian of the Institute for kindly allowing me to make use of it.—A.J. B.

of Kempt's brigade on our right—and some of the French troops, who were still fording the Amato when our men came up. Here Captain Malcolm McLean fell at the head of his company shot through the heart: the only British officer who lost his life in the battle.

Reynier began by a demonstration against the British left; but the first really serious development of the action took place on the other wing, and on that wing it was practically decided. As the light brigade advanced, the *shakoes* of the 1st Léger appeared through the brushwood. At this moment it must probably have been, that one of the most dramatic incidents in modern warfare took place. Kempt's men had been marching for some hours over rough ground, under the blazing sun of a Calabrian midsummer. The uniform of those days was not designed with much reference to the soldier's ease in marching, and, in addition, each man had his blanket strapped on his shoulders. Light companies, it must be remembered, were besides composed for the most part of smaller and lighter men, whose activity would be seriously hampered by having to carry bulky objects on their backs. Kempt, himself a little man, was doubtless all the more alive to the state of affairs, and ordered his men to halt and throw down their blankets. The Calabrian spectators, as one of them told an English visitor ten years later, "sweated cold; for," he added, "we thought the English were going to run." The 1st Léger thought the same and pressed forward with a cheer; but the English troops, freed from their encumbrances, were already coming to meet them. Neither side fired till they were within a hundred yards of each other; then a few rounds were exchanged, and the two corps, in perfect silence, advanced upon each other with the bayonet. Of late years this had been the favourite weapon of Napoleon's veterans. Our readers will not have forgotten the advance of Suchet's division at Austerlitz. But this time they had met their match; and though bayonets are said to have been actually crossed, the 1st Léger as a body shrank from the shock, nor could they be rallied by any efforts of their officers. They broke and fled in the direction of Maida, pursued by the light brigade. Almost simultaneously Acland's brigade had routed the corps opposed to it; and Reynier, seeing that his left wing was hopelessly beaten, made an effort to retrieve the fortune of the day on his right. Bringing his cavalry up to that wing, where Cole's brigade was offering a sturdy resistance to the 42nd Regiment of Imperial Grenadiers, he attempted to outflank and turn the British left. But an opportune succour was at hand. As has been mentioned, the 20th Regiment had been despatched on a special duty, from which it had not returned when the expedition started. Just when Stuart's men were standing to their arms, the transport bearing the 20th had anchored in St. Eufemia Bay, it would seem, off the mouth of the river Sant' Ippolito. Here it was hailed by Sir Sidney Smith and informed of General Stuart's intention to attack that morning. An officer of the 20th (or XX, as its members like to write it) describes what followed:

"Without waiting for orders, our gallant chief. Colonel Ross, gave directions for the regiment to disembark soon after daylight. General Stuart had landed with a small army a few days previously, and they were now engaged, for we could hear the firing and see the smoke. We therefore cheerfully obeyed the order, and landed forthwith, after filling our haversacks and canteens; for officers as well as men carried their three days' provisions, and their blankets and change of linen. We hurried across the country through woods and marshes, in the direction in which the music of cannon and musketry was heard, and we reached our little army just at the nick of time, for we came through a wood upon the left of the British line which the French cavalry were trying to turn. We immediately formed, and they attempted to turn our left; but Colonel Ross threw back the left wing of the 20th, and after giving them a few shots, they relinquished the attempt. For a long time, however, they kept hovering about us, and made us change our position several times, but we were always ready to receive them."

In fact, the 20th contributed very materially to the success of the day, and the sprig of myrtle which for years afterwards used to ornament the caps of the regiment on July 4th, in memory of the Calabrian myrtle thickets, was a well-earned decoration. Maida, it is interesting to observe, is the only pitched battle that British troops have ever fought on Italian soil.

The repulse of the French cavalry ended the action. Reynier, in spite of the intrepidity with which he exposed himself in the effort to check defeat—for if he was an unlucky and injudicious commander, he was a thoroughly brave man—could only join in the flight of his routed army, leaving over 3,000 killed, wounded, and prisoners, the English loss being barely 300. Headlong they fled, losing many stragglers, and scarcely halting till they reached Catanzaro, at the head of the Gulf of Tarantum, and well on the other side of the Apennines. For the moment, the district known as Further Calabria was abandoned by the French. Several of the smaller fortresses on the coast fell into Sir John Stuart's hands; and with an adequate force he might have cleared South Italy of the invader, and possibly anticipated or accelerated the results of the war which was soon to begin in the other peninsula; but divided counsels still prevailed in England. It had not yet become clear to our statesmen that until Napoleon was crushed Europe could not be tranquil or England safe, and no steps were taken to reinforce the heroic little army until just after it had been compelled, for want of support, to quit Calabria. Before many months had passed,

the total collapse of the Prussian monarchy at Jena and Auerstadt had withdrawn attention from the remoter parts of Europe; and then the French invasion of the Peninsula pointed to that region as the vulnerable point upon which all efforts must be concentrated.

Yet Maida was not a battle without results. When Parliament met in December, the thanks of both Houses were voted to General Stuart, his brigadiers, and the whole army; and on this occasion Mr. Windham, the Secretary for War, pointed out how the victory of Maida had broken the spell of invincibility that for so long had been attached to French troops. The effect was all the greater that just at that moment no fighting was going on elsewhere, so that the armies which had been engaged on the little Calabrian plain might be regarded as the champions of their respective causes. The news, we know, had the effect of making Napoleon extremely angry; and French writers were for a long time driven to distort the facts considerably in order to account for what seemed to them, on any supposition even of equality of forces, an inexplicable disaster. On the other hand, the spirit Maida inspired in English troops had no small share in producing the confidence which, in spite of untoward events at the outset, never failed them throughout the Peninsular campaign; and the half-forgotten and apparently almost isolated battle fought in a remote corner of Europe, when rightly understood, takes its place in the glorious roll which comprises Vimiero, Talavera, Salamanca, and Toulouse.

Walcheren

Captain Owen Wheeler

It is instructive, though scarcely gratifying, to note how largely the British fighting-man depends, for due appreciation of his exploits by land or sea, upon circumstances which in common fairness ought not to be taken into account in settling claims upon the national regard. The British public is much too prone to gauge military and naval valour by the measure of success ultimately attained by the operations in connection with which that valour was specifically displayed. Thus, while we are at all times ready to exalt moderate achievements when arising out of notable surroundings or leading up to brilliant consequences, we often sadly underestimate really praiseworthy work because its associations are humdrum or its results disagreeable. Of the latter class of injustice no more striking example could be found than the comparative obscurity in which is shrouded much, if not all, of the genuine heroism displayed in the ill-starred enterprise that forms the subject of this sketch. That the Walcheren expedition was disastrously marred by faulty conception, imperfect strategy, and miserable delays, is habitually accounted quite sufficient reason for denying to the gallant sailors and soldiers engaged in it the full meed of credit due to them for a notable exhibition of energy and pluck. No doubt this is human nature, and nothing will ever succeed like success. But it is not in the eternal fitness of things that the merest hanger-on of Trafalgar or Waterloo should go down to posterity as a popular hero, while the fine fellows who faced the Flushing batteries in 1809 should be forgotten, merely because their government and commander alike were to be blamed for procrastination and ineptitude.

Advancing from this brief introduction into the region of fact, it may be noted, for the benefit of those whose geography is a "negligible quantity," that Walcheren is one of a group of very low-lying islands which have been formed by alluvial deposits at the mouth of the Scheldt, and now constitute the Dutch province of Zeeland. Walcheren is separated by very narrow channels from the adjacent islands of North and South Beveland: it is about thirteen miles long by eleven broad, and lies about a hundred miles due east from the English coast. Inland it contains the considerable town of Middleburg, and on the south the important seaport of Flushing, the batteries of which in 1809 closed the passage of the western or principal branch of the Scheldt to any but the most powerful of hostile fleets. On the north of the island the fortress of Veere commanded at the same period the Veeregat, the channel separating Walcheren from North Beveland, while at the eastern extremity of South Beveland, Fort Bahtz—or, as it is now commonly called, Bath—barred the East Scheldt, and so still further blocked for an enemy's ships the waterway to Antwerp. The latter port—the key to the great estuary which, as has been justly observed, is the natural rival to that of the Thames—although fallen indeed from its former commercial grandeur, was in 1809 fast rising, under the magic hand of Napoleon, to fresh importance as a great naval stronghold. Already an arsenal and vast wet-docks had been created, and various other steps taken with the obvious intent of rendering Antwerp an excellent base for

246

a future great attack upon England. But, owing to distractions on the Danube and in the Peninsula, these preparations were temporarily in abeyance, and in the meantime Antwerp was being quite inadequately garrisoned by about 2,000 invalids and coastguards, the majority of the French troops still remaining in these parts being thrown forward, to the number of 9,000 or thereabouts, for the manning of Flushing and other forts on the islands of the Scheldt.

The immediate *raison d'être* of the Walcheren expedition is to be found in the memorable effort made by Austria in the spring and early summer of 1809 to stem the torrent of Napoleon's career of European conquest. Although hostilities in that connection were not actually commenced until April, 1809, the resolution of. the Austrians to declare war had been communicated to the British Government in November, 1808, and simultaneously the cabinet of Vienna had impressed upon that of St. James's the desirability of a British diversion, more particularly by a land force in northern Germany. But England, although fully alive to the necessity for such action, and, moreover, fully equal, as regards resources, to the part it was proposed she should play, was lamentably slow in rising to the occasion. Instead of taking the field simultaneously with Austria in April, the government allowed itself to be at any rate temporarily discouraged by the failure of Sir John Moore's Spanish expedition, and did not even commence to take preliminary steps until quite the end of May. Meanwhile, the Austrians had been badly beaten at Echmuhl, and had triumphed somewhat doubtfully at Aspern. Throughout June and July, an English expedition to the Scheldt having been finally decided upon, the work of getting ready ships, battering-trains, and

men, went slowly forward—so slowly that the preparations were not complete until news had reached this country of Napoleon's rout of the Austrians at Wagram. Thus, at the outset, the expedition failed to accomplish its original object—the creation, namely, of a. diversion calculated to assist a friendly Power in opposing the Napoleonic supremacy. Henceforth it was little more than a blow aimed at Napoleon's back by Great Britain on her own account, and never was blow more portentously delivered or more feebly followed up.

The expedition which left the Downs on the 28th July, 1809, *en route* for the Scheldt, was, from both a naval and a military point of view, one of the largest and finest ever despatched from these or any other shores. It consisted of thirty-seven ships of the line, twenty-three frigates, and eighty-two gunboats, besides transports having on board over 40,000 of all arms, including two complete battering-trains. The naval force was commanded by Sir Richard Strachan, the troops, and to some extent the expedition generally, being placed in charge of Lord Chatham, son of the great earl and brother of William Pitt, "a respectable veteran, not without merit in the routine of official duty at home," but " totally destitute of the activity and decision requisite in an enterprise in which success was to be won rather by rapidity of movement than deliberation of conduct." According to Lord Chatham's instructions, the object of the conjoint expeditions was the capture or destruction of the enemy's ships, either building or afloat, at Antwerp or Flushing, or afloat in the Scheldt; the destruction of the arsenals and dockyards at Antwerp, Terneuze, and Flushing; the reduction of the Island of Walcheren; and the closing of the Scheldt, if possible, to navigation by ships of war.

On the 29th July the left wing of Lord Chatham's force, under Lieutenant-General Sir Eyre Coote, arrived off Domburg, on the north side of Walcheren Island, and on the following day was landed on the sand hills in the vicinity of Fort Veere. On the morning of the 31st a deputation was received from Middleburg stating that the French garrison had retired into Flushing, and offering terms of capitulation, which were accepted. Fort Veere, after in obstinate defence by a garrison some 600 strong, was captured on the 1st of August. Meanwhile, a division under Sir John Hope had landed on South Beveland and had taken possession of the whole island, including Fort Bath. The enemy's ships, which, when the English expedition arrived off Holland, were moored off Flushing, had by this time retired up the river, and on the 4th August were lying some at Antwerp, others at Fort

Lillo, between Antwerp and Bath. On the 5th a strong detachment of the enemy's flotilla—consisting of two frigates, thirty brigs, eight luggers or schooners, and fourteen gunboats—made a determined effort to recapture Fort Bath, but after a smart cannonade were forced to retire. Returning to Walcheren we find Lord Chatham's headquarters fixed from the 2nd of August at Middleburg, the troops being engaged in getting guns into position and otherwise making vigorous preparations for the reduction of Flushing.

The activity and zeal of the naval force throughout the whole of these proceedings were beyond all praise. Loyally subordinating his own action to that of Lord Chatham in the first essential of getting the troops safely disembarked, Sir Richard Strachan subsequently lost no opportunity of rendering his hold upon the East and West Scheldt up to Fort Bath as secure as he could make it both by general ubiquity and judicious concentration of force at points of importance. Nor was anything left undone that could be done in the way of useful minor bombardment, cutting communications, and preventing supplies from being thrown into Flushing. One specially fine performance was the forcing of the entrance to the West Scheldt, under the fire of the Flushing batteries, by ten frigates,[1] under the orders of Lord William Stuart, captain of the *Lavinia*. This squadron was under fire for two hours, and the gallant and seamanlike manner in which it was conducted, and its steady and well-directed fire, were greeted with roars of applause by the English troops which were able to watch the action from the shore. But, notwithstanding these diversions, some of Sir Richard Strachan's despatches seem to indicate that the operations were regarded as unduly extensive and complicated, and that the protracted delay caused by the military preparations for the bombardment of Flushing was producing a certain amount of naval misgiving.

It is to the delay in question that the ultimate failure of the expedition is commonly attributed; and, indeed, there is much to support this view. Lord Chatham, at the time the expedition entered the Scheldt, was in possession of authentic information to the effect that Antwerp was practically undefended. If the division which landed in South Beveland under Sir John Hope, and captured Fort Bath without striking a blow, had, after leaving a sufficient garrison for the latter, pushed on to Antwerp at once, it would probably have captured both that town and Fort Lillo *en route* without any difficulty. Such a course, moreover, if promptly taken, would have had the effect of cutting off the French fleet, for, as noted above, when the expedition arrived off Holland the enemy's ships were moored off Flushing, and would probably have remained there or returned thither had Antwerp been carried by a *coup de main* and both Forts Lillo and Bath been in the hands of English garri-

---

1. *Lavinia. Heroine. Amethyst. Rota. Nymphen, l'Aigle. Euryalus. Statira, Dryad,* and *Perlen.*

sons. As it was, the French squadron escaped up the river, and Sir John Hope's division remained inactive in South Beveland, being joined on the 9th August by the divisions under the Earl of Rosslyn and the Marquis of Huntley.

On the evening of the 7th August a notable sortie was made from Flushing upon the right of our line, the attack being directed chiefly upon our advanced picquets, which were supported by the 3rd Battalion of the Royals—the 5th and the 35th—which, together with detachments of. the Royal Artillery, the 95th, and the eight battalions of the King's German Legion, engaged the enemy with great gallantry, and forced him to retire. Subsequently the besieged garrison endeavoured to cause some embarrassment by opening the sluices at Flushing and letting in the sea upon the island; but adequate precautions had been taken to render this ingenious attempt at inundation ineffectual, and the preparations for the bombardment were steadily pushed forward.

On the 13th August, the land batteries before Flushing being completed, and Lord Chatham having duly notified the fact to his naval colleague, the latter caused his bombs and gun-vessels to take up suitable stations at the south-east and south-west ends of the town; and at half-past one p.m. the bombardment was commenced, the enemy promptly and vigorously responding. At the outset we had on land alone fifty-two pieces of heavy ordnance, and an additional battery of six 24-pounders was completed the same night, the whole continuing to play upon the town till late the following day. On the evening of the 13th an entrenchment in front of the right of our line was brilliantly forced by the 14th Regiment, now the Prince of Wales's Own (West Yorkshire), and detachments of the King's German Legion, under Lieutenant-Colonel Nicolls, who drove the enemy out, and effected a lodgement within musket-shot of the walls of the town, taking one gun and thirty prisoners. But otherwise no great impression appears to have been made on the gallant defenders till the following day.

On the morning of the 14th August Sir Richard Strachan, with the *St. Domingo*, *Blake*, *Repulse*, *Victorious*, *Denmark*, *Audacious*, and *Venerable* line-of-battle ships, got under weigh, and, ranging up along the sea-line of defence, kept up for several hours a tremendous cannonade, with the result that by four o'clock in the afternoon the town was almost everywhere in flames, and the enemy's fire had for the time entirely ceased. Lord Chatham, who describes the scene of destruction as "most awful," hereupon summoned the place to surrender, but no satisfactory reply being given, hostilities were resumed with the utmost vigour. About eleven o'clock at night one of the enemy's advanced batteries was carried at the point of the bayonet by detachments from the 36th, 71st, and light battalions of the King's German Legion, opposed to great superiority of numbers; and about two in the morning of the 15th August the enemy demanded a suspension of arms for forty-eight hours. This was refused, only two hours being granted, when General Monnet, commanding the French troops, agreed to surrender on the basis of the garrison becoming prisoners of war. On the 16th, articles of capitulation were ratified, and the English troops took possession of the town. The return of the garrison which surrendered includes 16 officers of the staff, 101 officers, 3,773 non-commissioned officers and soldiers, 489 sick and wounded—total, 4,370. In addition to these the original garrison included, besides the number killed during the siege, which must have been very large, upwards of 1,000 wounded who had been removed to Cadsand previously to the complete investment of the town.

With the fall of Flushing the Walcheren expedition practically came to an end, but not in the manner that might have been expected from such a glorious beginning. Instead of being rapidly followed by the seizure of Antwerp and the destruction of the enemy's fleet, the siege, successful as it had been, had changed the whole aspect of affairs by giving to both the French and Dutch Governments time to place Antwerp in an excellent state of defence, to withdraw the fleet into a place of security, and to assemble 30,000 troops within striking distance of the Scheldt. This does not seem to have dawned on Lord Chatham until, with ridiculous tardiness, he had advanced his headquarters to Fort Bath, which he only reached on the 26th August, ten days after Flushing—barely thirty miles distant—had surrendered! Meanwhile the marsh fever was beginning to tell most seriously upon the troops, of whom little short of 3,000 were in hospital. A council of war was accordingly called, and it was unanimously decided that a further advance was impossible. Orders then followed indicating a gradual withdrawal from the advanced position in South Beveland and the embarkation of such troops as remained, after providing a substantial garrison for Walcheren, which it was hoped might still be permanently retained.

Had the retention of Walcheren been feasible, the expedition might

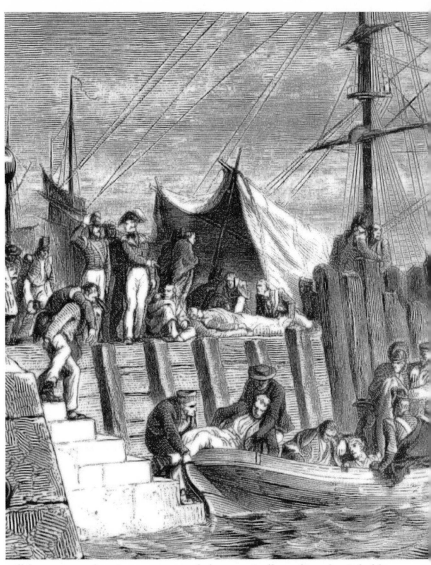

still have secured an important result by practically sealing the Scheldt, and the garrison detailed—some 15,000 strong—was apparently ample for the purpose. But fate and fever were too strong for the "respectable veteran" and his unfortunate soldiers. The Walcheren malaria soon caught the Englishmen in its fell grip, and did not readily release its victims. By the middle of September—about a fortnight after the rest of the expedition had returned home—half the garrison were in hospital, and the death-rate was running up to two and three hundred a week.

After two months of ghastly misery the final order for evacuation was given and carried out—one can imagine, with gloomy cheerfulness—after the works and naval basin of Flushing had been carefully destroyed.

Thus ended "Walcheren, 1809," an expedition which cost us 7,000 British lives, not to speak of nearly twice that number who were invalided home, and thousands more who brought back constitutions so shattered by malaria that they never fully regained their strength. What lessons are to be gained from such a colossal failure are writ sufficiently large in the foregoing simple narrative; but, at least, it is comforting to reflect that, serious as those lessons are, they involve no sort of slur upon the courage and discipline of the British naval and military services. As a great stroke of Continental policy the Walcheren expedition was radically culpable, in that it started at least three months too late. Strategically speaking, it was characterised by utter want of enterprise and sinful waste of time. But it included a very fair modicum of what Mr. Kipling's Terence Mulvaney calls "sumpshuous fightin'," and there is plenty of evidence to show that in this respect the British troops engaged, as well as their gallant opponents—who for thirty-six hours maintained their hold on Flushing against one of the most terrible bombardments ever recorded—worthily upheld the best traditions of their respective nations.

Albuera

Colonel W. W. Knollys

The Battle of Albuera, because of its sanguinary nature, and the fact that Napier, the historian of the Peninsular War, has enwreathed its memory with some of his most picturesque sentences, stands out as one of the prominent and popular episodes of war. If the eloquent Napier has described it so ably, it may be asked, why repeat a well-told tale? Napier, though anxious to be just and accurate, often allowed himself to be influenced by prejudices for or against corps and persons, and has not been free from this defect in his account of Albuera. Many think that he displayed prejudice, not to say virulence, towards Beresford; and, as a matter of fact, a violent and heated controversy between the commander and the historian followed the publication of the *Peninsular War*.

Before we come to the battle and the events which led up to it, let us glance for a moment at the antecedents and personalities of the two opponents. Marshal Soult and Lord—then Sir William—Beresford.

Soult, universally recognised as one of the ablest of Napoleon's lieutenants, born in 1760, was the eldest son of a provincial notary. Fairly well brought up, he was destined for the law; but his father's death, when he was still only a boy, caused the idea to be abandoned. He is said by some to have been of Jewish origin; but we can find no confirmation of the statement. In 1785 he enlisted in the regiment of "Royal Infantry," and, thanks to his education, he became six years later a sergeant. The revolution gave him an opening, and, in 1791, he was appointed instructor to the 1st Battalion of the Volunteers of the Bas Rhin. He soon obtained the rank of adjutant-general, and in

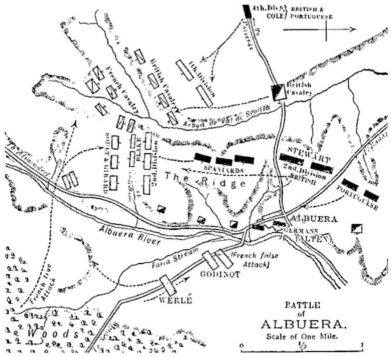

BATTLE
of
ALBUERA.

Scale of One Mile.

1794, after the Battle of Fleurus, he was made general of brigade. During the following four years he saw much service in Germany under Jourdan, Moreau, Kleber, and Lefebvre. In 1790, promoted to general of division, he distinguished himself in Massena's Swiss campaign, especially at the Battle of Zürich. In the following year he was second in command to Massena when that general conducted his magnificent defence of Genoa. In 1802 he was appointed one of the four generals holding the position of colonel in the Consular Guard. Though one of Moreau's officers he was discreet, acute, and pliable enough to attach himself to his old chief's rival. Napoleon; and in 1803 was given by the latter the command of the camp of Boulogne. In 1804 he was one of the first marshals created, and in the following year mainly contributed to the victory of Austerlitz. He subsequently greatly distinguished himself in Germany and Spain; and when, in 1813, Wellington was about to invade France, he was sent to withstand him, and carried out an offensive-defensive campaign with remarkable energy and ability. At the first abdication of Napoleon, Marshal Soult—Duke of Dalmatia—declared himself a royalist, and was appointed Minister of War by Louis XVIII. On the emperor's return from Elba Soult joined him, and was major-general—or chief of the staff—during the Waterloo Campaign. On the second restoration of Louis XVIII. Soult was exiled, but was, after a short time, allowed to return to France, was recreated marshal in 1820, and again played the part of a fervent royalist. After 1830 he became a partisan of constitutional royalty; but in 1848 he again changed, and was once more a republican. This was his last tergiversation, for in 1851 he died. The Duke of Wellington had a great respect for his talents as a commander, and was doubly cautious when opposed to him.

Beresford, the illegitimate son of the first Marquis of Waterford, was born in 1768. Having spent a year at the military academy of Strasburg, he was in 1785 gazetted ensign to the 6th Foot, which regiment he joined in Nova Scotia. While out shooting in that colony, he met with an accident which caused the loss of his left eye. He took part in the defence of Toulon, and also served in Corsica, but it could not be said that during his first ten years of soldiering that he had gained much experience in the field. Ten years, however, from the date of his first commission, and at the early age of twenty-seven, he found himself lieutenant-colonel commanding the 88th Regiment. Money and interest had pushed him on. In 1800 he landed in Bombay, and, having become full colonel, was appointed brigadier in the force despatched to Egypt under Sir David Baird. When, however, after a

long voyage and a terrible march across the desert Sir David arrived at Cairo, the struggle was over. In Sir David Baird's expedition to the Cape of Good Hope Beresford accompanied his old chief as brigadier, but in the conquest of the Dutch dependency he saw no fighting.

In the following year, however. Sir Home Popham, without any orders from government, prevailed on Sir David to send a small force with him to effect the conquest of Buenos Ayres. Beresford obtained the command of the land forces, which were brought up by troops at St. Helena to 1,025 men, besides a naval brigade, 800 strong. Ascending the River Plate, he landed twelve miles from that city on June 26th, behaved with the audacity and courage of a Cortez, and was everywhere victorious. On the day of disembarkation he drove off an opposing force, capturing four guns, and on the morrow entered the city, expelling its garrison of Spanish militia. The Spaniards, however, rallied from the blow, and, collecting troops, compelled Beresford, after a short struggle in which he showed the personal courage for which he was always conspicuous, to capitulate. Arriving in England, he was fortunate enough to find that the enthusiasm at his original success had not been altogether extinguished by his subsequent ill-fortune. Promoted to the rank of major-general, he was sent to hold Madeira for Portugal. A year later he was ordered to Portugal and commanded a brigade in Sir John Moore's glorious but unfortunate campaign. In 1809 he was appointed to the command of the Portuguese Army. It was not an unsuitable appointment. He was in the prime of life, was of commanding stature and fine presence, had seen—if not much actual fighting—a great deal of active service, was a good disciplinarian, and possessed some acquaintance with the Portuguese and their language. His success in organising and disciplining the Portuguese army is universally admitted. He took part in the campaign of 1809 in Northern Portugal, and in September, 1810, was present at Busaco. In December of that year, Hill having gone home on sick leave, Beresford was given by Wellington the command of the Anglo-Portuguese troops on the left bank of the Tagus. At the end of the following March he was ordered to relieve Campo Maior and besiege Olivenza and Badajoz. His force consisted of 20,000 infantry, 2,000 cavalry, and eighteen guns. His enterprise opened well. It is true that Campo Maior had been captured by the French on March 21st, but Beresford, thinking that he might surprise the captors, moved towards it on the 23rd. On the 25th his advanced guard, consisting of cavalry supported by some infantry under that gallant and capable man Colonel Colborne—afterwards

Lord Seaton—who commanded a brigade in the second division, arrived unexpectedly in sight of the town.

Latour-Maubourg, learning that the British were close at hand,
evacuated the place in haste and confusion, his force consisting of
some 1,200 cavalry, three battalions, a few horse-artillery guns, and a
battering-train of thirteen pieces. The advanced guard followed in hot
pursuit, Colborne being on the right at some distance, while the 13th

Light Dragoons, under Colonel Head, supported by two squadrons of Portuguese cavalry under Colonel Otway, took the shortest line. The heavy cavalry, *i.e.* the 3rd Dragoons and 5th Dragoon Guards, under Major-General the Hon. Sir William Lumley, were mustered on the left, but at first close up. With the 13th Light Dragoons, Colonel Head had only five troops with an aggregate of 203 of all ranks with him, one troop being detached to skirmish. When he drew near, two bodies of French cavalry appeared from the rear of their infantry, one body charging the Portuguese under Otway, the other the 13th. The former appear to have held their own, but there is no record of their performances. With respect to the 13th, they and their opponents charged with such fierceness that they rode right through each other, many men on both sides being dismounted in the collision. Both French and English sought at once to re-form, but the British being quicker, were among their adversaries before the latter had got into order, and a severe hand-to-hand fight ensued. One French squadron wheeled inwards and fell on the flank of the 13th, but were driven off. Finally the French cavalry, though largely superior in number to those immediately opposed to them, were, for all practical purposes, disposed of. The French infantry squares had with their fire taken part in the combat, but without any substantial effect. Disregarding this fire, the 13th, believing that they would be supported by the heavy cavalry, threw themselves on the French artillery, cutting many of them down, and then galloped forward in pursuit of the fugitives, partly of design with a view to cutting off the whole party, partly carried away by the excitement of their success. Reaching the bridge of Badajoz, they were fired on by the guns of the fortress, and obliged to fall back. On their return they encountered the flying French artillery. Sabring many drivers, they captured both guns and baggage. Continuing their retreat, the 13th found themselves in face of the unbroken French infantry and the remnants of the beaten French cavalry. Seeing no appearance of support, being now few in number, and men and horses alike being exhausted, the gallant Light Dragoons abandoned all, save one, of the captured guns, and, making a detour, escaped.

Their loss in this brilliant scuffle was 12 men killed and 33 of all ranks wounded, and 20 of all ranks missing, amounting to within a fraction of 30 *per cent,* of their total strength. The loss of the French on this occasion was 300 of all ranks killed, wounded, or prisoners. Among the killed was Colonel Chamarin, of the 26th Dragoons, who was slain in single combat by Corporal Logan, of the 13th. The corporal had killed two men of the French 26th Dragoons, which so enraged the colonel that he dashed forward and attacked him. Both adversaries were well mounted and good swordsmen, and seem to have been allowed to fight the matter out without aid or interference by their comrades. The deadly duel was short but sharp. Probably the hard hitting of the Englishman was too much for the scientific swordsmanship of the Frenchman, who, after the manner of his countrymen, preferred the point to the edge. Twice did the corporal cut the colonel across the face, and on the second occasion the latter's helmet came off, leaving his head exposed. The Englishman's opportunity had come, and with one mighty blow he nearly cleft the Frenchman's skull asunder, the edge of the sword passing through the brains as far as the nose.

It has been held that Beresford on this occasion neglected to follow up this success. His excuse was that it was reported to him that the 13th had been cut off; he would not therefore risk further loss in his small force of cavalry by allowing the Heavy Dragoons to charge. The information was incorrect, and even had it been accurate surely the last chance of saving the regiment would have been to have at all events made a demonstration with the two heavy regiments.

Though the affair had not been so successful as it might have been owing to Beresford's moral timidity, it must nevertheless have exercised a depressing effect on the French. Instead, however, of profiting by that effect and following up his blow, he contented himself with blockading Elvas, alleging the want of supplies, shoes, and bridging material. There never yet was wanting a plausible excuse for doing little or nothing. Be in this case, however, the argument valid or not, the effect was that the French had time given them for placing Badajoz in a state of defence.

Beresford, ordered by Lord Wellington to cross the Guadiana at Jerumenha, encountered great difficulty from the want of materials for a bridge. However, his commanding engineer. Captain Squire, was a man of energy and resource. With timber obtained from the neighbouring villages he constructed a trestle pier on each bank, filling the interval with five Spanish boats. The bridge was completed on the 3rd April, and the troops were assembled with a view to crossing at daybreak on the 4th. Unfortunately, during the night there was a freshet, which swept away the trestles and rendered the neighbouring ford impassable. No more materials were to be found. Squire, however, did not recognise the word "impossible." With the

boats, therefore, he constructed a flying bridge for the cavalry and artillery, while with the few pontoons in his possession and some casks found in the neighbouring villages, he made a light bridge for the infantry. Beresford's force commenced the passage late on the 5th April, and by the evening of the 6th all the troops were across the river. On the 7th, Latour-Maubourg, who had hitherto occupied himself mainly in collecting food, forage, and money contributions, took the alarm, and advanced to prevent Beresford from crossing the Guadiana, but found his adversary not only over the river but occupying a strong position on the eastern side of it. The French commander was therefore compelled to fall back. Beresford was at this time either joined or came practically into close communication with several fragments of the Spanish armies, but he was cautious, and prudently was not thereby stimulated into undertaking a vigorous campaign, for the success of which he would have been dependent on the loyal co-operation of allies whom a bitter experience had proved to be unreliable. He therefore constructed entrenchments at the bridge head, and directed that the bridge itself should be solidly reconstructed. Having taken these precautions to secure his communications, he invested Olivenza with a portion of his army, while with the remainder he advanced to Albuera. On the 15th April Olivenza surrendered, on which Beresford advanced towards Zafra, his object being to drive Latour-Maubourg over the Sierra Morena and to cut off General Maransin, who, having defeated Ballasteros, was pursuing him towards Salvatierra. Receiving, however, information of the approach of the allies, Maransin managed to elude the columns which were threatening to prevent his retreat.

Whilst these movements were taking place, a smart cavalry action occurred on April 16th near Los Santos between two regiments of French cavalry, advancing from Llerena to collect contributions, and the British cavalry. The brigade consisted of the 4th Dragoon Guards, the 3rd Dragoons (now 3rd Hussars), and the 13th Light Dragoons, the brigadier being Colonel the Hon. G. de Grey. The accounts of this spirited cavalry action are very meagre. The numbers were about equal, but the French were broken and hunted for six miles with a loss in prisoners alone of 200 men, every attempt made to rally being baffled. The regimental records of the 13th Light Dragoons—which, by the way, claim all the merit for that regiment says nothing about the casualties, but the records of the 3rd Dragoons admit some loss but say that it was "very little." That the 13th Light Dragoons were, if not chiefly, at all events hotly engaged is proved by the fact that the French commander, whose gallantry excited the admiration of his opponents, was killed by Private James Beard of the regiment.

On the 18th April, Latour-Maubourg fell back to Guadalcanal. About this time the army was joined by General Alten with his brigade of two light infantry battalions of the King's German Legion. On the 21st Lord Wellington himself arrived at Elvas, and Beresford hastened to meet him. The commander-in-chief, drawing the infantry nearer to Badajoz, demanded that the Spanish troops should co- operate in carrying on and covering the siege, and laid it down that, if Soult advanced to the relief of the place, he was to be fought at Albuera. The Spaniards, in accordance with their usual practice, were slow in carrying out an agreement. Lord Wellington therefore hurried northward again in order to withstand Massena on the Agueda, leaving directions with Beresford that he was not to undertake the siege until he was reinforced by him or obtained the co-operation of the Spaniards.

After his departure Beresford fixed his headquarters at Almendralejos, and, finding that the French were sweeping the country between the two armies of forage, he sent Penne Villamur with a brigade of Spanish cavalry, reinforced by five squadrons, and Colonel Colborne with his brigade, to which had been added two Spanish guns and two squadrons, to put a stop to these French parties. Colborne and Penne Villamur not only accomplished this object, but also induced Latour-Maubourg himself to fall back. On the 5th May, the Spaniards having at length consented to perform their part in the siege of Badajoz, the investment of the town was begun, and, being completed on the 7th, batteries and trenches were constructed with energy. Owing to the want of proper siege materials and a sufficient number of trained sappers and miners, the operations were carried on at a disadvantage and at the cost of much loss of life.

Soult, on the 10th May, started from Seville with the view of relieving the beleaguered fortress. He had with him 3,000 heavy dragoons, two regiments of light cavalry, a division of infantry, and a battalion of grenadiers. On the following day he was joined by Marasin, and on the 13th picked up Latour-Maubourg, who was at once appointed to the command of the heavy cavalry. On the 14th he was within thirty-miles of Badajoz, and on the 15th arrived at Santa Marta. Beresford's information was good, for on the night of the 12th of May he received intelligence of Souk's approach. He at once suspended all operations against Badajoz, and on the following day, in spite of the remonstrances of his engi-

neers, he raised the siege under cover of the 4th division and a body of Spaniards. On the same day, after a conference with Blake at Valverde, he finally decided on giving battle to Soult at Albuera, the Spanish commander promising to bring his army into line before noon on the 15th. On the morning of that day the British army occupied the left of the selected position, but there was no sign of the approach of Blake. About 3 p.m. on that day the whole of the allied cavalry came in hurriedly and in some confusion, closely followed by the French light cavalry. In plain English, the allied cavalry were driven in, effect-

ing their retreat in so unmilitary a fashion that they only sought to reach the main army, and abandoned the wooded heights in front of the position. Yet on two recent occasions the British cavalry brigade had displayed the most heroic valour, and the discredit of the manner in which Beresford's horsemen rejoined him may fairly be attributed to the incapacity of General Long, commanding the whole of the allied cavalry, who, feeling the responsibility too much for him, surrendered that day his command to General Lumley.

Beresford promptly formed a temporary right wing, and at once sent to hasten Blake and his own detached troops. Blake was so slow that his main body did not reach the ground till 11 p.m., and his rear-guard not till 3 a.m. on the 16th. Orders were at once sent to call in Cole and Madelen's Portuguese brigade. By some mischance the message did not reach Madelen at once, but Cole with his two brigades, the infantry of the 5th Spanish army, and two squadrons of Portuguese cavalry, arrived at 6 a.m. on the 16th. The Spanish infantry joined Blake's army, the Portuguese cavalry joined Otway's bri-

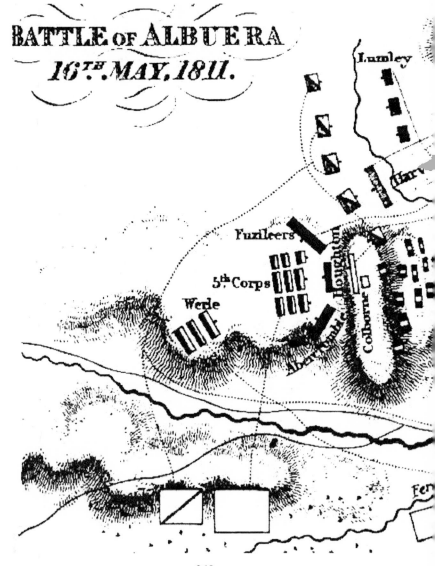

gade of Portuguese cavalry in advance of the left, while Cole formed up in rear of the 2nd division. Colonel Kemmis's brigade of the 4th division marched to join Beresford *viâ* Jerumenha, and consequently did not arrive till the 17th.

The position occupied by the allies consisted of a ridge about 4½ miles long, having the Aroya de Val de Sevilla in rear and the Albuera River in front. In front of the right of the position of the allies was a wooded hill, lying in a fork formed by the junction of the Faria

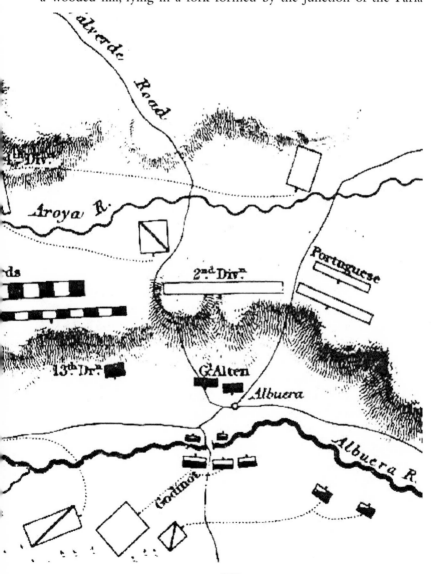

stream with the Albuera river. All these streams seem to have been easily passable above the village, but there was a bridge near Albuera in front of the left centre of the allies, where the road to Valverde crossed, and another where the same road crossed the Aroya de Val de Sevilla, commonly called in English descriptions Aroya. The position was first occupied as follows:—On the extreme left came General Hamilton's division of Portuguese with their left on the road, which at Albuera quits the Valverde road to go to Badajoz. On the right of the Portuguese came the 2nd division, under Major-General the Hon. W. Stewart, and consisting of the brigades of Colonel Colborne, Major-General Houghton, and Colonel the Hon. A. Abercrombie. On the extreme right, on the highest, broadest, steepest part of the position, were the Spaniards under Blake. The allied cavalry were drawn up, the main body across the Valverde road in rear of the Aroya and the 2nd division. The remainder of the cavalry were distributed along the Albuera River from in front of the allies' right to a spot beyond the Badajos road and below the village of Albuera. Major-General Alten, with his brigade of Germans, held the village.

The numbers on both sides were approximately as follows: The allies at—Spaniards 12,000, Portuguese 8,000, British 7.500, guns 30; French, 20,000 infantry, 3,000 cavalry, and 40 guns.

About 9 a.m. on the 16th a heavy force of French light cavalry and Godinot's division of infantry were seen, accompanied by artillery, advancing to attack the bridge in front of the village of Albuera. This force was followed by Werlé's division. The assailants were stoutly resisted by Alten's Light Brigade and the four guns of D Troop Royal Horse Artillery—two guns had been left at Lisbon—under Captain Lefebure. It soon became evident, however, that the real attack was on the right, not the left of the allies, for Werlé did not follow Godinot closely. Indeed, soon after 8 a.m., some French cavalry had issued from the Ilex wood, opposite the prolongation of the allies' right, and crossed the Albuera. Beresford therefore sent an order to Blake, as a measure of precaution, to form all his second and part of his first line on the broad elevated plateau running at right angles to the general direction of the allies' position. He at the same time directed Stewart with the 2nd division to take ground to his right in order to support Blake. General Hamilton was ordered to move to his right and, while sending one brigade forward to support Alten at the village and bridge, to hold the other in readiness to carry assistance to any part of the field where it might be needed. The two Portuguese

regiments of light infantry under Colonel Collins were attached to
General Hamilton's division. The heavy cavalry, 3rd Dragoon Guards
and 4th Dragoons, and D Battery Royal Horse Artillery under the
personal direction of Major-General Hon. William Lumley, the briga-

Colonel the Hon. G. de Grey, were placed on a small plain
e magnificent brook called the Aroya de Val de Sevilla. The
was drawn up in *échelon* to the cavalry about 100 yards to
ir. The 13th Light Dragoons were posted above the bridge
to watch the enemy, while Otway's cavalry were drawn up below the
bridge on the extreme left watching the French.

Napier says that the Albuera was fordable both above and below
the bridge, but there are other statements to the effect that below the
bridge it was not fordable on that day. At all events, even if the French
did not try and cross below the bridge, Otway was well posted to fall
on their flank should they pass at the bridge.

While these changes of position were taking place, the rain came
down and helped to screen the advance of the French infantry through
the wood and over the Albuera on the right; but Beresford was soon
shown clearly what the intentions of Soult were, for Werlé, leaving
only a battalion of grenadiers and a few squadrons to watch Otway,
rapidly countermarched and hastened to join the main body of the
French army, while the light cavalry, galloping along the bank of the
Albuera, crossed it and placed themselves on the right of Latour-Maubourg's heavy cavalry. Godinot, however, continued the fight at the
bridge either with the view of distracting the attention of the allies
or watching for a chance to cross the river. Beresford, as soon as he
saw Werlé's countermarch, rode in all haste to Blake, who, vain and
punctilious, had refused to obey the first order carried by Colonel
Hardinge, whom he told with great heat that the vital attack was at
the village and bridge. He had similarly disregarded a second message,
and, when Beresford arrived in person, the Spaniards still occupied
their original position. At this moment, however, the obstinate old
don had it pointed out to him by a German officer' on his staff that
heavy French columns were appearing on his right. Yielding to the
evidences of his eyesight, Blake proceeded to change front, but, to
quote Napier's words:

"With such pedantic slowness, that Beresford, impatient of his folly,
took the direction in person."

Unfortunately, the movement was too late, and, before the Spaniards could be drawn up in order on the summit of the before-men-
tioned plateau, the French were upon them. Whatever may have been
the conduct of the Spaniards later in the day, it is conceded that at this
period of the battle they behaved gallantly, and fell back fighting and
in fairly good order. Beresford strove to induce them to recapture the

plateau, but failed; so ordered Stewart's division to pass through the Spaniards and drive away the French. Colborne's brigade was at the head of the division. It is difficult to ascertain in what formation the brigade advanced. We know that every regiment was in column of companies, but whether in a line of contiguous columns or in mass, *i.e.* one regiment in rear of another, we cannot say. Colborne, a cool, skilful, and experienced soldier, wished to deploy before ascending the hill, but General Stewart, full of ardour, would not wait for this manoeuvre, and the brigade advanced in column of companies, each regiment deploying in succession as it reached the summit. The Buffs on the right were first formed, and opened fire; the 48th on their left were the next to deploy, then the 66th. Somehow or another the 66th, while still in column, were rear rank in front. Though under a heavy artillery fire, they counter-marched on the move with the utmost precision, and then wheeled into line and opened fire on the enemy, who were in close column. The 66th were ordered to charge, but had not advanced far when the "halt," followed by the "retire," was sounded. Immediately afterwards the order was given to advance again. Probably the 48th likewise fired and advanced at the same time. We know that the Buffs did. Suddenly a fearful catastrophe occurred. It would seem that the Buffs were ordered to re-form column and with their right wing to cover the rear of the brigade. They were consequently faced about, when suddenly four regiments of Polish lancers and light cavalry fell on the right flank of the brigade and swept along it. The authority for this statement is the late Colonel Clarke, who commanded a company of the 66th in the battle. He says that in his regiment the men formed groups of six or eight, the officers snatching up muskets and joining them. A fierce hand-to-hand fight ensued, the French infantry having taken advantage of the confusion to take part in the struggle. In a few minutes two-thirds of the brigade were killed, disabled, or captured, and six of our guns taken. Fortunately, the 31st was still in column at the moment, and was thus able to hold its ground. The French cavalry owed their success to the fact that, owing to the thickness of the atmosphere and the cloud of smoke, they had been able to approach unseen, and, even when perceived, were mistaken at first for Spanish cavalry. The conduct of the Polish lancers—as afterwards at Waterloo—was most brutal. They gave no quarter, and even speared the disabled. One young officer. Ensign Hay of the 66th, was first pierced right through the body by a Polish lancer, who afterwards repeated the thrust; this time, however, the point of the weapon was

caught on the breast-bone. Another lancer attacked Beresford himself, but the latter, being a powerful man, avoided the thrust, and, seizing, cast him from his saddle. According to the narrative of the Marquis of Londonderry in his history of the Peninsular War, another lancer, who attacked the Portuguese staff, was disposed of with more difficulty. To quote the exact words:

"A very different fate attended the personal exertions of the Portuguese staff. They, too, were charged by a single lancer, who knocked

down one with the butt of his pike, overset another man and horse, and gave ample employment to the entire headquarters before he was finally despatched. These heroes declared that the man seemed possessed by an evil spirit, and that, when he fell at last, he literally bit the ground."

The Buffs, being on the right of the brigade, were the first to suffer from the furious rush of the French cavalry, and an heroic defence was made of their colours. Ensign Thomas that day carried the regimental colour: called upon to surrender his precious charge, he replied sternly that he refused to do so, but, being thereupon mortally wounded, the colour was captured. Ensign Walsh carried the king's colour, and, when the regiment was broken, the sergeants of the colour party were slain valiantly defending it. Left alone and anxious to preserve his charge, he made an attempt to carry the colour to the rear. Pursued by several lancers, he was overtaken, surrounded, wounded, and taken prisoner. At that instant Lieutenant Latham, who had seen his peril, rushed up, and, before the French could carry off the colour, had seized it. A host of foes, emulous of the glory of capturing a standard, fell eagerly upon the gallant Latham, who was soon bleeding from several wounds, but who, defending himself valiantly with his sword, refused to yield. A French hussar grasped the colour staff with his left hand, and, rising in his stirrups, aimed a vigorous blow at his head. He failed to cut him down, but inflicted a grievous wound, severing one side of his face and nose. The indomitable Englishman, however, would not even then give in. The French horsemen, crowding round, strove to drag the colour from him, calling fiercely on him to yield the trophy. His reply was, "I will surrender it only with my life." His words were unintelligible, but his meaning was plain, and a hussar with a vigorous cut severed his left arm. Not vanquished yet,

Latham dropped his sword, seized the colour with his right hand, and continued the struggle, which must have ended quickly and fatally for him, had it not been that his adversaries in their eagerness to secure the prize jostled and impeded each other. He was, however, at length thrown down, trampled on by horses, and pierced by lances. At this critical moment a charge of British cavalry took place, and the French horsemen fled without having attained their object. Latham, though desperately wounded, exerted what little strength remained to him in tearing the silk from the staff and concealing the former under his body. He then swooned. A little later in the day the 7th Fusiliers passed over the spot where Latham lay apparently dead, and Sergeant Gough, espying the colour, took it up and eventually restored it to the Buffs. After a time Latham came to himself, and, crawling down to the brook, was found striving to quench his thirst. Removed to a neighbouring convent, his wounds were dressed, and he ultimately recovered. Ensign Walsh managed to escape and rejoin his regiment, when he told the story of Lieutenant Latham's conduct. The officers of the regiment, proud of the intrepidity of their comrade, subscribed 100 guineas for a gold medal commemorating Lieutenant Latham's exploit, and this medal he was allowed by the Horse Guards to wear. He was promoted for his heroism to a company in another regiment, and brought back to the Buffs as a captain.

The Prince Regent granted him an interview when he arrived in London, and, with that graciousness of manner which distinguished him, and that nobility of mind which he occasionally displayed, induced Latham to undergo an operation by an eminent surgeon for the diminution of the disfigurement caused by the wound in his face, His Royal Highness undertaking to pay the heavy fee. It is a singular

fact that, though few men have ever been so seriously injured and survived, in the official returns of the Battle of Albuera Latham was returned as "slightly wounded."

It is always difficult to follow the course of a battle and give the correct sequence of events. The difficulty is particularly great with regard to Albuera. Napier's account is eloquent, brilliant, and full of dramatic force, but it is not clear. Nor are other accounts more intelligible, and there has been much controversy with regard to certain points. After consulting many books, we have come to the conclusion that the story is in the main as we are about to tell it.

Colborne's brigade having been cut to pieces alike by the musketry and grape from their front as by the charge of cavalry on their flank and along their rear, the confusion was excessive. So great, indeed, was the disorder that the Spanish persisted in firing straight to their front, though there were British soldiers between them and the enemy. Indeed, at one period of the action a Spanish battalion and a British battalion exchanged shots for some time under the belief that they were foes. Beresford did his utmost to induce the Spaniards to advance, but they would not move; and it is stated in all accounts of the battle that Beresford, having appealed to the officers in vain, at length seized a Spanish ensign and carried him with the colour he bore some distance to the front, but the fellow ran back as soon as released. To have actually carried him Beresford must have dismounted; so what probably really took place was that the marshal, while on horseback, seized the ensign by the collar and dragged him forward. Whilst this was going on, the French cavalry had pretty well surrounded the remains of Colborne's brigade, which, as we have mentioned above, it had broken up with the exception of the 31st on the extreme left. Among other damage Captain Cleeve's battery, having accompanied Colborne's brigade on its right, was ridden over and the six pieces captured; they were, however, all, except one howitzer, eventually recovered.

It was at this critical moment that General Lumley sent four squadrons of the heavy brigade, supported by the fire of Captain Lefebure's four horse-artillery guns, to fall on the French cavalry. The latter apparently did not wait for the shock, but retreated. The next act in the drama was the advance of General Houghton's brigade, accompanied by General Stewart, who, warned by the catastrophe which had just occurred, deployed the regiments before they advanced, the 29th being on the right, the 48th on the left, and the 57th in the centre. The weather, which had been wet and misty, now cleared a

little. Houghton's brigade established itself on the hill, and the 31st fought by its side. The fire was dreadful, musketry being fired at close, and grape at half, range. Stewart was twice wounded; Houghton, after having been several times wounded, at length, struck by three bullets, fell and died; Colonel Duckworth, of the 1st battalion of the 48th, was killed: Colonel White, of the 29th, was mortally wounded; Colonel Inglis, of the 57th, was severely wounded, and the 29th men fell in swathes. Two-thirds of each of the three regiments were on the ground; ammunition was beginning to run short. Werlé's division was coming up in support of the French. Lumley, powerfully aided by his four horse-artillery guns, made valiant efforts against the superior numbers of the French cavalry, but could only just manage to hold them in check. Lefebure's battery was from time to time ridden through, and one of its guns was for a short time in the possession of the enemy; it was, however, soon recovered.

The battle, by all the rules of the game of war, was lost, and Beresford himself was of that opinion. From the vague and somewhat conflicting accounts it would seem that Beresford, having ridden to the bridge in front of Albuera to ascertain why a brigade of General Hamilton's Portuguese division for which he had sent had not arrived, found that it had been moved further to the east—the left of the line. He then ordered Colonel Collins to advance to the attack of the hill.

We have the positive assurance of the late Sir Alexander—then

Major—Dickson, commanding the Portuguese artillery, and who was at the bridge at the moment, that he was ordered to retreat with his artillery towards Valverde, and Baron Alten by order withdrew from the village for a moment. Fortunately, Colonel Hardinge (afterwards Lord Hardinge) was, at his elbow, and, gathering from his manner and orders what his intentions were, he said, "I think, sir. I ought to tell you that you have a peerage on the one hand and a court-martial on the other," and Beresford, after a moment's reflection, said, "I will go for the peerage." Either on general instructions or on his own initiative, knowing what the general wanted, he directed General Cole to attack with the 4th division, and, as soon as he saw his left brigade—the Fusilier brigade—approaching the left of Houghton's brigade:

"I went to Abercrombie," (commanding Stewart's 3rd brigade), "and authorised him to deploy and move past Houghton's left. While Houghton's brigade held the hill, Myers and Abercrombie passed the flanks on the right and left, and made a simultaneous attack on the enemy, who began to waver and then went off to the rear. Myers and Abercrombie, in my opinion, decided the fate of the day."

The above is a literal extract from Lord Hardinge's own journal.

The Fusilier brigade was on the left of Cole's division, and Hervey's Portuguese brigade of Cole's division on the right. We are told that Colonel Hawkshawe, with a battalion of the Lusitanian Legion, flanked the advance. Cole brought his division up somewhat obliquely, his right being thrown forward. What the position of Captain Sympher's battery, belonging to the 4th division, was we are nowhere told, but we know that, when Cleeve's battery was captured by the French cavalry, three guns of a British battery were also captured. The only British field-battery was Captain Hawker's. It must have been, then, three of his four guns, which fell temporarily into the hands of the enemy.

An interesting little book, called *Rough Notes of Several Campaigns*, by Sergeant S. Cooper, of the 7th Royal Fusiliers, who was present at Albuera, says that six nine-pounders were on the right of the division. Now, either there were only four guns, in which case they constituted Captain Hawker's battery, or there were six guns, in which event they were Captain Braun's Portuguese battery of Hamilton's division. Colonel Collins's brigade was probably somewhere in this part of the field, for we know that he himself was badly wounded.

Hervey's Portuguese brigade of Cole's division behaved with great gallantry, and repulsed a charge of the French cavalry; but the brunt of the fighting was borne by the Fusilier brigade, consisting of two

battalions of the 7th, and one battalion of the 23rd Fusiliers had been previously deployed, and advanced steadily in line under a heavy fire of musketry and artillery. As they neared the hill, the French executed a charge on some Spanish cavalry in front of the brigade. A volley fired into the mass of the combatants checked the French, and the

Spaniards, galloping round the left flank of the brigade, took no further part in the action. The brigade, continuing its progress, gained the
summit of the hill, and then ensued a furious duel. The French guns
vomited forth grape in a continuous stream, while under cover of
their fire the heavy French columns strove to deploy, but the musketry

of the brigade swept away the heads of their foes' formations, though not without suffering fearful loss themselves. Myers, the brigadier, fell stricken to death. Cole, the commander of the division, and Colonels Ellis, Blakeney, and Hawkshawe were all disabled, and many other officers, together with hundreds of men, were killed or wounded.

The brigade, indeed, seemed on the point of being vanquished by annihilation. To quote Napier's eloquent words:

"The Fusilier battalions, struck by the iron tempest, reeled and staggered like sinking ships. But, suddenly and sternly recovering, they closed on their terrible enemies, and then was seen with what a strength and majesty the British soldier fights."

Firing and advancing, the brigade pressed steadily but slowly onward, leaving behind it a constantly expanding field of dead and wounded men. In vain did Soult encourage his splendid troops; in vain did the latter fight with the historical gallantry of their race; in vain did the reserve, pushing to the front, strive to stem the ebbing tide. Our men were not to be denied, the French reserve was swept away by the fragments of the leading combatants, and, again to quote Napier:

"The mighty mass gave way, and like a loosened cliff went headlong down the steep. The river flowed after in streams discoloured with blood, and fifteen hundred unwounded men, the remnant of six thousand unconquerable British soldiers, stood triumphant on the fatal field."

It is but common justice to record that the conduct of Abercrombie's brigade at the crisis was as gallant as that of the Fusiliers. Indeed, all the British, Portuguese, and German troops behaved splendidly. The battle began a little before 9 a.m., and ended about 2 p.m., the fighting during the remainder of the day being confined to a desultory distant cannonade and an occasional exchange of musket shots between the advanced troops. Beresford, though he had driven his adversary' over the river, had suffered too heavily to permit of following up the victory. Indeed, he was in some apprehension of a renewed attack on the morrow.

The field of battle presented a dreadful sight. Major Dickson, writing of the scene, said that on the hill, where the battle chiefly ranged on a space of 1,000 by 1,200 yards, "there were certainly not less than 6,000 dead or wounded." In Colborne's brigade the Buffs lost 4 officers and 212 men killed, 13 officers and 234 men wounded, and 2 officers and 176 men missing. The 29th had only 2 captains, a few subalterns, and 96 men left. The 48th and the 66th also suffered heavily. In Houghton's brigade, as we have seen, the general was slain, as was also Colonel Duckworth; whilst Colonel White was mortally, and Colonel Inglis and Major Wray were severely, wounded. In fact, every field-officer of the brigade was either killed or wounded, so that at the close of the action the brigade was commanded by Captain Cemétière—strange to say, of French origin—of the 48th Regiment. In this brigade the 29th lost 7 officers and 77 men killed, 13 officers and 232 men wounded, and 11 men missing. The 1st battalion 48th Regiment also lost heavily. The 57th lost, out of 30 officers and 570 men, 20 officers and 420 men, and was brought out of action by the adjutant, who in the morning had been fourteenth in seniority.

The last-named regiment received on this occasion the honourable name of the "Die Hards," which has survived till this day. At Inkerman, at a critical period of the battle, when a heavy Russian column threatened the weak remnants of the 57th, Captain Stanley, who commanded, called out, "Die Hards, remember Albuera!" and the men, responding, made a gallant and successful effort. The sobriquet was gained under the following circumstances:—The regiment, when on the top of the fatal hill, was losing officers and men every second. The regimental colour had twenty-one holes in it, the queen's colour seventeen, the latter also having its staff broken. Ensign Jackson, who carried it, being hit in three places, went to the rear to have his wounds dressed. On his return he found Ensign Kitch, who had succeeded him, severely wounded but obstinate in refusal to give up his charge. Many companies had all their officers killed or wounded, and, owing to the heavy losses, the line presented the appearance of a chain of skirmishers. There is a tradition in the regiment that on the following morning after the battle the rations of No. 2 company were drawn by a drummer, who carried them away in his hat. Captain Ralph Fawcett, a young officer of only twenty-three years of age, although mortally wounded, caused himself to be placed on a small hillock, whence he continued to command his company, calling out from time to time to the men to fire low and not to waste their cartridges. Colonel Inglis, commanding the regiment, being struck by a grape-shot which penetrated his left breast and lodged in his back, refused to be carried to the rear, and remained where he had fallen in front of the colours, urging the men to keep up a steady fire and to *"die hard."*

Marshal Beresford, in his despatch, said that the dead, particularly those of the 57th, were to be seen "lying as they had fought in the ranks, and every wound in front."

General Stewart was twice hit, but would not quit the field. General Houghton, who had received several wounds without shrinking,

at last fell dead, as we have mentioned, pierced by three bullets, whilst cheering on the men of his brigade. Early in the morning, hearing of the enemy's advance, he hurriedly turned out in a green frock-coat. Whilst on horseback in front of his brigade, his servant came up with

the general's red coat. Without dismounting, Houghton with the utmost coolness made the exchange of garments, though at the time he was under the fire of the French artillery.

In the Fusilier brigade the Royal Fusiliers went into action with 31 officers in each battalion. Of these the 1st battalion lost 4 killed or died of their wounds and 10 wounded; while in the 2nd battalion there were 3 officers killed and 13 wounded, 1 sergeant and 63 men were killed, and 14 sergeants and 263 men were wounded. In the 2nd battalion, which went into action 435 non-commissioned officers and men strong, the losses were—killed, 1 sergeant and 46 men; wounded, 16 sergeants, 1 drummer, and 269 men. From the account of the late Sergeant Cooper of this regiment, we learn that, when the fusiliers had mounted the hill, there were constant cries of "Close up!" "Close in!" "Fire away!" "Forward!" Sergeant Cooper relates as an illustration of the great opinion which the army even then entertained of their illustrious leader that, when he (Cooper) was going into action, a comrade said to him, "'Where's Arthur?' meaning Wellington. I said, 'I don't know. I don't see him.' He replied, 'Aw wish he were here.' So did I."

The 23rd Fusiliers lost 2 officers and 74 men killed, 12 officers—of whom 2 died subsequently of their wounds—and 245 men wounded, and 6 men missing. At the end of the action one company was commanded by a corporal.

The gallant leader of the Fusilier brigade, Lieutenant-Colonel Sir William Myers, Bart., was among the slain. Through the interest of his father, who was a lieutenant-general, he was granted a commission while still a child, and in 1800, when barely sixteen, joined the Coldstream Guards from half-pay. Wounded at the landing in Egypt in 1801, in the following year he became a lieutenant-colonel, and very sensibly spent the next two years at the senior department of the Royal Military College. At the end of 1804, being only twenty years of age, he obtained the command of the 2nd battalion Royal Fusiliers. The two battalions of the regiment being sent to Portugal in 1809, they were, with a battalion of the 23rd Fusiliers, formed into a brigade, the command of which was given to Sir William Myers, scarcely then twenty-five years of age. At Talavera the brigade and its young brigadier played a distinguished part, and Sir William was recognised as one of the most rising officers in the army.

Albuera cut short his promising career, and it is asserted that his letters betray a presentiment of his approaching fate. When ordered to advance, he turned to his brigade, exclaiming with exultation, "It will be a glorious day for the Fusiliers." His horse being shot under him, he proceeded on foot till a second horse was brought. He had scarcely mounted the latter when he received a bullet which struck him in the hip, passing obliquely upwards through the intestines. He did not fall, but kept on encouraging his men. At length it became necessary to take him from the saddle, and he was borne off the field by a party of fusiliers. He wished a hut to be erected over him, but his servants, anxious to obtain for him the comfort of a bed, carried him to Valverde, a distance of ten miles. On the road he passed by a mule carrying the body of General Houghton to be buried at Elvas. He thereupon expressed a wish to be buried where he died. He did not, however, expire till the next day, when he breathed his last at the age of twenty-six, and was buried close to Valverde.

It may here be mentioned that a company of the 5th battalion of the both Rifles was at the Battle of Albuera, attached to the 4th division, and suffered some loss on the occasion.

The total casualties of the British and Portuguese was 984 of all ranks killed, 2,095 wounded, and 565 missing. The loss of the Spaniards was nearly 2,000; that of the French was about 9,000, including five generals.

During the night of the 18th, Soult retreated, much to Beresford's relief, for the circumstances of his victory had brought with them little exhilaration.

LEONAUR

ALSO FROM LEONAUR
AVAILABLE IN SOFTCOVER OR HARDCOVER WITH DUST JACKET

A HISTORY OF THE FRENCH & INDIAN WAR *by Arthur G. Bradley*—The Seven Years War as it was fought in the New World has always fascinated students of military history—here is the story of that confrontation.

WASHINGTON'S EARLY CAMPAIGNS *by James Hadden*—The French Post Expedition, Great Meadows and Braddock's Defeat—including Braddock's Orderly Books.

BOUQUET & THE OHIO INDIAN WAR *by Cyrus Cort & William Smith*—Two Accounts of the Campaigns of 1763-1764: Bouquet's Campaigns by Cyrus Cort & The History of Bouquet's Expeditions by William Smith.

NARRATIVES OF THE FRENCH & INDIAN WAR: 2 *by David Holden, Samuel Jenks, Lemuel Lyon, Mary Cochrane Rogers & Henry T. Blake*—Contains The Diary of Sergeant David Holden, Captain Samuel Jenks' Journal, The Journal of Lemuel Lyon, Journal of a French Officer at the Siege of Quebec, A Battle Fought on Snowshoes & The Battle of Lake George.

NARRATIVES OF THE FRENCH & INDIAN WAR *by Brown, Eastburn, Hawks & Putnam*—Ranger Brown's Narrative, The Adventures of Robert Eastburn, The Journal of Rufus Putnam—Provincial Infantry & Orderly Book and Journal of Major John Hawks on the Ticonderoga-Crown Point Campaign.

THE 7TH (QUEEN'S OWN) HUSSARS: Volume 1—1688-1792 *by C. R. B. Barrett*—As Dragoons During the Flanders Campaign, War of the Austrian Succession and the Seven Years War.

INDIA'S FREE LANCES *by H. G. Keene*—European Mercenary Commanders in Hindustan 1770-1820.

THE BENGAL EUROPEAN REGIMENT *by P. R. Innes*—An Elite Regiment of the Honourable East India Company 1756-1858.

MUSKET & TOMAHAWK *by Francis Parkman*—A Military History of the French & Indian War, 1753-1760.

THE BLACK WATCH AT TICONDEROGA *by Frederick B. Richards*—Campaigns in the French & Indian War.

QUEEN'S RANGERS *by Frederick B. Richards*—John Simcoe and his Rangers During the Revolutionary War for America.

LEONAUR

ALSO FROM LEONAUR
AVAILABLE IN SOFTCOVER OR HARDCOVER WITH DUST JACKET

JOURNALS OF ROBERT ROGERS OF THE RANGERS *by Robert Rogers*—The exploits of Rogers & the Rangers in his own words during 1755-1761 in the French & Indian War.

GALLOPING GUNS *by James Young*—The Experiences of an Officer of the Bengal Horse Artillery During the Second Maratha War 1804-1805.

GORDON *by Demetrius Charles Boulger*—The Career of Gordon of Khartoum.

THE BATTLE OF NEW ORLEANS *by Zachary F. Smith*—The final major engagement of the War of 1812.

THE TWO WARS OF MRS DUBERLY *by Frances Isabella Duberly*—An Intrepid Victorian Lady's Experience of the Crimea and Indian Mutiny.

WITH THE GUARDS' BRIGADE DURING THE BOER WAR *by Edward P. Lowry*—On Campaign from Bloemfontein to Koomati Poort and Back.

THE REBELLIOUS DUCHESS *by Paul F. S. Dermoncourt*—The Adventures of the Duchess of Berri and Her Attempt to Overthrow French Monarchy.

MEN OF THE MUTINY *by John Tulloch Nash & Henry Metcalfe*—Two Accounts of the Great Indian Mutiny of 1857: Fighting with the Bengal Yeomanry Cavalry & Private Metcalfe at Lucknow.

CAMPAIGN IN THE CRIMEA *by George Shuldham Peard*—The Recollections of an Officer of the 20th Regiment of Foot.

WITHIN SEBASTOPOL *by K. Hodasevich*—A Narrative of the Campaign in the Crimea, and of the Events of the Siege.

WITH THE CAVALRY TO AFGHANISTAN *by William Taylor*—The Experiences of a Trooper of H. M. 4th Light Dragoons During the First Afghan War.

THE CAWNPORE MAN *by Mowbray Thompson*—A First Hand Account of the Siege and Massacre During the Indian Mutiny By One of Four Survivors.

BRIGADE COMMANDER: AFGHANISTAN *by Henry Brooke*—The Journal of the Commander of the 2nd Infantry Brigade, Kandahar Field Force During the Second Afghan War.

BANCROFT OF THE BENGAL HORSE ARTILLERY *by N. W. Bancroft*—An Account of the First Sikh War 1845-1846.

LEONAUR

ALSO FROM LEONAUR

AVAILABLE IN SOFTCOVER OR HARDCOVER WITH DUST JACKET

AFGHANISTAN: THE BELEAGUERED BRIGADE *by G. R. Gleig*—An Account of Sale's Brigade During the First Afghan War.

IN THE RANKS OF THE C. I. V *by Erskine Childers*—With the City Imperial Volunteer Battery (Honourable Artillery Company) in the Second Boer War.

THE BENGAL NATIVE ARMY *by F. G. Cardew*—An Invaluable Reference Resource.

THE 7TH (QUEEN'S OWN) HUSSARS: Volume 4—1688-1914 *by C. R. B. Barrett*—Uniforms, Equipment, Weapons, Traditions, the Services of Notable Officers and Men & the Appendices to All Volumes—Volume 4: 1688-1914.

THE SWORD OF THE CROWN *by Eric W. Sheppard*—A History of the British Army to 1914.

THE 7TH (QUEEN'S OWN) HUSSARS: Volume 3—**1818-1914** *by C. R. B. Barrett*—On Campaign During the Canadian Rebellion, the Indian Mutiny, the Sudan, Matabeleland, Mashonaland and the Boer War Volume 3: 1818-1914.

THE KHARTOUM CAMPAIGN *by Bennet Burleigh*—A Special Correspondent's View of the Reconquest of the Sudan by British and Egyptian Forces under Kitchener—1898.

EL PUCHERO *by Richard McSherry*—The Letters of a Surgeon of Volunteers During Scott's Campaign of the American-Mexican War 1847-1848.

RIFLEMAN SAHIB *by E. Maude*—The Recollections of an Officer of the Bombay Rifles During the Southern Mahratta Campaign, Second Sikh War, Persian Campaign and Indian Mutiny.

THE KING'S HUSSAR *by Edwin Mole*—The Recollections of a 14th (King's) Hussar During the Victorian Era.

JOHN COMPANY'S CAVALRYMAN *by William Johnson*—The Experiences of a British Soldier in the Crimea, the Persian Campaign and the Indian Mutiny.

COLENSO & DURNFORD'S ZULU WAR *by Frances E. Colenso & Edward Durnford*—The first and possibly the most important history of the Zulu War.

U. S. DRAGOON *by Samuel E. Chamberlain*—Experiences in the Mexican War 1846-48 and on the South Western Frontier.

LEONAUR

ALSO FROM LEONAUR
AVAILABLE IN SOFTCOVER OR HARDCOVER WITH DUST JACKET

THE 2ND MAORI WAR: 1860-1861 *by Robert Carey*—The Second Maori War, or First Taranaki War, one more bloody instalment of the conflicts between European settlers and the indigenous Maori people.

A JOURNAL OF THE SECOND SIKH WAR *by Daniel A. Sandford*—The Experiences of an Ensign of the 2nd Bengal European Regiment During the Campaign in the Punjab, India, 1848-49.

THE LIGHT INFANTRY OFFICER *by John H. Cooke*—The Experiences of an Officer of the 43rd Light Infantry in America During the War of 1812.

BUSHVELDT CARBINEERS *by George Witton*—The War Against the Boers in South Africa and the 'Breaker' Morant Incident.

LAKE'S CAMPAIGNS IN INDIA *by Hugh Pearse*—The Second Anglo Maratha War, 1803-1807.

BRITAIN IN AFGHANISTAN 1: THE FIRST AFGHAN WAR 1839-42 *by Archibald Forbes*—From invasion to destruction-a British military disaster.

BRITAIN IN AFGHANISTAN 2: THE SECOND AFGHAN WAR 1878-80 *by Archibald Forbes*—This is the history of the Second Afghan War-another episode of British military history typified by savagery, massacre, siege and battles.

UP AMONG THE PANDIES *by Vivian Dering Majendie*—Experiences of a British Officer on Campaign During the Indian Mutiny, 1857-1858.

MUTINY: 1857 *by James Humphries*—Authentic Voices from the Indian Mutiny-First Hand Accounts of Battles, Sieges and Personal Hardships.

BLOW THE BUGLE, DRAW THE SWORD *by W. H. G. Kingston*—The Wars, Campaigns, Regiments and Soldiers of the British & Indian Armies During the Victorian Era, 1839-1898.

WAR BEYOND THE DRAGON PAGODA *by Major J. J. Snodgrass*—A Personal Narrative of the First Anglo-Burmese War 1824 - 1826.

THE HERO OF ALIWAL *by James Humphries*—The Campaigns of Sir Harry Smith in India, 1843-1846, During the Gwalior War & the First Sikh War.

ALL FOR A SHILLING A DAY *by Donald F. Featherstone*—The story of H.M. 16th, the Queen's Lancers During the first Sikh War 1845-1846.

LEONAUR

ALSO FROM LEONAUR
AVAILABLE IN SOFTCOVER OR HARDCOVER WITH DUST JACKET

THE FALL OF THE MOGHUL EMPIRE OF HINDUSTAN *by H. G. Keene*—By the beginning of the nineteenth century, as British and Indian armies under Lake and Wellesley dominated the scene, a little over half a century of conflict brought the Moghul Empire to its knees.

LADY SALE'S AFGHANISTAN *by Florentia Sale*—An Indomitable Victorian Lady's Account of the Retreat from Kabul During the First Afghan War.

THE CAMPAIGN OF MAGENTA AND SOLFERINO 1859 *by Harold Carmichael Wylly*—The Decisive Conflict for the Unification of Italy.

FRENCH'S CAVALRY CAMPAIGN *by J. G. Maydon*—A Special Correspondent's View of British Army Mounted Troops During the Boer War.

CAVALRY AT WATERLOO *by Sir Evelyn Wood*—British Mounted Troops During the Campaign of 1815.

THE SUBALTERN *by George Robert Gleig*—The Experiences of an Officer of the 85th Light Infantry During the Peninsular War.

NAPOLEON AT BAY, 1814 *by F. Loraine Petre*—The Campaigns to the Fall of the First Empire.

NAPOLEON AND THE CAMPAIGN OF 1806 *by Colonel Vachée*—The Napoleonic Method of Organisation and Command to the Battles of Jena & Auerstädt.

THE COMPLETE ADVENTURES IN THE CONNAUGHT RANGERS *by William Grattan*—The 88th Regiment during the Napoleonic Wars by a Serving Officer.

BUGLER AND OFFICER OF THE RIFLES *by William Green & Harry Smith*—With the 95th (Rifles) during the Peninsular & Waterloo Campaigns of the Napoleonic Wars.

NAPOLEONIC WAR STORIES *by Sir Arthur Quiller-Couch*—Tales of soldiers, spies, battles & sieges from the Peninsular & Waterloo campaigns.

CAPTAIN OF THE 95TH (RIFLES) *by Jonathan Leach*—An officer of Wellington's sharpshooters during the Peninsular, South of France and Waterloo campaigns of the Napoleonic wars.

RIFLEMAN COSTELLO *by Edward Costello*—The adventures of a soldier of the 95th (Rifles) in the Peninsular & Waterloo Campaigns of the Napoleonic wars.

LEONAUR

ALSO FROM LEONAUR
AVAILABLE IN SOFTCOVER OR HARDCOVER WITH DUST JACKET

AT THEM WITH THE BAYONET *by Donald F. Featherstone*—The first Anglo-Sikh War 1845-1846.

STEPHEN CRANE'S BATTLES *by Stephen Crane*—Nine Decisive Battles Recounted by the Author of 'The Red Badge of Courage'.

THE GURKHA WAR *by H. T. Prinsep*—The Anglo-Nepalese Conflict in North East India 1814-1816.

FIRE & BLOOD *by G. R. Gleig*—The burning of Washington & the battle of New Orleans, 1814, through the eyes of a young British soldier.

SOUND ADVANCE! *by Joseph Anderson*—Experiences of an officer of HM 50th regiment in Australia, Burma & the Gwalior war.

THE CAMPAIGN OF THE INDUS *by Thomas Holdsworth*—Experiences of a British Officer of the 2nd (Queen's Royal) Regiment in the Campaign to Place Shah Shuja on the Throne of Afghanistan 1838 - 1840.

WITH THE MADRAS EUROPEAN REGIMENT IN BURMA *by John Butler*—The Experiences of an Officer of the Honourable East India Company's Army During the First Anglo-Burmese War 1824 - 1826.

IN ZULULAND WITH THE BRITISH ARMY *by Charles L. Norris-Newman*—The Anglo-Zulu war of 1879 through the first-hand experiences of a special correspondent.

BESIEGED IN LUCKNOW *by Martin Richard Gubbins*—The first Anglo-Sikh War 1845-1846.

A TIGER ON HORSEBACK *by L. March Phillips*—The Experiences of a Trooper & Officer of Rimington's Guides - The Tigers - during the Anglo-Boer war 1899 - 1902.

SEPOYS, SIEGE & STORM *by Charles John Griffiths*—The Experiences of a young officer of H.M.'s 61st Regiment at Ferozepore, Delhi ridge and at the fall of Delhi during the Indian mutiny 1857.

CAMPAIGNING IN ZULULAND *by W. E. Montague*—Experiences on campaign during the Zulu war of 1879 with the 94th Regiment.

THE STORY OF THE GUIDES *by G.J. Younghusband*—The Exploits of the Soldiers of the famous Indian Army Regiment from the northwest frontier 1847 - 1900.

LEONAUR

ALSO FROM LEONAUR
AVAILABLE IN SOFTCOVER OR HARDCOVER WITH DUST JACKET

ZULU:1879 *by D.C.F. Moodie & the Leonaur Editors*—The Anglo-Zulu War of 1879 from contemporary sources: First Hand Accounts, Interviews, Dispatches, Official Documents & Newspaper Reports.

THE RED DRAGOON *by W.J. Adams*—With the 7th Dragoon Guards in the Cape of Good Hope against the Boers & the Kaffir tribes during the 'war of the axe' 1843-48'.

THE RECOLLECTIONS OF SKINNER OF SKINNER'S HORSE *by James Skinner*—James Skinner and his 'Yellow Boys' Irregular cavalry in the wars of India between the British, Mahratta, Rajput, Mogul, Sikh & Pindarree Forces.

A CAVALRY OFFICER DURING THE SEPOY REVOLT *by A. R. D. Mackenzie*—Experiences with the 3rd Bengal Light Cavalry, the Guides and Sikh Irregular Cavalry from the outbreak to Delhi and Lucknow.

A NORFOLK SOLDIER IN THE FIRST SIKH WAR *by J W Baldwin*—Experiences of a private of H.M. 9th Regiment of Foot in the battles for the Punjab, India 1845-6.

TOMMY ATKINS' WAR STORIES: 14 FIRST HAND ACCOUNTS—Fourteen first hand accounts from the ranks of the British Army during Queen Victoria's Empire.

THE WATERLOO LETTERS *by H. T. Siborne*—Accounts of the Battle by British Officers for its Foremost Historian.

NEY: GENERAL OF CAVALRY VOLUME 1—1769-1799 *by Antoine Bulos*—The Early Career of a Marshal of the First Empire.

NEY: MARSHAL OF FRANCE VOLUME 2—1799-1805 *by Antoine Bulos*—The Early Career of a Marshal of the First Empire.

AIDE-DE-CAMP TO NAPOLEON *by Philippe-Paul de Ségur*—For anyone interested in the Napoleonic Wars this book, written by one who was intimate with the strategies and machinations of the Emperor, will be essential reading.

TWILIGHT OF EMPIRE *by Sir Thomas Ussher & Sir George Cockburn*—Two accounts of Napoleon's Journeys in Exile to Elba and St. Helena: Narrative of Events by Sir Thomas Ussher & Napoleon's Last Voyage: Extract of a diary by Sir George Cockburn.

PRIVATE WHEELER *by William Wheeler*—The letters of a soldier of the 51st Light Infantry during the Peninsular War & at Waterloo.

LEONAUR

ALSO FROM LEONAUR

AVAILABLE IN SOFTCOVER OR HARDCOVER WITH DUST JACKET

OFFICERS & GENTLEMEN *by Peter Hawker & William Graham*—Two Accounts of British Officers During the Peninsula War: Officer of Light Dragoons by Peter Hawker & Campaign in Portugal and Spain by William Graham .

THE WALCHEREN EXPEDITION *by Anonymous*—The Experiences of a British Officer of the 81st Regt. During the Campaign in the Low Countries of 1809.

LADIES OF WATERLOO *by Charlotte A. Eaton, Magdalene de Lancey & Juana Smith*—The Experiences of Three Women During the Campaign of 1815: Waterloo Days by Charlotte A. Eaton, A Week at Waterloo by Magdalene de Lancey & Juana's Story by Juana Smith.

JOURNAL OF AN OFFICER IN THE KING'S GERMAN LEGION *by John Frederick Hering*—Recollections of Campaigning During the Napoleonic Wars.

JOURNAL OF AN ARMY SURGEON IN THE PENINSULAR WAR *by Charles Boutflower*—The Recollections of a British Army Medical Man on Campaign During the Napoleonic Wars.

ON CAMPAIGN WITH MOORE AND WELLINGTON *by Anthony Hamilton*—The Experiences of a Soldier of the 43rd Regiment During the Peninsular War.

THE ROAD TO AUSTERLITZ *by R. G. Burton*—Napoleon's Campaign of 1805.

SOLDIERS OF NAPOLEON *by A. J. Doisy De Villargennes & Arthur Chuquet*—The Experiences of the Men of the French First Empire: Under the Eagles by A. J. Doisy De Villargennes & Voices of 1812 by Arthur Chuquet .

INVASION OF FRANCE, 1814 *by F. W. O. Maycock*—The Final Battles of the Napoleonic First Empire.

LEIPZIG—A CONFLICT OF TITANS *by Frederic Shoberl*—A Personal Experience of the 'Battle of the Nations' During the Napoleonic Wars, October 14th-19th, 1813.

SLASHERS *by Charles Cadell*—The Campaigns of the 28th Regiment of Foot During the Napoleonic Wars by a Serving Officer.

BATTLE IMPERIAL *by Charles William Vane*—The Campaigns in Germany & France for the Defeat of Napoleon 1813-1814.

SWIFT & BOLD *by Gibbes Rigaud*—The 60th Rifles During the Peninsula War.

LEONAUR

ALSO FROM LEONAUR
AVAILABLE IN SOFTCOVER OR HARDCOVER WITH DUST JACKET

ADVENTURES OF A YOUNG RIFLEMAN *by Johann Christian Maempel*—The Experiences of a Saxon in the French & British Armies During the Napoleonic Wars.

THE HUSSAR *by Norbert Landsheit & G. R. Gleig*—A German Cavalryman in British Service Throughout the Napoleonic Wars.

RECOLLECTIONS OF THE PENINSULA *by Moyle Sherer*—An Officer of the 34th Regiment of Foot—'The Cumberland Gentlemen'—on Campaign Against Napoleon's French Army in Spain.

MARINE OF REVOLUTION & CONSULATE *by Moreau de Jonnès*—The Recollections of a French Soldier of the Revolutionary Wars 1791-1804.

GENTLEMEN IN RED *by John Dobbs & Robert Knowles*—Two Accounts of British Infantry Officers During the Peninsular War Recollections of an Old 52nd Man by John Dobbs An Officer of Fusiliers by Robert Knowles.

CORPORAL BROWN'S CAMPAIGNS IN THE LOW COUNTRIES *by Robert Brown*—Recollections of a Coldstream Guard in the Early Campaigns Against Revolutionary France 1793-1795.

THE 7TH (QUEENS OWN) HUSSARS: Volume 2—1793-1815 *by C. R. B. Barrett*—During the Campaigns in the Low Countries & the Peninsula and Waterloo Campaigns of the Napoleonic Wars. Volume 2: 1793-1815.

THE MARENGO CAMPAIGN 1800 *by Herbert H. Sargent*—The Victory that Completed the Austrian Defeat in Italy.

DONALDSON OF THE 94TH—SCOTS BRIGADE *by Joseph Donaldson*—The Recollections of a Soldier During the Peninsula & South of France Campaigns of the Napoleonic Wars.

A CONSCRIPT FOR EMPIRE *by Philippe as told to Johann Christian Maempel*—The Experiences of a Young German Conscript During the Napoleonic Wars.

JOURNAL OF THE CAMPAIGN OF 1815 *by Alexander Cavalié Mercer*—The Experiences of an Officer of the Royal Horse Artillery During the Waterloo Campaign.

NAPOLEON'S CAMPAIGNS IN POLAND 1806-7 *by Robert Wilson*—The campaign in Poland from the Russian side of the conflict.

LEONAUR

ALSO FROM LEONAUR
AVAILABLE IN SOFTCOVER OR HARDCOVER WITH DUST JACKET

COLBORNE: A SINGULAR TALENT FOR WAR *by John Colborne*—The Napoleonic Wars Career of One of Wellington's Most Highly Valued Officers in Egypt, Holland, Italy, the Peninsula and at Waterloo.

NAPOLEON'S RUSSIAN CAMPAIGN *by Philippe Henri de Segur*—The Invasion, Battles and Retreat by an Aide-de-Camp on the Emperor's Staff.

WITH THE LIGHT DIVISION *by John H. Cooke*—The Experiences of an Officer of the 43rd Light Infantry in the Peninsula and South of France During the Napoleonic Wars.

WELLINGTON AND THE PYRENEES CAMPAIGN VOLUME I: FROM VITORIA TO THE BIDASSOA *by F. C. Beatson*—The final phase of the campaign in the Iberian Peninsula.

WELLINGTON AND THE INVASION OF FRANCE VOLUME II: THE BIDASSOA TO THE BATTLE OF THE NIVELLE *by F. C. Beatson*—The final phase of the campaign in the Iberian Peninsula.

WELLINGTON AND THE FALL OF FRANCE VOLUME III: THE GAVES AND THE BATTLE OF ORTHEZ *by F. C. Beatson*—The final phase of the campaign in the Iberian Peninsula.

NAPOLEON'S IMPERIAL GUARD: FROM MARENGO TO WATERLOO *by J. T. Headley*—The story of Napoleon's Imperial Guard and the men who commanded them.

BATTLES & SIEGES OF THE PENINSULAR WAR *by W. H. Fitchett*—Corunna, Busaco, Albuera, Ciudad Rodrigo, Badajos, Salamanca, San Sebastian & Others.

SERGEANT GUILLEMARD: THE MAN WHO SHOT NELSON? *by Robert Guillemard*—A Soldier of the Infantry of the French Army of Napoleon on Campaign Throughout Europe.

WITH THE GUARDS ACROSS THE PYRENEES *by Robert Batty*—The Experiences of a British Officer of Wellington's Army During the Battles for the Fall of Napoleonic France, 1813 .

A STAFF OFFICER IN THE PENINSULA *by E. W. Buckham*—An Officer of the British Staff Corps Cavalry During the Peninsula Campaign of the Napoleonic Wars.

THE LEIPZIG CAMPAIGN: 1813—NAPOLEON AND THE "BATTLE OF THE NATIONS" *by F. N. Maude*—Colonel Maude's analysis of Napoleon's campaign of 1813 around Leipzig.

LEONAUR

ALSO FROM LEONAUR
AVAILABLE IN SOFTCOVER OR HARDCOVER WITH DUST JACKET

BUGEAUD: A PACK WITH A BATON *by Thomas Robert Bugeaud*—The Early Campaigns of a Soldier of Napoleon's Army Who Would Become a Marshal of France.

WATERLOO RECOLLECTIONS *by Frederick Llewellyn*—Rare First Hand Accounts, Letters, Reports and Retellings from the Campaign of 1815.

SERGEANT NICOL *by Daniel Nicol*—The Experiences of a Gordon Highlander During the Napoleonic Wars in Egypt, the Peninsula and France.

THE JENA CAMPAIGN: 1806 *by F. N. Maude*—The Twin Battles of Jena & Auerstadt Between Napoleon's French and the Prussian Army.

PRIVATE O'NEIL *by Charles O'Neil*—The recollections of an Irish Rogue of H. M. 28th Regt.—The Slashers—during the Peninsula & Waterloo campaigns of the Napoleonic war.

ROYAL HIGHLANDER *by James Anton*—A soldier of H.M 42nd (Royal) Highlanders during the Peninsular, South of France & Waterloo Campaigns of the Napoleonic Wars.

CAPTAIN BLAZE *by Elzéar Blaze*—Life in Napoleons Army.

LEJEUNE VOLUME 1 *by Louis-François Lejeune*—The Napoleonic Wars through the Experiences of an Officer on Berthier's Staff.

LEJEUNE VOLUME 2 *by Louis-François Lejeune*—The Napoleonic Wars through the Experiences of an Officer on Berthier's Staff.

CAPTAIN COIGNET *by Jean-Roch Coignet*—A Soldier of Napoleon's Imperial Guard from the Italian Campaign to Russia and Waterloo.

FUSILIER COOPER *by John S. Cooper*—Experiences in the 7th (Royal) Fusiliers During the Peninsular Campaign of the Napoleonic Wars and the American Campaign to New Orleans.

FIGHTING NAPOLEON'S EMPIRE *by Joseph Anderson*—The Campaigns of a British Infantryman in Italy, Egypt, the Peninsular & the West Indies During the Napoleonic Wars.

CHASSEUR BARRES *by Jean-Baptiste Barres*—The experiences of a French Infantryman of the Imperial Guard at Austerlitz, Jena, Eylau, Friedland, in the Peninsular, Lutzen, Bautzen, Zinnwald and Hanau during the Napoleonic Wars.

LEONAUR

ALSO FROM LEONAUR
AVAILABLE IN SOFTCOVER OR HARDCOVER WITH DUST JACKET

THE LIFE OF THE REAL BRIGADIER GERARD VOLUME 1—THE YOUNG HUSSAR 1782-1807 by *Jean-Baptiste De Marbot*—A French Cavalryman Of the Napoleonic Wars at Marengo, Austerlitz, Jena, Eylau & Friedland.

THE LIFE OF THE REAL BRIGADIER GERARD VOLUME 2—IMPERIAL AIDE-DE-CAMP 1807-1811 by *Jean-Baptiste De Marbot*—A French Cavalryman of the Napoleonic Wars at Saragossa, Landshut, Eckmuhl, Ratisbon, Aspern-Essling, Wagram, Busaco & Torres Vedras.

THE LIFE OF THE REAL BRIGADIER GERARD VOLUME 3—COLONEL OF CHASSEURS 1811-1815 by *Jean-Baptiste De Marbot*—A French Cavalryman in the retreat from Moscow, Lutzen, Bautzen, Katzbach, Leipzig, Hanau & Waterloo.

THE INDIAN WAR OF 1864 by *Eugene Ware*—The Experiences of a Young Officer of the 7th Iowa Cavalry on the Western Frontier During the Civil War.

THE MARCH OF DESTINY by *Charles E. Young & V. Devinny*—Dangers of the Trail in 1865 by Charles E. Young & The Story of a Pioneer by V. Devinny, two Accounts of Early Emigrants to Colorado.

CROSSING THE PLAINS by *William Audley Maxwell*—A First Hand Narrative of the Early Pioneer Trail to California in 1857.

CHIEF OF SCOUTS by *William F. Drannan*—A Pilot to Emigrant and Government Trains, Across the Plains of the Western Frontier.

THIRTY-ONE YEARS ON THE PLAINS AND IN THE MOUNTAINS by *William F. Drannan*—William Drannan was born to be a pioneer, hunter, trapper and wagon train guide during the momentous days of the Great American West.

THE INDIAN WARS VOLUNTEER by *William Thompson*—Recollections of the Conflict Against the Snakes, Shoshone, Bannocks, Modocs and Other Native Tribes of the American North West.

THE 4TH TENNESSEE CAVALRY by *George B. Guild*—The Services of Smith's Regiment of Confederate Cavalry by One of its Officers.

COLONEL WORTHINGTON'S SHILOH by *T. Worthington*—The Tennessee Campaign, 1862, by an Officer of the Ohio Volunteers.

FOUR YEARS IN THE SADDLE by *W. L. Curry*—The History of the First Regiment Ohio Volunteer Cavalry in the American Civil War.

LEONAUR

ALSO FROM LEONAUR
AVAILABLE IN SOFTCOVER OR HARDCOVER WITH DUST JACKET

LIFE IN THE ARMY OF NORTHERN VIRGINIA by *Carlton McCarthy*—The Observations of a Confederate Artilleryman of Cutshaw's Battalion During the American Civil War 1861-1865.

HISTORY OF THE CAVALRY OF THE ARMY OF THE POTOMAC by *Charles D. Rhodes*—Including Pope's Army of Virginia and the Cavalry Operations in West Virginia During the American Civil War.

CAMP-FIRE AND COTTON-FIELD by *Thomas W. Knox*—A New York Herald Correspondent's View of the American Civil War.

SERGEANT STILLWELL by *Leander Stillwell* —The Experiences of a Union Army Soldier of the 61st Illinois Infantry During the American Civil War.

STONEWALL'S CANNONEER by *Edward A. Moore*—Experiences with the Rockbridge Artillery, Confederate Army of Northern Virginia, During the American Civil War.

THE SIXTH CORPS by *George Stevens*—The Army of the Potomac, Union Army, During the American Civil War.

THE RAILROAD RAIDERS by *William Pittenger*—An Ohio Volunteers Recollections of the Andrews Raid to Disrupt the Confederate Railroad in Georgia During the American Civil War.

CITIZEN SOLDIER by *John Beatty*—An Account of the American Civil War by a Union Infantry Officer of Ohio Volunteers Who Became a Brigadier General.

COX: PERSONAL RECOLLECTIONS OF THE CIVIL WAR--VOLUME 1 by *Jacob Dolson Cox*—West Virginia, Kanawha Valley, Gauley Bridge, Cotton Mountain, South Mountain, Antietam, the Morgan Raid & the East Tennessee Campaign.

COX: PERSONAL RECOLLECTIONS OF THE CIVIL WAR--VOLUME 2 by *Jacob Dolson Cox*—Siege of Knoxville, East Tennessee, Atlanta Campaign, the Nashville Campaign & the North Carolina Campaign.

KERSHAW'S BRIGADE VOLUME 1 by *D. Augustus Dickert*—Manassas, Seven Pines, Sharpsburg (Antietam), Fredericksburg, Chancellorsville, Gettysburg, Chickamauga, Chattanooga, Fort Sanders & Bean Station.

KERSHAW'S BRIGADE VOLUME 2 by *D. Augustus Dickert*—At the wilderness, Cold Harbour, Petersburg, The Shenandoah Valley and Cedar Creek..

LEONAUR

ALSO FROM LEONAUR
AVAILABLE IN SOFTCOVER OR HARDCOVER WITH DUST JACKET

THE RELUCTANT REBEL *by William G. Stevenson*—A young Kentuckian's experiences in the Confederate Infantry & Cavalry during the American Civil War..

BOOTS AND SADDLES *by Elizabeth B. Custer*—The experiences of General Custer's Wife on the Western Plains.

FANNIE BEERS' CIVIL WAR *by Fannie A. Beers*—A Confederate Lady's Experiences of Nursing During the Campaigns & Battles of the American Civil War.

LADY SALE'S AFGHANISTAN *by Florentia Sale*—An Indomitable Victorian Lady's Account of the Retreat from Kabul During the First Afghan War.

THE TWO WARS OF MRS DUBERLY *by Frances Isabella Duberly*—An Intrepid Victorian Lady's Experience of the Crimea and Indian Mutiny.

THE REBELLIOUS DUCHESS *by Paul F. S. Dermoncourt*—The Adventures of the Duchess of Berri and Her Attempt to Overthrow French Monarchy.

LADIES OF WATERLOO *by Charlotte A. Eaton, Magdalene de Lancey & Juana Smith*—The Experiences of Three Women During the Campaign of 1815: Waterloo Days by Charlotte A. Eaton, A Week at Waterloo by Magdalene de Lancey & Juana's Story by Juana Smith.

TWO YEARS BEFORE THE MAST *by Richard Henry Dana. Jr.*—The account of one young man's experiences serving on board a sailing brig—the Penelope—bound for California, between the years 1834-36.

A SAILOR OF KING GEORGE *by Frederick Hoffman*—From Midshipman to Captain—Recollections of War at Sea in the Napoleonic Age 1793-1815.

LORDS OF THE SEA *by A. T. Mahan*—Great Captains of the Royal Navy During the Age of Sail.

COGGESHALL'S VOYAGES: VOLUME 1 *by George Coggeshall*—The Recollections of an American Schooner Captain.

COGGESHALL'S VOYAGES: VOLUME 2 *by George Coggeshall*—The Recollections of an American Schooner Captain.

TWILIGHT OF EMPIRE *by Sir Thomas Ussher & Sir George Cockburn*—Two accounts of Napoleon's Journeys in Exile to Elba and St. Helena: Narrative of Events by Sir Thomas Ussher & Napoleon's Last Voyage: Extract of a diary by Sir George Cockburn.

LEONAUR

ALSO FROM LEONAUR
AVAILABLE IN SOFTCOVER OR HARDCOVER WITH DUST JACKET

ESCAPE FROM THE FRENCH *by Edward Boys*—A Young Royal Navy Midshipman's Adventures During the Napoleonic War.

THE VOYAGE OF H.M.S. PANDORA *by Edward Edwards R. N. & George Hamilton, edited by Basil Thomson*—In Pursuit of the Mutineers of the Bounty in the South Seas—1790-1791.

MEDUSA *by J. B. Henry Savigny and Alexander Correard and Charlotte-Adélaïde Dard* —Narrative of a Voyage to Senegal in 1816 & The Sufferings of the Picard Family After the Shipwreck of the Medusa.

THE SEA WAR OF 1812 VOLUME 1 *by A. T. Mahan*—A History of the Maritime Conflict.

THE SEA WAR OF 1812 VOLUME 2 *by A. T. Mahan*—A History of the Maritime Conflict.

WETHERELL OF H. M. S. HUSSAR *by John Wetherell*—The Recollections of an Ordinary Seaman of the Royal Navy During the Napoleonic Wars.

THE NAVAL BRIGADE IN NATAL *by C. R. N. Burne*—With the Guns of H. M. S. Terrible & H. M. S. Tartar during the Boer War 1899-1900.

THE VOYAGE OF H. M. S. BOUNTY *by William Bligh*—The True Story of an 18th Century Voyage of Exploration and Mutiny.

SHIPWRECK! *by William Gilly*—The Royal Navy's Disasters at Sea 1793-1849.

KING'S CUTTERS AND SMUGGLERS: 1700-1855 *by E. Keble Chatterton*—A unique period of maritime history-from the beginning of the eighteenth to the middle of the nineteenth century when British seamen risked all to smuggle valuable goods from wool to tea and spirits from and to the Continent.

CONFEDERATE BLOCKADE RUNNER *by John Wilkinson*—The Personal Recollections of an Officer of the Confederate Navy.

NAVAL BATTLES OF THE NAPOLEONIC WARS *by W. H. Fitchett*—Cape St. Vincent, the Nile, Cadiz, Copenhagen, Trafalgar & Others.

PRISONERS OF THE RED DESERT *by R. S. Gwatkin-Williams*—The Adventures of the Crew of the Tara During the First World War.

U-BOAT WAR 1914-1918 *by James B. Connolly/Karl von Schenk*—Two Contrasting Accounts from Both Sides of the Conflict at Sea During the Great War.

LEONAUR

ALSO FROM LEONAUR

AVAILABLE IN SOFTCOVER OR HARDCOVER WITH DUST JACKET

IRON TIMES WITH THE GUARDS *by An O. E. (G. P. A. Fildes)*—The Experiences of an Officer of the Coldstream Guards on the Western Front During the First World War.

THE GREAT WAR IN THE MIDDLE EAST: 1 *by W. T. Massey*—The Desert Campaigns & How Jerusalem Was Won---two classic accounts in one volume.

THE GREAT WAR IN THE MIDDLE EAST: 2 *by W. T. Massey*—Allenby's Final Triumph.

SMITH-DORRIEN *by Horace Smith-Dorrien*—Isandlwhana to the Great War.

1914 *by Sir John French*—The Early Campaigns of the Great War by the British Commander.

GRENADIER *by E. R. M. Fryer*—The Recollections of an Officer of the Grenadier Guards throughout the Great War on the Western Front.

BATTLE, CAPTURE & ESCAPE *by George Pearson*—The Experiences of a Canadian Light Infantryman During the Great War.

DIGGERS AT WAR *by R. Hugh Knyvett & G. P. Cuttriss*—"Over There" With the Australians by R. Hugh Knyvett and Over the Top With the Third Australian Division by G. P. Cuttriss. Accounts of Australians During the Great War in the Middle East, at Gallipoli and on the Western Front.

HEAVY FIGHTING BEFORE US *by George Brenton Laurie*—The Letters of an Officer of the Royal Irish Rifles on the Western Front During the Great War.

THE CAMELIERS *by Oliver Hogue*—A Classic Account of the Australians of the Imperial Camel Corps During the First World War in the Middle East.

RED DUST *by Donald Black*—A Classic Account of Australian Light Horsemen in Palestine During the First World War.

THE LEAN, BROWN MEN *by Angus Buchanan*—Experiences in East Africa During the Great War with the 25th Royal Fusiliers—the Legion of Frontiersmen.

THE NIGERIAN REGIMENT IN EAST AFRICA *by W. D. Downes*—On Campaign During the Great War 1916-1918.

THE 'DIE-HARDS' IN SIBERIA *by John Ward*—With the Middlesex Regiment Against the Bolsheviks 1918-19.

CPSIA information can be obtained at www.ICGtesting.com
Printed in the USA
LVOW06s1159300514

387910LV00001B/75/P